Explore the World

NELLES

GW00320375

U.S.A.

THE WEST, ROCKIES AND TEXAS

Authors:
Jürgen Scheunemann, Margarete Batt, Arturo Gonzalez,
Sara Hare, Anita King, Gary McKechnie, Anne Midgette

*An Up-to-date travel guide
with 144 color photos
and 21 maps*

Dear Reader: Being up-to-date is the main goal of the Nelles series. Our correspondents help keep us abreast of the latest developments in the travel scene, while our cartographers see to it that maps are also kept completely current. However, as the travel world is constantly changing, we cannot guarantee that all the information contained in our books is always valid. Should you come across a discrepancy, please contact us at: Nelles Verlag, Schleissheimer Str. 371 b, 80935 Munich, Germany, tel. (089) 3571940, fax. (089) 35719430, e-mail: Nelles.Verlag@T-Online.de

Note: Distances and measurements, including temperatures, used in this guide are U.S. Standard. For conversion information, see the *Guidelines* section of this book.

LEGEND

✻	Place of Interest	▬▬ National Border	▬▬	Interstate
▨	Public or Significant Building	*Venice* Place Mentioned in Text	▬▬	Toll Expressway
◼	Hotel	✈ International Airport	▬▬	Four-lane Highway
●	Restaurant	☀ Beach	▬▬	Connecting Highway
▨	Shopping Center	··♣·· National Park	▬▬	Main Highway
○	Market	--♣-- National Forest	───	Railway
▨	High-rise	▲ Campsite	⑨⑤	Interstate Highway
✝ ✡	Church, Synagogue	\ 25 / Distance in Miles	⚊①	U.S. Highway
Ⓢ	Underground Station	**Mt. Baker** 10778 Mountain Summit (Height in Feet)	⑨	State / Provincial Highway

U.S.A. – The West, Rockies and Texas
© Nelles Verlag GmbH, 80935 Munich
   All rights reserved

Second Revised Edition 2000
ISBN 3-88618-147-2
Printed in Slovenia

Publisher:	Günter Nelles	**Translation:**	Marton Radkai
Managing Editor:	Berthold Schwarz	**Cartography:**	Nelles Verlag GmbH
Project Editor:	Jürgen Scheunemann	**Color**	
English Edition		**Separation:**	Priegnitz, Munich
Editor:	Chase Stewart	**Printed by:**	Gorenjski Tisk

TABLE OF CONTENTS

TRAVEL INFORMATION

LIST OF MAPS
(Legend see page 2)

GO WEST!

A Journey through the Promised Land

America is at its most American where it is farthest from Europe: in the metropolises of the West Coast, in the canyons of Utah and Colorado, in the valleys of the Rocky Mountains, in the gambling casinos of Las Vegas, in the pueblos of Arizona, and, last but not least, in the gold-mining towns of Nevada. The American West is a myth, a legend, an idea, one could even say an ideology. But the West that was considered so wild and treacherous had already become history before the turn of the 20th century.

This left much breathing space for the growing myth. Back then, the American historian Frederick Jackson Turner published his famous thesis on the American frontier. Turner's essay stated that the new European immigrants could only become genuine Americans by experiencing the wilderness of the frontier, which was steadily moving westwards. This new species of human being would then no longer have anything to do with old Europe; instead, he would be individualistic and incorruptible – and hence more democratic. Modern historians refute this thesis that life on the frontier automatically led to one's becoming Americanized; in fact, real life on the border between wilderness and civilization had been idealized into pleasant, but fictional, legend.

The Conquest of the Wild West

The glorification of the frontier conceals a darker side of American history.

Previous pages: Fascinating play of colors in Bryce Canyon, Utah. Loafing in Venice (Los Angeles). Left: Navajo Indian woman in Navajo Tribal Park.

The Wild West was by no means an unpopulated tract of land. Long before the white man cast his shadow on the New World, an estimated four to ten million Native Americans lived on the North American continent. By the year 1890, they numbered a mere 300,000. The first expeditions out west – the most famous one being that of Lewis and Clark in 1804-06 – made friendly contact with most of the tribes they encountered. However, the following generations of westward-bound settlers, gold-miners and ranchers conducted a virtual war of extermination. The genocide of the indigenous Americans – the Sioux, the Apaches, the Cheyennes and the Nez Percés – remains to this day the darkest chapter in American history.

An interesting note is that in recent censuses an increasing number of Americans have given their origins as Indian: around two million in 1990, which represents a tidy 0.8 percent of the population, and twice as many as 20 years before. Be that as it may, the Indian wars remain a controversial national topic.

By the 19th century, Northerners, at least, were keenly aware of the social injustice represented by the southern institution of slavery; but, apart from a few sporadic outbreaks of outrage at some of the army's more blatant atrocities, the intellectual elite of the East Coast maintained a rather disinterested attitude toward the Indian wars. This is hardly surprising in light of the widespread belief in "Manifest Destiny" since the 1840s. It was, so ran the theory, the divinely-ordained destiny of the United States to expand to take over the entire continent; a destiny the country's citizens, accordingly, hastened to fulfill.

Historically, America has tended to define "The West" as those territories that had not yet been annexed beyond the westernmost point of settlement. If, in the 18th century, the "Northwest Territories" lay to the south of the Great Lakes, the

same term was, a century later, applied to what are now the states of Washington and Oregon in the Pacific Northwest.

In 1763, American expansion was abruptly checked at the Appalachians after the end of the colonial war between France and England; however, after the American colonists successfully waged their War of Independence in 1776, the young nation began expanding again, down to Florida in the south and to the Great Lakes in the north. In 1803, the Louisiana Purchase doubled the size of the U.S.A. As a historical footnote, it should be mentioned that negotiators had planned only to discuss the purchase of New Orleans with Napoleon; but the French Emperor offered them the entire territory between the Mississippi and the Rocky Mountains for a mere 15 million dollars. The frontier moved 1,000 miles westward in one fell swoop.

Above: Ghost town of Goldfield. Right: Lively border exchange with Mexico in El Paso. Far right: Chicanos – much in demand as laborers.

After the largest real estate buy in the history of mankind, a continuous flow of settlers poured into the West. In 1830, only one-quarter of all Americans lived beyond the Appalachians; by 1850, it was half. The U.S. government continued signing sales agreements with the Indians, only to break them a few years later. The annexing of the Republic of Texas and the end of the war with Mexico gave the U.S.A. the entire Southwest.

It was around this time that the myth of the Wild West came into being. Naturally, the standard Hollywood-style clichés of cowboys and Indians have little to do with reality, except, perhaps, in a very few cases. Daily life in the 19th century looked considerably different. For one thing, the settlers pushing their way westward along the Oregon Trail and other routes often found the soil conditions so poor that the land could only be used for grazing cattle. It was, in fact, gold that brought thousands of desperados into Colorado, Utah and California; but only a few got rich in this way. All

that remains of the heady days of the gold rushes are a few ghost towns in the salt deserts and the valleys of the Rocky Mountains.

The last great wave of settlers moved in between 1870 and 1900, when the new railways brought some two million newcomers to the frontier. The "iron horse," as the Native Americans called the steam locomotive out of respect and mistrust, galloped straight across the continent. On May 10, 1869, the tracks of the *Union Pacific* and *Central Pacific* companies were joined near Promontory Point in Utah to complete the United States' first transcontinental railway.

The trains brought hunters from the East Coast out to the prairie states, where they succeeded in virtually obliterating the great bison herds that had sustained the Indian tribes. In 1863, "Buffalo" Bill Cody, something of a national hero, boasted of having killed 4,300 bison in a mere eight months. By the turn of the century, nearly all of North America's estimated 32 million buffalo had been ex-

terminated. By the time Frederick Jackson Turner promulgated his theory of the frontier in 1893, therefore, the actual subject of his thesis had pretty much vanished.

But the myth has survived even to this day. Just as German and Scandinavian immigrants poured into Kansas and Wisconsin in the last century, so, today, do Mexicans come to California and Texas in droves to fulfill their own version of the American Dream. However, the realities of life in this western Horn of Plenty are anything but wine and roses. Instead of prosperity and growth, many *chicanos*, as the Mexicans are often referred to in the U.S., find themselves enmired in bitter poverty and hopelessness.

America and the West

It was in the West that America developed its unique identity and became the country it is today. "Go west, young man, and grow up with the country," were the words of politician and writer

15

Horace Greeley more than 150 years ago. Anyone who did go west came back a different person. The West exercised significant social and political influence on the country as a whole, and turned it into an economic (and, by extension, political) world power. The prairie, the Rocky Mountains and the Pacific Coast were new, exciting, young, untamed and merciless. Anyone who wanted to survive here as a settler, rancher or gold miner had to do so under his own steam. But if you could make it in the West, you could make it anywhere. The West had its own laws, both in a positive and negative sense, dictated by the harsh conditions of life in the wilds.

In this part of the country, women had the right to vote as early as the 1860s. After all, women had to put their shoulder to the wheel just as much as men had. At the same time, might made

Above: Individuality is highly prized. Right: The private initiative "Adopt a Highway" cleans up the country's roads.

right; in this virtually lawless country, you could carry the day either with a gun or, later, with a fistful of dollars. Survival of the fittest was the operative law: at first with regard to the indigenous inhabitants; later with new settlers; and finally with one's neighbors.

In a more general sense, as a metaphor for the American spirit, the frontier ideology has persisted into the 20th century. Those quintessentially American pioneer ideals were still alive and well when John F. Kennedy kicked off his 1959-60 campaign with "New Frontier" as his buzzword against the creaky Eisenhower administration. Kennedy was aspiring to a new philosophical and political frontier, filled with hope and opportunity. Both major parties, and a variety of other social groups, have invoked the frontier concept to introduce reforms, social change or new political directions in the years since.

The American Mentality

The turbulent and romantic history of the American West has influenced, indeed, shaped, the mind-set of those living beyond the Mississippi. And the legacy of this history is still very much in evidence today. Many of the American virtues and traits that strike a European visitor as noteworthy go straight back to the days of the pioneers.

One of the most remarkable aspects of the Western mentality is the paradox between an emphasis on independence and individuality on the one hand, and sometimes clannish social solidarity on the other. This is indeed a contradiction, but America is large enough to live with its contradictions.

This paradox derives directly from frontier life. If your neighbor lived 50 miles away in a wild country, only solidarity could help in the case of an emergency. As soon as the trouble was over, however, this same neighbor resumed his

status as a competitor in the search for land, natural resources or power.

There are plenty of concrete examples of this kind of duality today. Americans on the West Coast or in the Midwest, for example, are considered more friendly and hospitable than their East Coast counterparts: if you have the misfortune of breaking down on the highway, you can count on someone stopping to lend a hand. On the other hand, the hordes of homeless in such cities as Los Angeles cannot expect the least bit of social support. In the very same city, thousands of people spend their hard-earned dollars on the typical Californian youth and beauty cult, dedicating their free time to leisure pursuits carried to excess, only, it seems, to avoid the monster of boredom.

Yet these same self-absorbed individuals can suddenly crystalize into a united front, particularly when they feel that their rights as Americans or common interests are being threatened. Authentic American grass-roots democracy then springs to life, giving rise, for example,

to a drive to collect signatures for the building of a new school, or in protest of some issue or other. Americans become community-oriented and commit themselves unconditionally to the cause – even if the issue is only something as relatively tame as cleaning up a local segment of highway.

The relationship between the East and West Coasts is not exactly free of animosities, and neither side makes much effort to do away with them. The political and social establishment in the East tends to look down its nose at the farmers and ranchers in the Midwest as unpolished rednecks and hillbillies. States such as Oklahoma and Kansas are the butt of jokes from coast to coast. There's only truth to these stereotypes insofar as it is in the middle of the country that you find one hundred percent, God-fearing, hardworking, conservative, straight Americans. In fact, this part of the country is often referred to as the "heartland." It is indeed where America is at its most American.

Even the great cities on the West Coast – Los Angeles and San Diego in particular – have to suffer the witticisms of New Yorkers and Bostonians. According to Easterners, life in the California sun is artificial, superficial, and without restraints, standards, seriousness or morals. Los Angeles is often referred to as "La La Land," which derives from the short form of its name, L.A., and the supposedly somewhat lackadaisical attitude of its residents.

In the past few years, politicians in distant Washington have started pointing to Hollywood as being responsible for the moral decay of the entire country. Every evil that visits the U.S.A. seems to come from the West nowadays, even though some of the most outspoken politicians, such as Bob Dole or Phil Gramm, come from the West themselves (Kansas and Texas, respectively).

Above: Endlessly stretching highways cut through the land. Right: Harley drivers on Cabrillo Blvd. in Santa Barbara.

On the Road

One of the best ways to get to know America is from the front seat of a car. Driving along the long, ramrod-straight highways through this seemingly endless country lulls you into a state of relaxed meditation as you watch miles of scenery roll by. Unlike many Europeans, Americans tend to view driving as a pleasant way to travel, rather than a necessary and stressful evil. And Americans are constantly on the move. Just about all your errands can be taken care of "drive-thru"; in effect, you can conduct your whole life in passing, without ever having to stop and think things over.

Americans have lived this way in the West for over a century. If you got tired of life in one place, you simply packed up tools and baggage and went on to the next. Americans move house an average of seven times in a lifetime, and change jobs eight times. Being "on the move" is normal. One symptom of this is the many mobile homes, especially in the South-

west, and the countless, often oversized trailers in which retired couples travel across the country.

The automobile has become the metallic symbol of freedom and opportunity in the United States. The hobo travels about on freight trains looking for odd jobs; the tramp wanders around on any kind of moving vehicle; the hippie of yore used his thumb to get around and discover the country: all of these are modern nomads, legendary American types that could only have come to be in the West. These people are 20th century reincarnations of the cowboy. Hollywood used and abused the cliché of hard-riding cowboys and noble wilderness a thousand times and to the threshold of spectator endurance. The real Wild West suffered a second death in the process.

The entertainment industry in the U.S. has given a boost to the image of the driving cowboy with the genre of the road movie. The "Easy Rider" taking his Harley through the country, whether in pursuit of some evanescent goal or being pursued himself, is no more than a rehash of the archetypal American hero; as is the solitary cross-country trucker, or *Thelma and Louise.* Even some of the most vociferous critics of the American Way of Life, such as Jack Kerouac, could not refrain from living by the automobile (see his 1957 novel *On the Road*).

The Western States

The sheer expanse of the West overwhelmed the first Spanish settlers, and continued to astound subsequent arrivals. The strangeness was compounded by the region's unfamiliar fauna and flora, unlike anything in Europe or on the East Coast. Today, the country's incredible size can be seen in the population density: about ten people per square mile, as opposed to 140 in Germany, for example. One-fifth of the country's population lives in the 17 states between Kansas City and San Francisco, a surface area of 1.8 million square miles comprising half of the country.

19

California is the quintessential West Coast state, and a Promised Land if ever there was one. No other American state promised so much to its new arrivals and was then able to deliver the goods. Gold, fertile prairies and pastures, and well-supplied fishing grounds attracted conquerors and adventurers alike. Today, California, with its 32 million inhabitants, is the most important state in the Union in terms of economy. Its liberal political tradition, culminating in the Flower Power movement in the 1960s, became a kind of cultural and political beacon for the entire Western World.

Nowadays, the high-tech industry located between San Francisco and Los Angeles attracts new immigrants to the state, and technology developed in the area, in turn, has a powerful influence on the rest of the world. No one doubts that California, the epitome of the "sunshine

Above: Wupatki – document of an extinct Indian culture. Right: Financially successful – Asian immigrants.

state," also has its darker sides, but even a few earthquakes have not succeeded in clouding the allure of its golden dream.

The Southwest is generally arid and sparsely populated. Mountains and deserts in all variations of earth colors characterize the landscapes of Arizona, Utah, New Mexico and Nevada; sunrise and sunset especially bring out the region's reds, ochres and browns. The southwestern states also recall the vanished Indian cultures that have left only traces of their ancient civilization. In recent decades, the Southwest has developed its own distinctive culture, with a regional cuisine, its own fashion and even its own slang.

This sense of independence is even more pronounced in neighboring Texas. It's a good deal older as well, going back to the birth of the state in the middle of the 19th century. Texas is to Americans what Bavaria is to the Germans, Wales is to the British and Brittany is to the French. Everything is different here: language, lifestyle, ideology. Everything is bigger, more relaxed, and above all more

wealthy. Texas means business, ranches, oil wells, big cars, cowboy boots, and such flowering cities as Dallas/Fort Worth, Houston and Austin.

The Rocky Mountains, the country's longest mountain range, begins north of these states and stretches all the way to Canada, crossing Colorado, Idaho (arguably the most beautiful of all American states), Nebraska, Wyoming and Montana. In spite of growing environmental problems, the Rockies are also the most beautiful mountain range in the U.S.

Clear, remote and quiet mountain lakes and shores can still be found in the Pacific Northwest as well, notably in Oregon and Washington State. This part of the country has only recently been discovered by European tourists, and is therefore seldom as overrun as points south. Americans themselves only discovered the area a hundred years ago, which means you can still find tracts of unspoiled nature in the area. And even in the modern and increasingly popular cities of Portland and Seattle, you can

sense that the history of settlement here is relatively new.

The Future is in the West

The West still likes to see itself as young, unruly and forward-looking. The future of America perhaps does lie out here. It's in this half of the continent that you find the nation's economic and technical force. Kansas and South Dakota, for example, are the grain silos of the country; Texas, Nebraska and Oklahoma supply half the world with beef. Texas, California, Oklahoma and Wyoming produce twice as much crude oil as Alaska. The airplane industry has settled in Washington State, California and Texas. Computer giants (such as Microsoft in Seattle) and genetic research companies have their futuristic laboratories in the West, mostly in and around Los Angeles.

In the coming years, it's in the West that the face of America will be changing most; traveling here, therefore, means traveling into the nation's future.

FROM
LOS ANGELES
TO PHOENIX

LOS ANGELES
SAN DIEGO
PALM SPRINGS
ARIZONA DESERTS

Travelers wishing to adapt their fashion style to suit this world of the rich and beautiful will need two pairs of sunglasses: A designer pair for Los Angeles and a pair with UV-filter for desert driving. Viewed through impermeable shades, this desert world appears alien - an apparent virtual reality. In the shimmering hot waves of desert heat, the sights on this tour of dizzying contrasts might resemble a mirage. From opulent Beverly Hills to simple Spanish-era missions, from ritzy resorts to abandoned ghost towns, from pristine national parks to sprawling desert metropolises, this 390 mile (625 km) tour captures the legends of the Old West – legends still alive today.

LOS ANGELES

The journey begins along the California coast in **Los Angeles** - city of filmstars, which spreads out, like a giant octopus, over an area 80 miles in diameter. This city's character is revealed on it's six-lane freeways, which run through Los Angeles like arteries. Here, the coolest cars mingle - red Corvette convertibles,

Previous pages: Joshua Tree National Monument. Left: African-Americans dominate the basketball scene (Phoenix Suns).

vintage Chevies, "low-rider" El Caminos and long white limousines with dark tinted windows; welcome to **Los Angeles**, City of Angels – or "La La Land", depending on your perspective. Whether you love it or hate it, Los Angeles will be an unforgettable experience.

With its abundant sunshine and glamorous Hollywood image, Los Angeles appears as an unreal utopia rendered opaque by a thin layer of celluloid film - or is that just smog?. The beautiful people of this image-conscious city flash smiles, posing as if on camera. However, the specific risks of life in L.A. – the threat of earthquakes, racial unrest, drug-related crime and forest fires – can provide sleepless nights for even the wealthiest Angelinos in their otherwise perfect world.

Founded by just eleven Spanish families in 1781, the city today has grown to more than three million residents, with more than 14 million in the greater Los Angeles area. The quintessential American melting pot, L.A. boasts residents from every corner of the world. Therefore, it is little wonder that from Koreatown to Little Tokyo, from African-American Watts to the Hispanic *barrios* of East L.A., the city simmers, and every now and again, boils over. There are dangerous neighborhoods here,

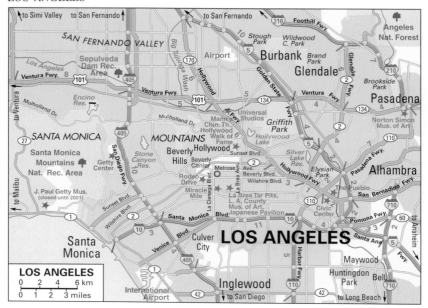

streets peppered with gangs and guns. Although much of the violence is over-blown media-hype, it's probably better to avoid short cuts through unknown areas and stay on the main roads.

Exploring Los Angeles by Car

Los Angeles doesn't seem to have evolved around a city center per se; it is made up more from a conglomeration of towns. Which is why L.A. should be explored by car. Distances, even within the city, can sometimes be enormous.

Perhaps even more so than San Francisco, this is the true cultural center of California. A row of impressive museums line Wilshire Boulevard, among them is the **Los Angeles County Museum of Art**, an architectural master-piece with an international showcase of art from pre-historic to present times. The

Right: Exclusive shopping in Beverley Hills. Far right: A stunt show in Universal Studios, Hollywood.

Isozaki-designed **Japanese Pavilion** is also a highlight. Next door, the **La Brea Tar Pits** attract oddity seekers; at this ar-cheological site more than 200 varieties of fossils have been unearthed.

Pueblo Park, where the oldest build-ings of the city are located, belongs to the historical center of L.A. Walking along **Olvera Street** you can sense the city's Spanish heritage, while in **Chinatown** and **Little Tokyo** a strictly Asian flair prevails.

South of the old city center is the **Civic Center** with **City Hall**, which offers a fine view over the town. Southwest of city hall, **Broadway** is a very popular street for shopping, and not far from here you will find the lively **Grand Central Market**, with more than fifty market stalls.

Famous since the 1930s, **Sunset Strip** has been exploding with nightlife for over six decades. Today, one can still cruise leisurely along and revel in this nostalgic stretch of road - preferably in a convertible of course, past monumental

billboards and bustling crowds. Sunset strip is a section of the legendary **Sunset Boulevard**.

Mulholland Drive, another famous Los Angeles street, winds from the Hollywood Hills across the ridge of the Santa Monica Mountains and almost to the Pacific Ocean. From its heights you can catch views of the city and the San Fernando Valley. To find Mulholland, follow Benedict Drive north from Sunset Boulevard. On the West Side, **Beverly Center** is a massive shopping mall between La Cienega and Beverly Boulevard, with parking and shops on alternate levels. As for the most elegant shopping street - Beverly Hills' **Rodeo Drive** is best explored on foot.

Melrose Avenue, a bustling in-crowd strip (especially at night) is where wanna-be rock 'n' rollers with post-punk hairdos pose. More boutiques and specialty shops abound between **Fairfax** and **La Brea**.

With new exhibits opening constantly, **Universal Studios Hollywood**, west of Griffith Park (access via the Hollywood Freeway), continues to invite visitors to board flight simulators and free-fall down volcanic tunnels. The five-hour tour is truly entertaining, with everything from King Kong replicas to the Castle of Count Dracula. The high-tech equipment alone makes the visit worthwhile.

Universal City Walk, an amusement and shopping area which seems more like a theater stage, sits just outside the front gates of Universal Studios. Storefronts spill out into this street, designed to recreate the neighborhoods of Los Angeles on a miniature scale. Teeming mobs on a Saturday night crowd the **twelve-screen cinema**, the **Museum of Neon Art** and dozens of restaurants and clubs which are filled with Angelinos.

Nearby is **Hollywood**, marked by its legendary hilltop sign. Its many sights include **Mann's Chinese Theater**, the most famous cinema in the world, where stars have immortalized themselves in the sidewalk's cement by ceremoniously leaving their hand and footprints . This is also where the **Hollywood Walk of Fame** on Hollywood Boulevard begins,

27

where bronze stars with the names of famous personalities are embedded in the sidewalk.

The district around **Wilshire Boulevard** and the **Miracle Mile** is a favorite route amongst Angelinos for cruising between Beverly Hills and Los Angeles.

The **J. Paul Getty Museum**, on the Pacific Coast Highway in Malibu, will remain closed until the year 2001. In the meantime, the museum's collection can be viewed at the **Getty Center**, a 50 hectare complex devoted to culture and the arts. Other interesting exhibits can be seen at the **Armand Hammer Museum** (including European painting from the 16th century on) and the **Norton Simon Museum of Art** in Pasadena (European and Southeast Asian art). The **Gene Autrey Western Heritage Museum** in Griffith Park recalls the Wild West. On a more foreboding note, the new **Museum of Tolerance** lets you walk back through

Above: Brightly illuminated L.A. nights.
Right: Street performers in Venice Beach.

time to witness the horrors of American racism and the Nazi Holocaust.

Coastal and Southern Los Angeles

The beach communities of **Santa Monica**, **Venice** and **Pacific Palisades** each have a special character of their own. The Santa Monica **Pier** offers shops, arcades and an old-fashioned carousel; another option is simply to stroll along Santa Monica's boutique-lined **Third Street Promenade**. **Ocean Front Walk** in **Venice** is a meeting place – as well as an exhibition stage – for body builders, roller skaters and all kinds of people who are into all kinds of things.

Heading south towards San Diego, you'll pass **Long Beach** (where the Queen Mary, one of the world's largest cruise ships with numerous shops, hotels and restaurants on board, is permanently anchored) and **Newport Beach**. Both are upmarket residential areas (but there are also several poverty-stricken quarters in Long Beach), which is why this stretch is

known as the "Californian Riviera". In between both places lies **Huntington Beach**, a haven for surfers. If you're traveling with kids, look in at **Knott's Berry Farm**, some 25 miles away; this amusement park features live "Peanuts" comic strip characters.

Only a few miles southeast of here, in **Anaheim**, is **Disneyland**, founded by film producer Walt Disney in 1955. Here you encounter not only a life-sized Mickey Mouse and his friends, but you can transcend space and time in one of the complex's seven theme parks: New Orleans and the pirates of the 18th century, perhaps, or a jungle expedition in *Adventureland*, or maybe a roller coaster trip into outer space in *Tomorrowland*. In **Yorba Linda**, north of Anaheim, the new **Richard M. Nixon Presidential Center** can be visited (featuring the president's birthplace in a museum).

The **Pacific Coast Highway** (Highway 1; called simply PCH by locals), the legendary coast road with its views, a symphony of foamy surf and sheer cliffs,

is quite breathtaking. In spring, pink and white ice plant blossoms blanket the bluffs.

Further south is the town of **San Juan Capistrano**, Orange County's oldest city. **Orange County** long had the dubious honor of being the fastest growing suburb in the U.S. – until 1994, when, thanks to fallacious real estate speculation, the city's treasurers managed to bankrupt the place.

The **Mission San Juan Capistrano** on the **Camino Real** (Spanish for "Royal Highway") is one of 21 missions built a day's horseback ride apart in the late 1700s by the Franciscan padres who claimed these lands for Spain. The Mission is famous for its swallows, arriving and departing on their annual migrations like clockwork - on the very same day every year. **Del Mar**, farther south, is the site of a popular annual county fair, the Del Mar Fair.

Continuing south and 14 miles north of San Diego the coast road winds into the picturesque university town of **La Jolla**,

which is home to the world-renowned **Scripps Institution of Oceanography**, the **Stephen Birch Aquarium and Museum** and the **University of California** in San Diego.

SAN DIEGO

With its Spanish architecture, views over the open sea, unspoiled nature and quiet streets, charming **San Diego** - the second-largest city in California, will soon help you forget monstrous Los Angeles. A simple cruise along the broad seaside boulevards of this sparkling city will intoxicate you with the captivating atmosphere.

Mission Bay, northwest of the city, is a true El Dorado for water sports fans. The Mediterranean-like climate here yields an abundance of palms, yuccas and flowering shrubs. No wonder, then, that

Above: On the beach at Mission Bay, San Diego. Right: Abundant variety of vegetation in Anza-Borrego Desert State Park.

San Diego's one million residents consider themselves very lucky to inhabit such a paradise – which boasts, incidentally, more golf courses per capita than any other U.S. city.

Known as the "the birthplace of California," San Diego traces its roots to 1542, when Portuguese explorer Juan Rodriguez Cabrillo sailed into San Diego's harbor. The maritime influence is still strong today: San Diego is an important naval base for the U.S. Coast Guard and Navy.

The **Cabrillo National Monument** on the summit of Point Loma offers an overwhelming view over the city and sparkling sea. Mexico's desert seems close enough to touch, and this could be a good opportunity to take a quick trip across the border to **Tijuana** for a couple of *burritos* and a *margarita* or two.

Don't miss the **Mission San Diego de Alcala**, a beautiful adobe church, nor the old town of San Diego with its **Gaslamp Quarter**, a predominantly Victorian neighborhood, and the **Junipero Serra**

Museum, named after the Franciscan founding father of California.

Balboa Park, a veritable jewel of emerald color, contains a number of museums (with exhibits on Pueblo Indians, photography and tropical flora, amongst other things), theaters and restaurants. Part of the park houses the world-famous **San Diego Zoo**, spreading over more than 1000 acres and containing more than 800 different species of exotic animals, from panda bears to long-billed New Zealand kiwi. Another site of interest, though somewhat controversial amongst animal rights activists, is **Sea World**, home to killer whales, dolphins and all manner of other marine animals.

The itinerary now veers inland on Interstate 8 to the **Anza Borrego Desert State Park**, 90 miles east of San Diego. Named after Mexican explorer Juan Bautista de Anza, this is the largest state park in the U.S. In this vast desert preserve, colorful displays of flowering cacti and wildflowers blanket the beige sand in the springtime. Ranging from sea level to 650 feet in elevation, the 600,000 acres of this park appear limitless. The sand dunes are great for off-road mountain biking and camping. There are no restricted campsites here. Just stop the car anywhere and pitch your tent.

From Anza-Borrega, our route winds north on state highways CA 78 and CA 86 past the **Salton Sea**, a saltwater lake created by the floodwaters of the Colorado River in 1905.

If you decide to skip San Diego, you can head east to Arizona through endless suburban cities, including **Riverside**, the citrus capital of California. Today, the "Parent Washington Navel Orange Tree," propagated in 1873, can be seen at the corner of Magnolia and Arlington avenues.

The Sonora Desert

Heading east on I-10 past Riverside, the urban landscape gradually gives way to the vast open spaces of the **Sonora Desert**, which spreads as far as the eye can see. This arid landscape, which spans the border between Arizona and California, comprises much of the American Southwest. Several million years ago this area was covered by sea. Nowadays, the isolated vegetation must try and capture the limited amount of moisture held in the sands. Many plants have very short lifespans and must reseed every year, the exception to this rule being, of course, the cactus - the great gatherer of water, which can survive for hundreds of years. Summer temperatures average above 100° F and only three inches of rain falls each spring.

There are two valleys in the *Colorado Desert*, as the Californian Sonora is known (because of the canal that runs though it), and today, with the miracle of modern irrigation methods, they have both blossomed into major agricultural areas: the **Coachella Valley** north of the Salton Sea and the **Imperial Valley**, south toward the Mexican border.

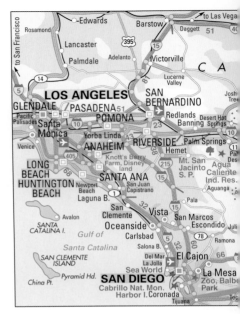

PALM SPRINGS

The agricultural oasis of the Coachella Valley is home to "America's foremost desert resort," **Palm Springs**. This glittering jewel has it all: golf (more than 70 golf courses in a 20 mile radius), tennis, bicycle and hiking tours, shopping galore, celebrities - but above all, plenty of sunshine.

Due to its proximity to Los Angeles, Palm Springs has been attracting celebrities since the 1930s. VIPs of entertainment such as Bob Hope, Frank Sinatra, Elvis Presley and Liberace have vacationed here, as have U.S. presidents Eisenhower, Kennedy, Johnson, Nixon and Ford (who built a home here). Therefore, this town became a popular destination for the rich and famous, and consequently also draws in the tourists.

Stop at the **Village Green Heritage Center** or the **Palm Springs Desert Museum** to explore Palm Springs' history.

Originally inhabited by the Cahuilla Indians, much of the city's land today is still owned by the tribe. The area was first discovered by Spanish explorers in 1774 and they named it Agua Caliente (Spanish for "hot water") due to its hot springs. In the 19th century Palm Springs served as a stagecoach and a Southern Pacific railroad stop.

Moorten's Botanical Garden, established more than 50 years ago by cactus buffs Patricia and Chester "Cactus Slim" Moorten, will amaze you with its array of desert vegetation in its relatively small nature park.

For a lesson on palm trees, head to **Palm Canyon**, four miles south in the **Agua Caliente Indian Reservation**. In this oasis, approximately 3,000 native fan palm trees line riverbeds surrounded by lush undergrowth. California palms here are estimated to be 2,000 years old and provide ideal shade for a picnic. Desert animals roam within their own natural and unspoilt ecosystem at the 1,200 acre **Living Desert Reserve** in Palm Desert .

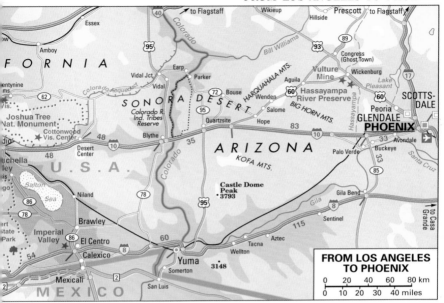

**FROM LOS ANGELES
TO PHOENIX**

| 0 | 20 | 40 | 60 | 80 km |
| 0 | 10 | 20 | 30 | 40 miles |

A few miles west, the Palm Springs **Aerial Tramway** will elevate you from the canyon floor to an altitude of 8,516 feet over rugged mountain terrain to the edge of the **Mount San Jacinto State Wilderness Area**. Nearby, in **Desert Hot Springs**, is **Cabot's Old Indian Pueblo Museum**, an enormous imitation pueblo dwelling filled with Indian artifacts (partly closed for renovation).

Joshua Tree National Park

East of Palm Springs the breathtakingly dramatic scenery of **Joshua Tree National Park** stretches out before you: An 870 square mile natural treasure, it has, since 1994, been dedicated to the preservation of California's Mojave and Colorado Deserts.

In the 1920s and 30s, conservationists lobbied in defense of the desert flora that was rapidly disappearing, partly due to the fact that many specimens were simply ripped out of the ground and re-planted in private gardens. As a result of

the International Desert Conservation League, Joshua Tree National Monument was established in 1936 to halt cactus poaching. The park is named after the Joshua tree, a giant yucca with outstretched limbs that attains heights of more than 30 feet. The tree was given its name by the Utah Mormons, who upon sight of it were reminded of Joshua the prophet: "Thou shalt follow the way pointed for thee by the trees." The park has virtual forests of Joshua trees.

The northern entrance to the park is reached via Highway 62, with the **Oasis Visitor Center**; the southern entrance is reached via I-10 and **Cottonwood**. Both entrances lead to the **Wonderland of Rocks**, with Ryan Mountain, Keys View and the Lost Horse Gold Mine. (A word of caution: without water and suitable clothing, the hot days and cold nights may prove intolerable – and dangerous.)

Just a few miles before the Arizona border, I-10 leads you into the town of **Blythe**, named after Thomas Blythe, the irrigation engineer and entrepreneur who

33

founded this community in the 1870s. Sights are few here, but those interested in canoeing may like to chance the nearby Colorado river.

ARIZONA DESERTS

Arizona has seen pre-historic Indian cultures, Spanish conquerors, Mexican rulers and American pioneers of the wild west. Long before Columbus discovered the "New World", the Anasazi, Hohokam and Mogollon tribes all lived here before mysteriously abandoning the region between 1100 and the arrival of the Spanish *conquistadors* in the 1500s. In the year 1540, Francisco Vasquez de Coronado led an expedition to the American Southwest in a desperate and futile quest for gold. Ore was scarce and Spain settled for native souls instead. By the late 1600s, missionaries had established set-

Above: Spanish history – San Xavier Mission near Tucson. Right: Saguaro National Monument (130 miles southeast of Phoenix).

tlements everywhere, under the Spanish flag.

When Mexico won independence from Spain in 1821, the Arizona region became part of Mexico. As its northern outpost, Arizona sat too far from Mexico City, and American traders, trappers, prospectors and settlers soon began "knocking on the door" in their relentless drive westward. The Apache, Papago and Pima Indians later inhabited these lands during an era marked by seemingly endless conflict between natives and settlers.

After the Gold Rush of 1849, Arizona served as a key trading post on the route to California. Statehood was not immediate for Arizona because federal authorities suspected that its inhabitants had sympathized with the Confederates during the Civil War. Finally, in 1912, Arizona became the 48th state of the Union. Composed largely of endless beige desert, it is the sixth largest state in the country, measuring 335 miles wide and 390 miles long.

After the California Gold Rush started

to subside, large numbers of settlers flocked to Arizona in their quest for gold and other precious metals. Farms and ranches prospered with improved irrigation methods, by digging channels. Later, rich copper deposits were discovered, bringing increased revenues and the nickname "The Copper State."

These frontier days ended with the building of the railroads, which, in the 1870s and 80s also pierced the Arizona border. Since then, this "capital of the Sun Belt" has continuously attracted residents and since 1940 the state's population has more than tripled.

Quartzsite

Just off I-10 is the town of **Quartzsite**. Named in 1896, this "site of quartz" and other rocks and minerals is a rockhound's paradise. In winter, this otherwise sleepy town attracts about a million *snowbirds* (pensioners) who flock here to enjoy the pleasant temperatures.

A local oddity is the pyramid-shaped

monument to **Hadji Ali**, a Middle Eastern camel driver employed by the U.S. Army in 1856 to test these "ships of the desert" for use in travel and communication across the American Southwest. In the end, the pony prevailed and the experiment was abandoned during the Civil War. "Hi Jolly" became a prospector.

North of Quartzsite the **Colorado River Indian Tribes Museum and Library** exhibits artifacts from prehistoric Indian cultures. The museum is part of the Indian reservation of the same name. The dirt road (Rte. 72) leading there from **Bouse** is an adventure in itself. Once you arrive, the well-preserved mines (which were abandoned in 1924) reward and make worthwhile your journey.

Mining and Ranching at Wickenburg

Wickenburg, an Old West mining town and modern dude ranch resort on the Hassayampa River northeast of Quartzsite, on US Hwy. 60, is named

35

after Prussian prospector, Henry Wickenburg, who in 1863 noticed shiny nuggets whilst hunting vulture.

The **Vulture Mine** turned out to be Arizona's richest in gold; part of a $30 million boom. Eighty mines once operated here, and Wickenburg was Arizona's third largest city. Today, mining for gold and other minerals here – celebrated each February in *Gold Rush Days* – is a popular activity. Nowadays, activities including horseback riding and cowboy vacations on real *dude ranches*, are simply a must for any proper Arizona vacation.

Historic buildings from the 1800s line **Frontier Street** in town. Don't miss the grim **Jail Tree**, where prisoners were kept chained during the 27 year long building of the town's first jail! The **Little Red Schoolhouse** is a typical example of the single-roomed schools used during the era of the "wild west".

Above: The Gila woodpecker feeds on cactus fruit.

The **Desert Caballeros Western Museum** depicts, amongst other things, street scenes of early Wickenburg in days gone by. Outside Wickenburg is the Vulture Mine, with veins of gold and silver, and the ghost town of **Vulture City**. Sturdy shoes are required to take the self-guided tour and to pan for gold. But do not drink from the Hassayampa River – Apache for "river that runs upside down" - legend has it that anyone who drinks from this river will never again tell the truth!

The **Hassayampa River Preserve** is situated three miles south of Wickenburg. The river banks of this wildlife sanctuary are flanked by nature trails through the very rare North American cottonwood forest that is home to numerous species of birds.

Central Arizona and Phoenix

From the Old West flavor of Wickenburg, Route 60 leads south to the **Valley of the Sun**, where the deserts are full of cacti – including the giant saguaro – and rugged mountains seem inviting for some hiking and camping. Further east, the tranquil desert peace suddenly yields to the big-city bustle of **Phoenix**, which seems nowadays to consist mainly of luxurious world-class vacation resorts and retirement communities.

Phoenix grew from the irrigation networks built by the ancestors of the current Pima Indians, a waterway that stretched across more than 300 miles drawing water from the Salt River into the desert. Here, water was as precious as gold and silver - at least until the American pioneers arrived. When the gold rush subsided, miners eventually turned to agriculture using the canal system to supply their farms, and this gave Phoenix its name. An early pioneer predicted that a great new city would rise from the settlement just as the mythical phoenix bird rose from its own ashes. Today, Phoenix has a population of more than 1.3 million.

LOS ANGELES
Area code 213
Accommodation
LUXURY: **Checkers Hotel**, 535 S. Grand Ave., L.A., Tel: 624-0000. *MODERATE:* **Beverly House Hotel**, 140 S. Lasky Dr., Beverly Hills, Tel: (310) 271-2145. *BUDGET:* **Sunset Dunes Motel**, 5625 Sunset Blvd., Hollywood, Tel: 467-5171.
Restaurants
EXPENSIVE: **Bel-Air Dining Room**, 701 Stone Canyon Rd., Bel Air, Tel: (310) 472-1211. Californian cuisine. *MODERATE:* **Campanile**, 624 S La Brea Ave., L. A., Tel: (323) 938-1447. Italian-Californian cuisine.
Sights and Museums
Disneyland, 26 miles south of L. A., Harbor Blvd., Anaheim, Tel: (714) 781-4000. **Griffith Park**, 4730 Crystal Springs Dr., L. A., 90027, Tel: (323) 665-5188. **J. Paul Getty Museum**, 17985 Pacific Coast Hwy., Malibu (closed until 2001). Alternative: **The Getty Center**, 1200 Getty Center Dr., L.A.; Highway 405, then exit at Getty Center Dr., Tel: (310) 440-7300. Open Tue-Wed 10 am-7 pm, Thurs-Fri 11 am-9 pm, Sat-Sun 10 am-6 pm, closed on Mondays. **L.A. County Museum of Art**, 5909 Wilshire Blvd., Tel: (323) 857-6000. **Mann's Chinese Theater**, 6925 Hollywood Blvd., Tel: (323) 464-8186. **The Museum of Tolerance**, 9760 W Pico Blvd., Tel: (310) 553-8403. **Universal Studios Hollywood**, Universal City, 100 Universal Dr., Tel: (818) 622-2801.
Tourist Information
Downtown L.A. Visitor Information Center, 685 Figueroa St., L.A. 90017, Tel: (213) 689-8822.

SAN DIEGO AND PALM SPRINGS
Area code 619 (San Diego) / 760 (Palm Springs)
Accommodation
LUXURY: **Hotel del Coronado**, 1500 Orange Ave., Coronado Island, Tel: (619) 435-6611. Victorian Grand Hotel, where many movie greats have stayed. *MODERATE:* **Dana Inn & Marina**, 1710 W Mission Bay Drive, San Diego, Tel: 222-6640. Welcomes families, close to Sea World, own pool. **Palm Canyon Resort**, 221 Palm Canyon Dr., Borrego Springs, Tel. (760) 767-5341. Beautifully situated amidst abundant nature, with RV park.
Restaurants
EXPENSIVE: **Chameleon Cafe**, 1301 Orange Ave., San Diego, Tel. 437-6677. Sophisticated creations with a distinctly Asian flair, great bar with large choice of tequila and vodka as well as a patio for smokers.
Sights and Museums
Balboa Park, Park Blvd., San Diego, Tel: 239-0512 with **San Diego Zoo**, Tel: 234-3153, **San Diego Museum of Art**, Tel: 232-7931, **Museum of Man**, Tel. 239-2002, **Natural History Museum**, Tel. 232-2821. **Birch Aquarium**, 2300 Expedition Way, La Jolla, Tel. 858-534FISH. **Cabot's Old Indian Pueblo Museum**, 67616 East Desert View, Desert Hot Springs, Tel: (760) 329-7610. **Cabrillo N. M.**, Point Loma, Tel: (619) 557-5450. **Indian Lore Monument**, 15 miles north of Blythe, US 95. **Joshua Tree N. P.**, 74485 National Park Dr., Twentynine Palms 92277, Tel: (760) 367-5500. **Living Desert Reserve**, by Palm Desert. **McCallum Adobe**, 221 South Palm Canyon Dr., Palm Springs. **Mission San Diego de Alcala**, 10818 San Diego Mission Rd., Tel: 281-8449. **Moorten's Botanical Garden**, 1701 S Palm Canyon Dr., Palm Springs, Tel: 327-6555. **Oasis Waterpark**, 5 miles south of I-10, by 1500 Gene Autry Trail, Tel: (760) 325-7873. **Palm Canyon**, 6.5 miles south of Palm Springs at S Palm Canyon Dr. **Palm Springs Aerial Tramway**, 2 miles north of Palm Springs, on CA 111, Tel: 325-1391. **Palm Springs Desert Museum**, 101 Museum Dr., Palm Springs, Tel: 325-7186. **Sea World**, 1720 South Shores Road, Mission Bay, Tel: (619) 226-3901. **Village Green Heritage Center** with **Cornelia White House**, 221 South Palm Canyon Dr., Palm Springs, Tel: 323-8297. **Del Mar Fair** (fair), mid-June to beginning of July.
Tourist Information
International Information Center, Horton Plaza, 1st Ave./F Street, San Diego, Tel: 236-1212, http://www.sandiego.org **C & V Office Palm Springs**, 69930 CA 111, Suite 201, Rancho Mirage, 92270, Tel: 770-9000.

QUARTZSITE AND WICKENBURG
Area code 520
Accommodation
CAMPING: **Western Hills RV Park**, Tel: 684-5271. *GUEST RANCH:* **Flying E Ranch**, Box EEE, Wickenburg, AZ 85358, Tel: 684-2690. Family-run Dude and Cattle Ranch, ideal for wild west vacations. **Rancho de los Caballeros** (October-May), Box 1148, Wickenburg, AZ 85358, Tel: 684-5484. Luxurious Dude Ranch with tennis courts, pool and a great golf course.
Sights and Museums
Colorado River Indian Tribes Museum and Library, southwest of Parker on 2nd Ave./Mohave Rd., Tel: 669-9211. **The Desert Caballeros Western Museum**, 20 North Frontier St., Wickenburg, Tel: 684-2272. **Hassayampa River Preserve**, 3 miles south of Wickenburg, on US 60, close to MP 114, Tel: 684-2772.
Tourist Information
Quarzsite Chamber of Commerce, Tel: 927-5600. **Wickenburg Visitor Center** at Santa Fe Depot, 216 N Frontier St., Tel: 684-5479.

FROM PHOENIX TO SANTA FE

PHOENIX
TOUR OF SOUTHERN ARIZONA
INDIAN COUNTRY
NEW MEXICO
SANTA FE

Cowboys and Indians don't just exist in the movies, and the sights along this route prove it. Although this 500 mile, ten day journey spotlights Hollywood-style sets fit for the movies - bohemian New Age communes, ancient Anasazi Indian cliff dwellings, luxury resorts and the shimmering space age greenhouses of Biosphere 2 – these scenes are just backdrops for the real Great Southwest.

Although historically distinct, the shared contemporary culture of Arizona and New Mexico has produced a near craze in the U.S. since the late 1980s. In everything from architecture to art, furniture to food, the "Southwest style" is hot – as hot as the chili peppers so popular in the local cuisine. Visitors come from far and wide to see Santa Fe's adobe houses and shops, and to check out the resorts and golf courses of Phoenix.

PHOENIX – THE DESERT CITY

Situated in the famed Valley of the Sun, the desert city of **Phoenix** is Arizona's state capital and the modern center of the Southwest. This booming metropolis offers a thriving downtown business center, burgeoning retirement com-

Left: Indian powwow at Tusuque Pueblo, New Mexico.

munities, and more than 300 days of sunshine per year. Phoenix and the adjacent city of Scottsdale abound in luxury hotels and outdoor recreational activities – from golf to hot air ballooning.

The history of the Wild West comes to life in Phoenix museums. The **Arizona Mining and Mineral Museum** traces the history of gold and silver mining by American pioneers. Samples of copper and precious stones, from azurite to turquoise, are displayed. Rock and mineral shows in the area draw thousands from all across the country.

The **Heard Museum** offers perhaps the most impressive and expertly displayed Southwestern Indian collection anywhere, with prehistoric artifacts to contemporary crafts. The *kachina* collection (the sacred dolls of the Hopi and Zuni tribes) fills an entire room.

The frontier era comes to life at the **Pioneer Arizona Living History Museum**, a recreated village featuring costumed actors portraying the lifestyles of early pioneers. The **Desert Botanical Garden** will lead you into the thorny world of desert flora, and the nearby mountains of **Camelback** and **Squaw Peak** reward hikers with sweeping panoramic views of the city - only to be surpassed, of course, by a breathtaking flight in a hot air balloon.

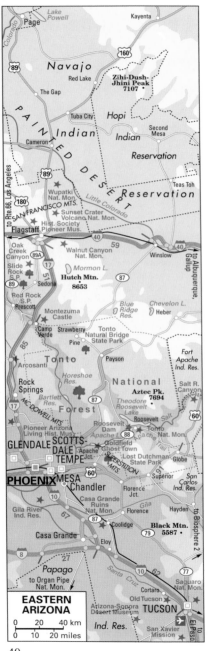

EASTERN
ARIZONA

| 0 | 20 | 40 km |
| 0 | 10 | 20 miles |

TOUR OF SOUTHERN ARIZONA

Taliesin West is Frank Lloyd Wright's architectural settlement in Scottsdale, inviting students to study architecture in the middle of the **Sonora Desert**. They live in simple tents at the foot of the McDowell Mountains, as they learn to "grow" buildings from the landscape.

The **Apache Trail**, a winding passageway through the **Superstition Mountains** that was once a warpath for the Apaches, offers hair-raising rides and breathtaking scenery. From Phoenix, head east to **Apache Junction**, then head onto Route 88, where the 44 mile Apache Trail begins. Alternatively, you can take a round trip - the 200 mile long **Apache Trail Loop** - from Roosevelt.

North of Apache Junction, **Goldfield Ghost Town** offers a recreated underground mine tour and a chance to pan for gold. Nearby, the mysterious **Lost Dutchman State Park** is named after the miner Jacob Waltz, who was actually a German (the word *Deutsch* – or German – is often equated with *Dutch* in America). The location of his gold mine was never discovered, though many adventurers who tried to follow Waltz to his claim were later found dead.

Two miles north of here, look out for the prospectors' landmark known as **Weaver's Needle**, a 4,553 foot jagged pinnacle, which once provided miners with a point of orientation.

For an adventure in nature, enjoy a hike among the desert vegetation, wildflowers and high pines of the 159,700 acre **Superstition Wilderness** south of the Apache Trail. Yet another highlight on this route is the highest masonry dam in the world, **Roosevelt Dam** (280 feet). About 60 miles upstream, on **Salt River**, rafting and kayaking excursions twist through the Salt River Canyon – a thrilling outdoor experience. Guided trips are offered by several tour companies.

Near Roosevelt, **Tonto National Monument** has two well-preserved cliff dwellings of prehistoric Salado (Spanish for "salted") Indians, which can be viewed. They were talented craftspeople, as can be seen from their polychrome pottery and intricate cotton weaving, and they lived here in the early 1300s.

The small town of **Globe**, located near the **San Carlos Indian Reservation**, was part of Apache land until a 14 mile long silver vein was discovered here. Land near this claim was taken from the Indians, who relentlessly raided the settlement until the famous Apache chief Geronimo signed a peace treaty with the white man in 1886.

The silver ran out, but copper was abundant and the **Old Dominion Mine** became one of the most important in the country. The **Gila County Historical Museum** contains a reproduction of a section of a mine, period rooms, and arti-

Above: Artificial ecosystem under glass – Biosphere 2.

facts from the **Besh-Ba-Gowah Ruins** of the Salado Indians.

Farther south, not far from Route 77, stands the much discussed project known as **Biosphere 2**, an artificial, self-contained ecosystem; a miniature earth (31.5 acres) under glass, which is open to visitors.

Route 77 takes you further along to the city of Tucson, where the movie set Western town of **Old Tucson** draws in visitors with action packed stunt shows. From Tucson, Arizona's prettiest cactus parks can be visited to the west and east of the city; especially recommended are **Saguaro N.P.** and **Organ Pipe National Monument**. The **Kartchner Caverns** are a new tour attraction about 28 miles south of Tucson (for bookings phone (520) 586-CAVE). The zoo in the **Arizona-Sonora Desert Museum** is also well worth seeing.

From Tucson, the I-10 takes you to the town of **Casa Grande**. Twenty miles from here, just north of Coolidge, the **Casa Grande Ruins National Monu-**

ment is a reminder of the region's past civilizations. The four storey Casa Grande (Spanish for "Big House") is the largest building ever constructed by the Hohokam Indians and may have been used for astronomical observations. It was built around 1320, and consists of walls up to four and a half feet thick made of kalich, a hard subsoil of calcium carbonate. Over 600 floor and roof beams support the interior structure.

In February, **O'Odham Tash-Casa Grande's Indian Days** provide rodeos, parades and ceremonial dances for visitors. The **Gila River Arts and Crafts Center** on the Gila River Reservation has a great gift shop with exhibits and crafts from the Pima, Hopi, Navajo and Maricopa Indian tribes. The I-10 north brings you back to Phoenix.

North of Phoenix

Nature beckons to the east and west of Interstate 17 northbound, from cacti to cool forests. For architecture fans, another intriguing site is **Arcosanti** (60 miles north of Phoenix off I-17, exit 262), the bizarre brainchild of Italian-born Paolo Soleri, who came to Arizona to study architecture with Frank Lloyd Wright. This urban prototype, attempting to unify architecture and ecology, was dubbed "arcology." Arcosanti is home to some 5,000 people.

Further along, the I-17 runs through the Verde Valley. From **Camp Verde**, a road runs up to **Montezuma Castle**, with its rock apartments built into the cliffs. The six lakes and wilderness areas of the **Tonto National Forest** offer relaxation in the midst of this barren wilderness.

Back in 1881 it was the glitter of gold that attracted visitors to **Payson** – a town southeast of Camp Verde on Route 87.

Right: Skiing on the San Francisco Peaks near Flagstaff.

Sites around Payson include Arizona's oldest schoolhouse in **Strawberry**, the **Payson Zoo**, home to more than 60 retired four-legged movie stars, Western writer **Zane Grey's Lodge** and **Tonto Natural Bridge State Park**, the world's largest natural travertine bridge.

New Age Life in Sedona

One of the most scenic routes in the entire U.S.: Route 89A, runs west of and parallel to Interstate 17. Along this road lies the bohemian town of **Sedona**. This is a social and cultural mecca in the heart of "red rock country" and has developed into a popular New Age resort. Artists and tourists alike flock to **Bell Rock** and **Airport Mesa**, which are believed to be locations of strong psychic energy. The red rocks surrounding Sedona do indeed create a mystical and supernatural atmosphere – even if you're only hiking in **Red Rock State Park**, southwest of Sedona, driving along **Oak Creek Canyon** or sliding through a natural water chute in **Slide Rock State Park**. Major annual events include **Jazz on the Rocks** in late September and **Fiesta del Tlaquepaque**, a Mexican carnival in October.

Traveling westward from Sedona on Route 89A, you can take a trip through Oak Creek Canyon and over Mingus Mountain, passing the cities of Prescott and Wickenburg on your way back to Phoenix.

Flagstaff and the Legend of Route 66

The name **Flagstaff** dates back to July 4, 1876, America's centennial, when patriots stripped the branches from a tall pine tree and flew the U.S. banner from it. Only the historic buildings downtown serve to remind visitors of the frontier days in this now sprawling city of service stations, chain motels and restaurants.

Flagstaff nestles at the base of the **San Francisco Peaks**, Arizona's highest

mountains and a great base for hiking, camping, biking, skiing or just photographing and picnicking. Northwest of Flagstaff, Native American and American West history and artifacts can be explored at the **Museum of Northern Arizona**, an exhibition of life on the Colorado Plateau and Native American arts and crafts. The planet Pluto was discovered at the nearby **Lowell Observatory**, in 1930. The guided tours as well as night-time observations of the universe draw in the stargazers.

Whatever you do, don't miss a ride along **Route 66** (see page 218). Opened in 1926, this legendary route was the "Main Street of America," passing through every town on the way west from Chicago, Illinois, across 2,400 miles to Santa Monica, California. Sixty years later, Route 66 was too jammed, and interstate highways were built to funnel traffic away, bypassing the "mom and pop" motels, classic American diners and local color. Songsmith Bobby Troup immortalized this stretch of hardtop with

the famous line: "Get your kicks on Route 66." Look for historical markers along the original road. The section from Seligman to Kingman is worth recommending for the **Grand Canyon Caverns**, a 300 million year old network of caves.

Route 66 is an ideal place to dress *Southwestern style* in a pair of cowboy boots and a duster coat, or to visit a local curio shop or a Native American arts and crafts fair to find that perfect bolo tie or those silver and turquoise earrings. *Truck stops* provide the perfect local color for digging into tortilla chips and salsa, while corner bars are the place to enjoy a tequila with salt and lemon to the tune of authentic country tunes.

Canyons and Volcano Craters

In **Walnut Canyon National Monument**, 7.5 miles east of Flagstaff off I-40, there are about 300 small **cliff dwellings** of the prehistoric Sinagua (Spanish for "without water"), believed to be ances-

tors of the Hopi. The ledges of sandstone walls in this 400 foot deep canyon have protected the well-preserved ruins from erosion, which date to the 1100s. From the canyon rim, a steep trail descends past 25 cliff dwellings.

Fifteen miles north of Flagstaff on US 89 is **Sunset Crater Volcano National Monument** – the youngest of more than 400 dormant volcanoes in the San Francisco Mountains. Nearby, **Wupatki National Monument** features well-preserved Sinagua and Anasazi Indian ruins – Arizona's largest above-ground ruins. The Sinagua people lived here until Sunset erupted in A.D. 1064 and forced them to evacuate. The Wupatki Visitor Center has exhibits about this tribe and is a good place to pick up a brochure or a book. Rangers give archeological tours, but only a few of the 2,500 prehistoric sites within the 35,693 acres of this monument are open to the public: **Wupatki** (Hopi for "Tall House") with a restored ball court similar to Mayan ruins, **Wukoki** (Hopi for "Wide House"), **Citadel** and **Lomaki** (Hopi for "Beautiful House"). There are also overnight ranger-led backpack trips in April and October to **Crack-in-Rock Ruins**.

Further north, **Cameron Visitor Center** has information about the Navajo Indian Reservation. North and east of Cameron are the rainbow-hued hills of the **Painted Desert**, a vast landscape painting of the earth's colors. Dinosaur tracks and sandstone buttes (called Elephant's Feet) formed by erosion spread out near **Tuba City**.

INDIAN COUNTRY

Driving through Arizona and New Mexico means traveling Indian Country. But throughout history, the rights of Native Americans, the Southwest's original inhabitants, have been seriously impinged upon. Land conflicts led to a vir-

Above: A Navajo Indian woman sells necklaces she has strung herself. Right: Spider Rock in Canyon de Chelly.

tual genocide as the Pima, Hopi, Navajo and Apache revolted against Spanish, Mexican and finally American rule. Army forts were built to protect settlers and conduct an undeclared war of attrition against the Native Americans. Eventually outnumbered, they were forced to sign treaties consigning them to live on reservations.

Northeast Arizona is the heartland of Indian Country, and its parched desert hills, buttes and mesas are sacred to the Navajo, Hopi and Zuni tribes.

Living in harmony with nature is the basis of Native American culture. Strong religious beliefs in animistic spirits guide ritualized ceremonies for rain and harvests. Today, however, village elders worry about the survival of ceremonial knowledge as the younger generation, increasingly disinterested, moves off the reservation.

But one recent development is breathing new life into the void: gambling. Indian reservations are not subject to U.S. laws that ban gambling everywhere but in Nevada and Atlantic City. As a result, casinos now jingle on Indian reservations in 27 states. These casinos attract gamblers from miles around and are said to pull in an annual revenue estimated at nearly $4 billion.

In the **Pojoaque Pueblo** near Santa Fe, the unemployment level has dropped from 40 percent to zero in only a few years thanks to the influx of cash and the jobs created by the casinos.

Canyon de Chelly and Window Rock

Flagstaff is a starting point for canyon tourism and excursions into Navajo country. The sheer sandstone cliffs and more than 60 ruins make **Canyon de Chelly**, northeast of Flagstaff, with Spider Rock and White House Ruin, a detour not to be missed. Inhabited as early as 2,000 years ago, this magical

homeland of the Anasazi combines splendid natural beauty with tragic recent history.

In the late 1800s the canyon sheltered Indians against the bondage of white rule. From these cliffs, Christopher "Kit" Carson and 1,000 men forced 8,000 Navajo and other tribes to surrender and marched them on the infamous Long Walk to Fort Sumner, New Mexico (where they remained under guard for four years before being sent to the current reservation).

Named for the natural arch almost 50 feet wide in a nearby sandstone ridge, **Window Rock** is the Navajo tribal administration center. The world's largest American Indian fair is held here in September. The **Navajo Tribal Museum** in the Navajo Arts & Crafts Enterprise Building displays arts and crafts and historical exhibits.

Another interesting route leads to the ruins of an ancient Indian settlement in **Chaco Canyon** (Thoreau exit from Interstate 40), and further north to **Aztec National Monument**.

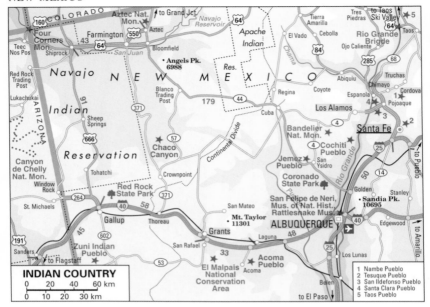

INDIAN COUNTRY
0   20   40   60 km
0   10   20   30 km

1 Nambe Pueblo
2 Tesuque Pueblo
3 San Ildefonso Pueblo
4 Santa Clara Pueblo
5 Taos Pueblo

NEW MEXICO

Crossing the border on I-40 into New Mexico, "The Land of Enchantment" as it is known in America, you may find the landscape of endless beige desert a little less than enchanting. A passing thunderstorm, however, can awaken New Mexico's magic. The innocuous looking white clouds approach over the plain and suddenly envelop you in blinding rain, thunder echoing off the canyons like the beating of an Indian drum. Then the clouds move on as they came, silence returns, and nothing seems to have happened at all.

In order to get a good feeling for the landscape hereabouts, you might pick up a novel by Tony Hillerman, a best-selling Navajo author who pens mysteries rich in Southwestern culture.

More of a modern-day trading post, **Gallup** attracts residents of the area, in-

cluding Navajo and Zuni Indians, who come here to shop. A picnic near the massive red sandstone buttes of **Red Rock State Park** provides a nice travel break. More than 50 tribes from the U.S., Canada and Mexico converge here for the **Intertribal Indian Ceremonial** which takes place every August. The **Navajo Nation Fair**, beginning the Wednesday after Labor Day (the first weekend in September), consists of five days of ceremonial dances, rodeos and an arts and crafts fair.

It's tempting to rush through western New Mexico on the Interstate as the anticipation mounts to reach much-lauded Santa Fe. But a more interesting route continues through Indian country on Route 53 via the **Zuni Indian Pueblo**, the largest of the state's 19 pueblos. The Zuni jewelry, pottery and carvings that can be purchased here make beautiful souvenirs. To the east, **El Malpais National Monument and National Conservation Area** spreads out over 376,000 acres of volcanic and sandstone canyons

Right: Embarrassed or curious? Indian children at Acoma Pueblo observe tourists.

hiding petroglyphs and inscriptions of prehistoric Indians, as well as of Spanish explorers.

Grants and Albuquerque

Don't blink while cruising along on the I-40 or you just might miss the north-south ridge of the **Continental Divide** (five miles from Thoreau).

Grants, a uranium mining town on the other side of the Continental Divide, is home to the **New Mexico Mining Museum**, with a unique display relating to uranium. **Acoma Pueblo**, the oldest continuously inhabited pueblo in North America, is 30 miles east of Grants.

At first glance, **Albuquerque** and Phoenix, which opened this chapter a few hundred miles ago, appear to have a lot in common. They are both valleys of desert urban sprawl shadowed by nearby mountains. The climate is hot, and curio shops and sand are everywhere. But the difference is acoustic: the language spoken most in Albuquerque is Spanish. New Mexico's Spanish colonial period lives on in Albuquerque's large Hispanic population. Visit the **Old Town Plaza** with its quaint adobe architecture to get a good idea of the city's Spanish influence. Around the plaza are souvenir shops, galleries and restaurants.

Other sites worth seeing include the massive **San Felipe de Neri** Spanish church on Old Town Plaza, the **New Mexico Museum of Natural History**, the **Indian Pueblo Cultural Center** and the **American International Rattlesnake Museum** – but only if you're feeling brave.

The big **Gathering of Nations** powow, with over 5,000 dancers, takes place in April, and the State Fair gets underway in September. Don't miss the Albuquerque **Hot Air Balloon Festival** if you happen to be here in October.

Traditional festivals, which are generally open to the public, are celebrated

throughout the year in the pueblos with colorful ceremonies and religious dances.

SANTA FE

Santa Fe is accessible via Interstate 25, passing **Coronado State Park**. Another possibility is a detour along the **Turquoise Trail**, east of Albuquerque on Route 14.

Settled more than 2,000 years ago and long the home of the Pueblo Indians, **Santa Fe** is still a Native American heartland, and the immensely popular "Santa Fe-style" adobe architecture recalls Pueblo Indian roots.

Although the Spanish conquistadors claimed the Santa Fe as the northernmost point of the Mexican empire, Santa Fe, unlike Albuquerque, has retained its Native American flavor.

After the San Pueblo Indians chased out the Spanish conquerors in 1680, Santa Fe served as a key trading post along the old east-west trading route - the **Santa Fe Trail**, until the "iron horse" –

the railroad – replaced the until then commonest form of transportation of stagecoach and covered wagon.

Over recent years, Santa Fe has become a tremendously popular place to visit, and the chic boutiques and galleries that have sprung up like mushrooms reflect the summer influx of well-heeled tourists. Still, there's a quaintness to the streets around **Santa Fe Plaza**, with historic sites, museums, boutiques, arts and crafts galleries, and restaurants housed in adobe buildings.

A focal point is the **Palace of the Governors**. This downtown landmark on the northeast side of the plaza is a grand reminder of Spanish presence. The Palace is the oldest public building in the United States and a past seat of government for all four flags that have flown over this city – those of Spain, Mexico, the Confederacy and the United States.

Above: Acoma is the oldest inhabited pueblo village in North America. Right: In a ceramics studio at Pueblo Ildefonso.

Santa Fe is an epicenter not only of Native American art, but increasingly for all American art. In fact, the city has earned a name as the third largest art market in the United States, after New York and Los Angeles. Proof of this are the galleries interspersed with the chic shops along **Canyon Road**, where you can view some of the abstract landscapes of a famous past resident, artist Georgia O'-Keeffe (1887 - 1986), to whom the **Georgia O'Keeffe Museum** was dedicated in 1997. In fact, all museums in this cultural haven are worth stopping into. The **Museum of International Folk Art** exhibits crafts from every corner of the world, while the **Wheelwright Museum of the American Indian** displays Native American art. Taking place in August, the *Santa Fe Indian Market* is the largest exhibition of Native American art in the entire Southwest.

Seven miles out of town is another cultural attraction, the **Santa Fe Opera**; in summer, thousands attend performances in this beautiful open-air theater. Santa

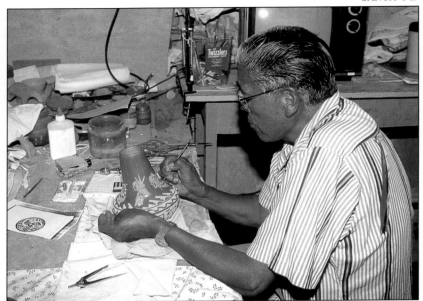

Fe has plenty of sports on offer, too, from summer *whitewater rafting* on the nearby Rio Grande to winter skiing in the **Santa Fe Ski Basin**.

Pueblos around Santa Fe

Southwestern architecture is not the only element of local culture to have spread throughout the country: the regional cuisine has also swept through North America. Some say the red chilis in New Mexico's spicy cuisine are reminiscent of the red New Mexican earth. Southwestern cuisine is characterized by spicy, smoky flavors – very different from either Tex-Mex or authentic Mexican cuisine. Some typical ingredients are blue corn, mild green chilis and smoked meats.

New Mexico is well known for its Pueblo Indians (believed to be descended from the Anasazi), including the Zuni, Acoma, Sandia, Taos and Jemez Indians. A pueblo is a self-contained, permanently settled Indian village.

In the canyons and along the Rio Grande to the north and south of Santa Fe are a number of Native American pueblos to visit, including **San Ildefonso Pueblo**, once the home of the famous potter Maria Martinez, whose works can be seen in many regional museums. At the **Santa Clara Pueblo**, the **Puye Cliff Dwellings** offer kiva sweat lodges and pit houses, considered the most spectacular in the area. Other interesting pueblos include **Tesuque**, **Jemez** and **Cochiti**.

The **Frijoles Canyon**, 45 miles northwest of Santa Fe on Route 4, carved into the volcanic ground of the Janey Mountains, conceals a number of remarkable Anasazi ruins.

The main attraction of the Frijoles Canyon is **Bandelier National Monument**, containing the remains of cliff dwellings and religious sites dating from the 13th to 16th centuries. The park was named after the Swiss-American ethnologist A.F. Bandelier (1840-1914), who studied and researched Pueblo Indians. It is well worth the drive and visit.

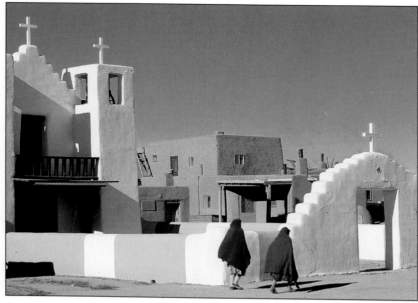

Also on Route 4 is the modern ghost town of **Los Alamos**, birthplace of the atomic bomb developed as part of the *Manhattan Project* by German-American scientist Robert Oppenheimer at **Los Alamos National Laboratories**. The first atom bomb was tested at the nearby **Trinity Site** on July 16, 1945. The huge mushroom cloud from the explosion could be seen from as far away as Santa Fe and El Paso.

The Road to Taos

The scenic road from Santa Fe to **Taos** passes **Nambe Pueblo**, where you can have a look at **Nambe Falls**, one of New Mexico's most spectacular waterfalls. In **Chimayo** is the **Santuario de Chimayo**, a church believed to be a site of miracle healing. The wall of the back room is covered with crutches and votive plaques, a testimonial to all those cured

Above: On the way to church (Taos Pueblo, New Mexico).

here. Generations of weavers once lived in Chimayo, and their crafts have lived on to this day. Woodcarving enthusiasts should head to **Cordova**. Nearby, Truchas is famous for being the site of the Robert Redford film *The Milagro Beanfield War* (*milagro* means "miracle"), based on the novel by New Mexican John Nichols.

Taos is best known for **Taos Pueblo**, one of the most beautiful and best preserved in all New Mexico. Taos has developed a reputation over the years as an artists' and spiritualists' enclave with a distinct New Age character, but it still has its fair share of exclusive shops and cozy, romantic restaurants located around the **Plaza**. The **Kit Carson Home and Museum** houses Hispanic and Indian art.

Ten miles northwest of Taos, the **Rio Grande Bridge**, 650 feet above the water, is one of the highest spans in the U.S. Northeast of the city, the **Taos Ski Valley** stretches out in the Sangre de Cristo Mountains.

PHOENIX AND SURROUNDINGS
SCOTTSDALE
Area code 602 (Phoenix) / 480 (Scottsdale)

Accommodation
LUXURY: **Marriott's Camelback**, 5402 E. Lincoln Dr., Scottsdale, Tel. 948-1700. It simply doesn't get more luxurious than this. Great location, golf, tennis, 3 pools, sauna and a superb spa.
BUDGET: **Holiday Inn**, 777 N Pinal Ave., Casa Grande, Tel. (520) 426-3500.

Sights and Museums
Arcosanti, Mayer, Tel. (520) 632-7135. **Arizona Mining and Mineral Museum**, 1502 W Washington St., Phoenix, Tel: 255-3791. **Biosphere 2 Center**, 120 miles south of Phoenix near Oracle, Tel: (520) 896-6200. **Casa Grande Ruins N. M.**, 1 mile north of Coolidge, Tel: (520) 723-3172. **Casa Grande Valley Historical Museum**, 110 W Florence Blvd., Casa Grande, Tel: (520) 836-2223. **Desert Botanical Garden**, 1201 N. Galvin Pkwy., Tel. (480) 941-1225. **Heard Museum**, 22 E Monte Vista Rd., Phoenix, Tel: 252-8840. **Karchner Caverns**, Tel. (520) 586-CAVE. **The Pioneer Arizona Living History Museum**, 3901 W Pioneer Rd., Phoenix, Tel: (623) 465-1052. **Pueblo Grande Museum**, 4619 E Washington St., Phoenix, Tel: 495-0900. **Rawhide 1880s Western Town**, 23023 N Scottsdale Rd., Scottsdale, Tel: 563-1880. Western town with live events. **Taliesin West**, northeast of Scottsdale, Tel: (480) 860-2700.

Tourist Information
Phoenix & Valley of the Sun, C & V Bureau, One Arizona Center, 400 East Van Buren, Suite 600, Phoenix, Tel: 254-6500, http://www.accessarizona.com/partners/phoenixcvb/ **Native American Tourism Center**, 4130 N Goldwater Blvd., Scottsdale, Tel: 945-0771.

SOUTHERN ARIZONA
PHOENIX AREA
Area code 520

Accommodation
MODERATE: **Ramada Limited**, 1699 E. Ash St., Globe, Tel. 425-5741. Good motel with 80 rooms and 2 suites for up to 6 guests. **Ghost Ranch Lodge**, 801 W. Miracle Mile, Tucson, Tel. 791-7565, good Best Western Motor Inn.
CAMPING: Along the Apache Trail Loop, Info: **Tonto Basin Ranger District** office in Roosevelt (at Roosevelt Lake Marina, Tel: 467-2236).

Sights and Museums
Arizona-Sonora-Desert Museum (Zoo), 2021 N. Kinney Rd., Tucson, Tel. 883-2702. **Goldfield Ghost Town** Tel: (480) 983-0333. **Lost Dutchman**

State Park, via AZ 88, 4 miles north of Apache Junction, Tel: 982-4485. **Superstition Wilderness**. **Tonto N. M.**, 5 miles beyond Roosevelt, Tel: 467-2241. **Montezuma Castle N. M.**, P.O. Box 219, Camp Verde, AZ 86322, Tel: 567-3322. **Saguaro N.P.**, 3693 S. Old Spanish Trail, Tel: 733-5158. **Old Tucson Studios**, 201 S. Kinney Rd., Tel: (520) 883-0100.

Sports and Recreation
For those interested in the kayaking and whitewater rafting facilities available on Salt River, contact: **Desert Voyages**, Box 9053, Scottsdale, AZ 85252, Tel: (480) 998-7238.

Tourist Information
Payson Chamber of Commerce, 100 W Main St., Payson, Tel: 474-4515.

SEDONA, FLAGSTAFF, GALLUP, INDIAN COUNTRY AND SANTA FE

Accommodation
LUXURY: **Bishop's Lodge**, Box 2367, Bishop's Lodge Rd., 3 miles north of Plaza, Santa Fe, Tel: (505) 983-6377, guest ranch.
MODERATE: **St. Francis**, 210 Don Gaspar Ave., Santa Fe, Tel: (505) 983-5700, Res.: 1-800-666-5700.
BUDGET: **Arizona Mountain Inn**, 685 Lake Mary Rd., Flagstaff, Tel: (602) 774-8959. **Best Western**, 3009 W US 66, Gallup, Tel: (505) 722-2221. **Canyon Villa B&B**, 125 Canyon Circle Dr., Sedona, Tel: (602) 284-1226. **Stage Coach**, 3360 Cerillos Rd., Santa Fe, Tel: (505) 471-0707.

Sights and Museums
El Morro N. M., 30 miles east of Zuni, Tel: (602) 783-4226. **Georgia O'Keeffe Museum**, 217 Johnson St., Santa Fe, Tel. (505) 995-0785. **Lowell Observatory**, 1400 W. Mars Hill Rd., Tel: (520) 774-2096. **Museum of Northern Arizona**, 3101 N. Fort Valley Rd., Tel. (520) 774-5213. **New Mexico Mining Museum**, 100 North Iron St., Grants, Tel: (505) 287-4802. **Sunset Crater Volcano N. M.**, Tel: (520) 526-0502. **Walnut Canyon N. M.**, 7.5 miles east of Flagstaff, Tel: (520) 526-3367. **Wheelwright Museum of the American Indian**, 704 Camino Lejo, Santa Fe, Tel: (505) 982-4636. **Wupatki N. M.**, 35 miles northeast of Flagstaff, via US 89, Tel: (520) 679-2365. **Zuni Pueblo**, 40 miles south of Gallup, Tel: (505) 782-4481.

Tourist Information
Flagstaff Chamber of Commerce/Visitor Center, 101 W Santa Fe Ave., Flagstaff, Tel: (602) 774-9541. **Gallup C & V Bureau**, 701 E Montoya Blvd., Gallup, Tel: (505) 863-3841. **Santa Fe C & V Bureau**, PO Box 909, Tel: (505) 984-6760, 1-800-777-2489. **Sedona-Oak Creek Canyon Chamber of Commerce**, Tel: (602) 282-7722.

FROM SANTA FE TO SAN ANTONIO

FROM SANTA FE
TO EL PASO
WEST TEXAS
TEXAS HILL COUNTRY
AUSTIN
SAN ANTONIO

Texas is the second largest state in the U.S.A. after Alaska, and everything, without exception, about this state is big. Big men wear big boots and big hats, they drive big trucks and stretched cars, eat big steaks, and talk about their big money earned from big ranches or oilfields.

Drivers coming from the midwest cannot truly understand the meaning of the word "big" until they are introduced to the "big distances" they will experience in Texas. Attuning yourself to the size, flatness, emptiness and light of the plains of West Texas is an important part of "seeing" this country. Some of the terrain here seems like phenomena from another geological age. As I-10 moves eastward through Texas, the landscape gradually gives way to the rolling green rises of Texas Hill Country. Here, you'll find the real heart of Texas: Austin, the state capital, and historic San Antonio, which manages to blend an Old Mexican flavor into its vital, contemporary atmosphere. From Santa Fe to San Antonio the drive is around 1,000 miles, which can be managed in about a week.

Previous pages: Rodeo – a rough man's sport; the bulls testicles are squeezed to make them behave wildly. Left: Guadalupe Mountains National Park.

FROM SANTA FE TO EL PASO

One Roswell couple used to amuse themselves on the drive home from Santa Fe by counting the trees along the way: On one trip, they arrived at a grand total of fifteen. Route 285 is a straight, bleak, desolate road. A main source of revenue for the deserted looking little towns of Encino and Vaughn are speeding tickets issued to passing drivers.

At **Vaughn**, Highway 54 runs down through Carrizozo into **Lincoln National Forest**, and the landscape rises from the plain into cool mountain air among the trees. Route 380 leads off into the **Capitan Mountains**, where there's good skiing at the **Ski Apache Resort**. This resort, as well as the race track at **Ruidoso Downs**, is run by the Native Americans of the Mescalero Apache Reservation. Further along 380 is **Lincoln**, once home to the legendary *Billy the Kid*.

Route 380 continues toward **Roswell**, a sprawling town put on the map by two space-related events: the early experiments of rocket pioneer Robert Goddard, and the "Roswell Incident" sighting of a UFO, both in the 1940s. Roswell has two small **UFO museums**, and Goddard's laboratories are displayed at its **Museum and Art Center**. The **Bitter Lake National Wildlife Refuge**, northeast of

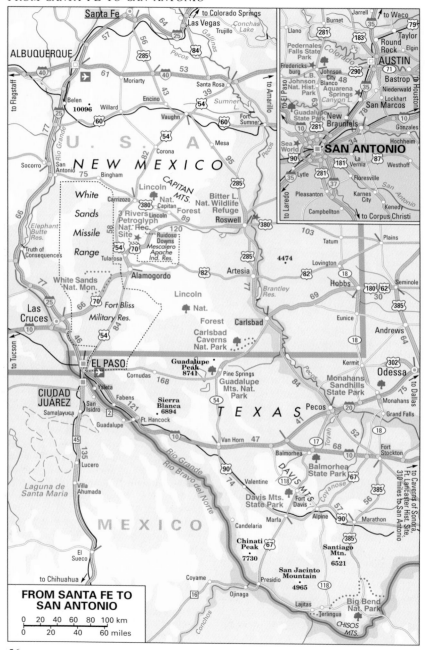

**FROM SANTA FE TO
SAN ANTONIO**

0 20 40 60 80 100 km

0   20   40   60 miles

town, is a stop on the migratory route of many species of birds: pelicans and Canadian geese are frequent guests to this region.

Farther south, in **Carlsbad**, the three mile long underground formations of **Carlsbad Caverns National Park** draw thousands of visitors each year. Huge stalagmites and stalactites thrust upward or hang ponderously from the ceiling, encrusted with drops of colored rock. A further highlight is the nocturnal activity hundreds of thousands of bats. In contrast, **Legoland California** has everything the (child's) heart could desire.

If, rather than detouring through Carlsbad, you elect to stay on Route 54 towards El Paso, you'll pass the **Three Rivers Petroglyph Site** before arriving at **White Sands National Monument**. The white gypsum sand dunes resemble a moonscape – as if dropped down randomly in the New Mexico plains, and can be explored in a 16 mile round trip. They're located in the midst of the weapons-testing grounds of **White Sands Missile Range**.

WEST TEXAS

In El Paso it is said "The most interesting thing about El Paso is Ciudad Juarez". This refers to its "twin" city across the border. In some ways, **Ciudad Juarez** and **El Paso** function as one city, separated only by the Rio Grande. Juarez is one of Mexico's main cities, and El Paso depends on it in no small measure for trade. For visitors, Juarez offers cheap goods in bargain shops, cheap drinks in its bars, racing at Juarez Track, Sunday afternoon bullfights, and an atmosphere more colorful and earthy than that available north of the border. Souvenir hunters should browse through FON-ART, a government sponsored market for

Above: Everything seems bigger in Texas – even the hats.

native artists which presents traditional art from all over Mexico.

Spanish missionaries were among the first settlers here. In Juarez, there's a 17th century mission next to the **Avenida Juarez cathedral**, while **San Isidro**, south of El Paso on the Rio Grande, is said to be the oldest mission in the entire United States. Missionaries came here to convert the original residents, the Tigua Indians, who claim that their reservation at **Ysleta** (open to tourists) is the oldest Indian community in the U.S. (although the Zuni in Arizona would dispute this).

The **Rio Grande**, called Rio Bravo by the Mexicans, used to frequently burst its banks. Today, it has been brought under control with concrete barriers. This was necessary for political reasons: after a flood, the river often changed its course, thereby changing the border between Mexico and the U.S. Running through the river is the fence known as the "Tortilla Curtain," erected to keep Mexicans from crossing illegally into America, and so called because people predicted that

the Mexicans would eat it up. Illegal immigrants are known as "wetbacks" (indicating that their backs are still wet from swimming the river), and there are plenty of them. Border patrols work to turn back the hordes, some of whom are kept overnight in border detention facilities or sanctuary houses before being returned.

Desert Mountains

From El Paso ("the pass" in the mountains), I-10 ie the only pass that runs through the mountains. It runs beside the Rio Grande before turning east to cut across the state. This area is one of the most deserted in Texas, sparsely dotted with tiny communities and ghost towns. Not much has changed here since early Spanish explorers dubbed it *despoblado*, "unpopulated place." Settlers tended to stay away from this terrain, one of the last

Above: Over the Mexican border in Boquillas del Carmen. Right: Big Bend National Park.

areas to be made "safe" from the local Apaches. The starkness of this territory led General Philip H. Sheridan to say, in 1866, "If I owned Texas and all hell, I would rent out Texas and live in hell."

The land is wrinkled with the southernmost outcroppings of the Rocky Mountain range. From I-10, Route 54 leads further on up to **Guadalupe Mountains National Park** on the New Mexico border, also the site of the state's highest mountain, **Guadalupe Peak** (8,749 feet). Further along Interstate 10, there's relief awaiting hot drivers at **Lake Balmorhea**, situated in the national park of the same name.

The mountains continue southward, where a detour of merely 130 miles along Routes 17 and 118 brings you to some of the most spectacular scenery in Texas. The **Davis Mountains** are in actual fact the only really mountainous area in the state. Near **Fort Davis**, Texas's highest town at 4,900 feet, is the **McDonald Observatory**; the altitude and clear skies make this an ideal site for stargazing.

From here, the 118 leads down to *the* West Texas highlight: **Big Bend National Park**. Big Bend is a region of rivers and waterfalls, canyons with bizarre stone formations, and the **Chisos Mountains**, formed by volcanic action 60 million years ago. Both gas stations here close daily at 5 p.m., so you should fill up in good time!

Raft trips and hikes are two preferred ways of exploring the area. Nearby are two little ghost towns: **Lajitas**, today in a tourist oriented incarnation, and **Terlingua**, where Texans gather every autumn for the *National Chili Cook-Off.*

After Balmorhea, Interstate 10 leads past the **Toyah** and **Coyanosa** rivers, an area where irrigation and soil conditions produce excellent canteloupe, pecans and hot peppers.

That West Texas is known as "oil country" – nearly half of the U.S.' oil output comes from Texas – can be seen in **Fort Stockton**, the largest and most modern town in the Far West Texas region. Before Fort Stockton, Route 1776

leads to **Monahans Sandhills State Park**, a 200 mile expanse of sand dunes where archeologists have found Indian artifacts and dinosaur bones.

Throughout this area, 19th century cavalry forts, built to control "Indian trouble," give insight into frontier life of the past. One such site is the ruin of **Fort Lancaster** on Route I-10. Further along, the **Caverns of Sonora** are one of Texas' longest cave systems.

TEXAS HILL COUNTRY

Texas Hill Country is a world apart from the barren plains of the western part of the state. Its greenery and live oaks are broken by rivers and lakes. Boating, fishing, canoeing and swimming are prime activities here at numerous state parks, some formed by damming the Colorado River west of Austin.

Texas Hill Country was made famous as the birthplace of Lyndon B. Johnson (1963-1968; born 1908 in Stonewall), John F. Kennedy's successor as president

. The area today is rife with Johnson memorials, including the LBJ National Historical Park near Stonewall.

Despite this presidential link and the beauty of the land, this region is generally poor. Until well into the 1800s it was by settlers as anything other than prime territory. The Mexicans, who won independence in 1821, were happy to let immigrants, many of them German, settle down around San Antonio because they formed a kind of buffer zone against the hostile Comanche Indians. This resulted in many German communities developing around the outskirts and the names of these towns have remained to this day: Hochheim, Waelder, Bergheim, Niederwald, New Braunfels or Luckenbach.

One of the best known of these settlements is **Fredericksburg**, east of I-10 on Route 290. Like many of the area's German settlements, Fredericksburg has kept

Above: A little chat while shopping at the general store in Luckenbach. Right: Austin – city center with Capitol Building.

its German flavor; in fact, you can still hear the language spoken in the old-time **County Store**, or visit the **Vereinskirche** church, while sausages and *schnapps* are produced throughout the area. More about the history of these settlers can be discovered at the **Admiral Nimitz Museum and Historical Center**, together with the **Bush Gallery** (opened in 1999) in which the war between U.S. and Japan is documented, and also the **Pioneer Museum Complex**. It was the Germans who brought the accordion to the region; the Mexicans then adopted it as an integral part of their own folk music.

Past **Johnson City**, where American president buffs can inspect Lyndon B. Johnson's home, the **Pedernales River State Park** is one of many popular water sports centers. Further south, **Guadalupe State Park** shows one of the loveliest sides of Hill Country. Popular with canoers eager to test its challenging rapids, the park is also an ideal spot for nature lovers and birdwatchers. About 20 miles west of Austin, **Hamilton Pool** is a favorite swimming hole; coursing down from its cliff-like walls is a 60 foot natural waterfall.

AUSTIN

Currently, **Austin** is one of the most popular and desirable places to live in the entire United States. Many young people come here because of the university or for the city's flourishing music scene, while others are attracted by Austin's physical beauty; the old oak trees shading the city's wide street and historic buildings, such as those standing along Sixth Street.

The **University of Texas** campus and **Old Pecan Street** in the historic quarter are popular meeting places. On the main university campus you'll find an abundance of student cafés and local musicians perform in popular blues bars, such as **Antone's**.

Near the university, the marble **Lyndon B. Johnson Library and Museum** contains yet more information and memorabilia relating to the President.

Another focus of the city is its government buildings. The **State Capitol Building** is, true to the Texas tradition of "big," a little bit taller than the Capitol Building in Washington, D.C., and is built of red granite, considered more prestigious than the more usual Texas limestone. Across the street is the slightly older building of the **Governor's Mansion**.

San Marcos, located south on I-35, is worth a detour for its **Aquarena Springs** water park and the huge **Wonder World** cave. Between San Marcos and San Antonio lies **New Braunfels**, founded by German immigrants in 1845. A thirty minute drive west of here is the **National Bridge Wildlife Park**, home to a number of exotic animals, including ostriches and giraffes. The impressive **Natural Bridge Caverns**, the largest stalactite caves in Texas, are also worth visiting.

SAN ANTONIO

Just like El Paso, San Antonio - which is Texas' oldest and perhaps most beautiful city - has tried to make its Mexican heritage an asset. With more than half of its residents of Mexican origin, their language and culture are an integral part of San Antonio life, reflected in everything from **El Mercado**, the United States's largest Mexican market, to the annual *fiesta*, to the vibrant neighborhood of **La Villita**, filled with Tex-Mex restaurants. San Antonian Henry Cisneros was the first U.S. mayor of Hispanic origin, until Bill Clinton summoned him to his Cabinet.

Spanish heritage goes back a long way and missions were already established here in 1718, which can be visited along the signposted Mission Trail south of town. Certainly San Antonio is bound up with state history in a special way.

Many traces of Texas' history can be seen in San Antonio, such as the **Alamo Chapel** in the heart of town, regarded by

many Texans as a shrine to the heroes who gave their lives for Texan independence in the famous Battle of the Alamo, in 1836 and lost against the forces of the mighty Mexicans. However, through their battle the Texans did manage to attain a time extension, but already in 1845, Texas became part of the United States.

San Antonio has been dubbed "the frontier Venice". Through the center of town, **Paseo del Rio**, or *River Walk*, winds along the banks of the San Antonio River, about 18 feet below street level. Tour boats depart from its banks on sightseeing or dining cruises under the arches of the river's 13 bridges. On holidays, especially Christmas and *fiesta*, the whole ensemble is strung with colored lights and *luminarios*, traditional Mexican paper lanterns.

Tourists often hear about the "*six flags over Texas*". This refers to the mixed heritage of an area that has at one time or another been under Spanish, French, Mexican, independent Texan, Confederate and American government. This colorful heritage is displayed in the **Institute of Texan Cultures**, behind the tall **Tower of the Americas** in **Hemis-Fair Park**. This history is also reflected in historical buildings: the Spanish **Governor's Palace**; the four Spanish missions along **Mission Trail** (south of downtown); and the French-Gothic style **San Fernando Cathedral**.

In **Brackenridge Park**, the art deco building of the **Witte Museum** houses exhibitions on local and natural history. Another notable building of slightly older vintage is the remarkable **Menger Hotel**, just across from the Alamo chapel. Opened in the mid 1800s, it has numbered Oscar Wilde, Sarah Bernhardt, and Robert E. Lee among its guests. A great family destination is the **Sea World of Texas** theme park, 18 miles north of town, which is home to some 12,000 sea creatures.

Above: The Alamo Chapel is a symbol for the Texan fight for liberty.

NEW MEXICO
Area code 505
Accommodation
MODERATE: **Best Western Caverns Inn** and **Guadalupe Inn**, 17 Carlsbad Caverns Hwy., White's City, Tel: 785-2291. Both hotels are ideally located for a visit to Carlsbad Caverns.

Sights, Museums and Parks
Bitter Lake National Wildlife Refuge, 13 miles northeast of Roswell (via US 70), Tel: 622-6755. **Carlsbad Caverns National Park**, 27 miles southwest of Carlsbad, via US 62/180, Tel: 785-2232. **Legoland California**, 1 Lego Dr., Carlsbad, Tel: 760-918 LEGO. **Lincoln National Forest**, close to Alamogordo, Tel: 437-7200. **Roswell Museum and Art Center**, 100 W 11th St., Tel: 624-6744. **Three Rivers Petroglyph National Recreation Site**, 36 miles south of Carrizozo, on US 54. **White Sands National Monument**, 15 miles to the southeast of Alamogordo, on US 70/82, Tel: 479-6124.

Tourist Information
Carlsbad C & V Bureau, 302 S. Canal St., Carlsbad, NM 88220, Tel: 887-6516.

WEST TEXAS
Area code 915
Accommodation
MODERATE: **Sunset Heights**, 717 W Yandell Ave., El Paso, Tel: 544-1743. Victorian B & B with a superb breakfast.
BUDGET: **Devil's River**, I10/Golf Course Rd. (US 277), Sonora, Tel: 387-3516. **El Parador**, 6400 Montana Ave., El Paso, Tel: 772-4231. **Sands**, 1801 W Dickinson Blvd., Fort Stockton, Tel: 336-2274 (near Big Bend N. P.).

Sights, Museums and Parks
Balmorhea State Park, 50 miles south., on TX 17, near the Davis Mountains., Tel: 375-2370. **Big Bend National Park**, 165 km south of Alpine, on TX 118, Information Tel: 477-2251. **Caverns of Sonora**, 8 miles southwest of Sonara, via I-10, on RM 1989, Tel: 387-3105. **Davis Mountains State Park**, Information Tel: 426-3337. **Fort Davis National Historic Site**, Tel: 426-3224. **Fort Lancaster State Historic Site**, 33 miles west on US 290. **Guadalupe Mountains National Park**, 15 miles north of Van Horn, via TX 54, Tel: 828-3251. **McDonald Observatory**, on Mt. Locke, Tel: 426-3640. **Monahans Sandhills State Park**, 6 miles east on I-20, exit MP 86, Tel: 943-2092. **Tigua Indian Reservation** with **Ysleta Mission**, Tel: 859-3916.

Tourist Information
El Paso Tourist Bureau, 1 Civic Center Plaza, El Paso, TX 79901, Tel: 534-0653.

TEXAS HILL COUNTRY
Area code 830
Accommodation
LUXURY: There are many B & B's in Fredricksburg: **Alte Welt Gasthof**, 142 East Main St., Tel: 997-0443. Romantic B & B with two beautiful suites. **The Back Fourty**, 457 Bob Moritz Dr., Tel: 997-6373. Outside town, rustical, comfortable, with massage and beauty services. *BUDGET:* **Save Inn Motel**, 107 US 281, Johnson City, Tel: 868-4044.

Sights, Museums and Parks
Admiral Nimitz Museum and Historical Center, 340 E Main St., Fredericksburg, Tel: 997-4379. **Lyndon B. Johnson National Historical Park**, Information Tel: 868-7128. **Pedernales Falls State Park**, 14 miles east, on Ranch Rd. 2766, Tel: 868-7304. **Vereinskirche**, Market Square, Fredericksburg, Tel: 997-7832.

Tourist Information
Fredericksburg Chamber of Commerce, 106 N Adams, Fredericksburg, TX 78624, Tel: 997-6523.

AUSTIN AND SAN ANTONIO
Area code 512 (Austin) / 210 (San Antonio)
Accommodation
LUXURY: **Menger Hotel**, 204 Alamo Sq., San Antonio, Tel: 223-4361. Beautifully renovated, elegant atmosphere. *MODERATE:* **Beauregard House**, 215 Beauregard St., San Antonio, Tel: 222-1198. Historical pension. *BUDGET:* **La Quinta North**, 7100 I-35N, Austin, Tel: 452-9401.

Sights, Museums and Parks
The Alamo, Alamo Plaza, San Antonio, Tel: 225-1391. **Brackenridge Park**, N Broadway (US 81), San Antonio. **Governor's Mansion**, 1010 Colorado St. (in the Capitol Complex), Austin, Tel: 463-5516. **Institute of Texan Cultures**, HemisFair Park, San Antonio, Tel: 458-2300. **Lyndon B. Johnson Library & Museum**, on campus of the Univ. of Texas, Austin, Tel: 9165137. **San Fernando Cathedral**, West Market/West Commerce Sts, San Antonio. **Spanish Governor's Palace**, 105 Military Plaza, San Antonio, Tel: 224-0601. **State Capitol**, 11th/Congress Ave., Austin, Tel: 463-0063. **Tower of the Americas**, HemisFair Park, San Antonio, Tel: 223-3101 (Restaurant). **Witte Museum**, 3801 Broadway/Tuleta St., San Antonio, Tel: 357-1900. **Sea World of Texas**, 10500 Sea World Dr., San Antonio, 78251, Tel: 523-3611.

Tourist Information
Austin C & V Bureau, 201 E 2nd St., PO Box 1088, Austin, TX 78767, Tel: 474-5171. **San Antonio C & V Bureau**, PO Box 2277, San Antonio, TX 78298, Tel: 207-6748.

FROM
SAN ANTONIO
TO HOUSTON

CORPUS CHRISTI
TEXAS COAST
GALVESTON
HOUSTON

At the beginning of the 16th century, Spanish explorer Alonso Alvarez worked his way along the coast of the Gulf of Mexico searching for a short cut to Cathay. Spanish geographer Pineda made a major contribution to his fledgling field by mapping out the broad, flat beaches and scrubby marshland of what is today the Texas shore.

In stark contrast to the seemingly hostile deserts of West Texas, there could hardly be a more pleasant landscape than this Texan coast. The 300 mile drive from San Antonio to Houston isn't long: a matter of hours. But if you want to soak up the sun and sand, explore the seashore or the charms of historic Galveston, waterfront towns on the Gulf Waterway, wildlife on Padre Island National Seashore or simply enjoy the legendary Texan friendliness of the locals, you'll find that the hours can easily stretch into days.

King Ranch

From San Antonio, I-37 leads southeast through a region that presents something of a gray area to the visitor. This scrubby mesquite terrain, between the

Left: Dubuffet sculpture amid the sky-scrapers of Houston.

center of the state and its salt coast, is neither fish nor fowl, so to speak – or perhaps one should say it's both fish and fowl, as it is a popular destination for sport hunters, who follow everything from whitewing dove to wild boar. The dry emptiness reaches down to the southernmost "point" of the state of Texas, the spur which follows the curve of the Rio Grande along the Mexican border. Citrus orchards are cultivated in this valley, and Mexican culture is reflected in the Spanish names of many of the towns near Brownsville.

While the area doesn't offer many tourist sites, it is increasingly popular with winter refugees from colder northern climates, and the trailer parks and citrus orchards create a fleeting resemblance to Florida. Near **McAllen**, the **Bentsen-Rio Grande State Park** is a draw for bird watchers. Bentsen is the name of a local family of citrus growers whose head is also a popular United States Senator, Lloyd Bentsen, one of Washington's most respected Democrats.

A large area south of I-37 is taken up by the fabled **King Ranch**, the largest working cattle ranch in the world, covering some 825,000 acres. Turn off south on Roue 77 toward **Kingsville**; west of town, on Route 141, is the headquarters of this family-owned expanse founded in

the middle of the last century by a steam-boat captain named Richard King. Visitors can follow a road around part of the territory to get an idea of the daily chores and the sometimes incredible bleakness of real cowboy life.

CORPUS CHRISTI

About two hours by car from San Antonio, **Corpus Christi** seems to be in another world. Pineda gave it this very Catholic name in the 16th century, but it is not known for its historic ambience or Old World flair. White sands and sport fishing, high-rise hotels and museums are the real draws here.

Corpus Christi isn't all about recreation, as the bustling Port of Corpus Christi shows. The city first flowered as an army base during the conflicts with Mexico at the dawn of Texas' statehood; the military fla-

vor persists in the many naval bases in the area, which can be toured. Maritime buffs can take a closer look at the workings of the U.S. Navy on the aircraft carrier *USS Lexington*, which saw plenty of duty in World War II and has been made into a naval museum. Another port attraction is the **Columbus Fleet**, full-sized replicas of the ships on which Columbus sailed to the New World in 1492.

Separating Corpus Christi Bay from the port is the huge **Harbor Bridge**, the tallest in the whole state. At its foot, **Bayfront Plaza** has become a new center of attraction for city visitors and residents alike. Anyone who is in Corpus Christi for work at the **Convention Center** can stroll through the **Watergarden** at lunchtime, look in at the **Art Museum of South Texas** (housed in a building designed by architect Philip Johnson), or learn about shipwrecks at the **Corpus Christi Museum**, all nearby. Not far away is the lovely old neighborhood of **Heritage Park** with its many beautifully restored historic houses.

Above: Lasso artistry. Right: Traditional hand-crafted saddle production for Western riders.

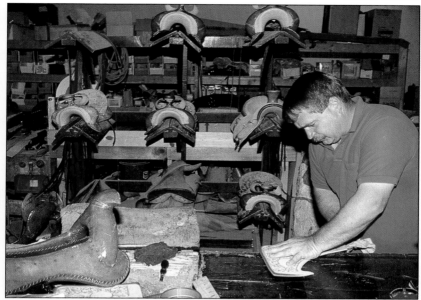

A more unusual museum is the **Museum of Asian Cultures**, which houses a fine collection of Japanese art. Corpus Christi may not be the first place you'd think to look for fine Japanese art and objects; in fact, the museum reflects the lifelong interest and involvement of a local resident named Billie Trimble Chandler, who spent a number of years in Japan as a teacher.

At the **Texas State Aquarium** on the other side of Harbor Bridge, the exhibits are alive and swimming; a collection of fish, eels, sharks, and other marine life, with a fine view over the beach.

Padre Island

Beach is a key word for Corpus Christi visitors. The city beach, also called **North Beach**, offers some real surf; by contrast, the sheltered **McGee Beach** to the south has calmer waters and is therefore better suited for families with small children. But the greatest beach attraction in all of Texas is undoubtedly the white sand of **Padre Island**, one of the nation's longest undeveloped beaches (about 70 miles). While some of the northern part of this expanse has paved roads and is crowded with condominiums, hotels and restaurants, the buildings thin out the farther south you get, and what then dominates the landscape are dunes, flat marshland, sea and sky. On the mainland side of the island, which is four miles across at its widest point, tidal inlets attract all manner of saltwater creatures seeking shelter in the warm mud, and 350 different bird species nest here. On the Gulf side of the island, sea treasures – shells, weathered beach glass, gleaming stones polished by the waves – lie along the waterline.

You can appreciate these all the more because the thick white sand makes for slow walking; for trips farther down the island, it's advisable to rent a jeep with four-wheel drive (driving on the beach is legal in Texas). Quite apart from the natural treasures here, it was gold that brought wealth to this coast: Three Spanish galleons full of gold and valuables sank in 1554 off the coast here (dubbed "the graveyard of the Gulf"). Much of their contents have been salvaged.

THE TEXAS COAST

All the developers who were banned from the National Seashore have set up shop at the southern end of Padre Island. A genuine resort atmosphere runs rampant here, near **Brownsville** and the mouth of the Rio Grande. Still, there are a couple of bastions of nature conservancy amidst the condos.

The **Gladys Porter Zoo** is in Brownsville, with more than 1,900 species of animals and plants displayed in quasi-natural habitats. This is a popular place to spend an afternoon for young and old alike.

East of Corpus Christi, the islands and parks don't stop. **Mustang Island State Park**, at the northern end of Mustang Island, offers great beaches and is famous for its fishing. At its very tip is **Port Aransas**, a once-sleepy little fishing village which has played up its "quaint" quotient for tourism in recent years, but which is still fine for exploring, browsing in shops, wandering along docks, or finding a fishing boat to take you out for some deep-sea action. On shore, the **Horace Caldwell Fishing Pier** gives a chance to angle from land; it extends 1,240 feet into the Gulf, and is open 24 hours a day. A town landmark, the **Tarpon Inn** exhibits details of the record-breaking successes of past fishermen on its walls.

From here, a free ferry runs to **Aransas Pass**, where not fish, but shrimp, are the order of the day; and this port is home to a huge working fleet of shrimp boats. Across the bay, the uninhabited island of "Saint Joe," or **San José Island**, affords some protection from hurricanes.

Conservation is the key word at the **Aransas National Wildlife Refuge**. This

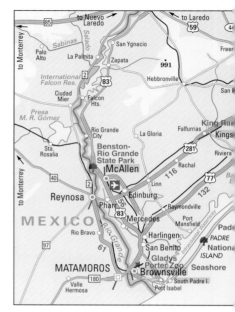

is the winter home of the whooping crane, an extremely endangered species which migrates south from Canada each year in early October. Nearly extinct a few decades ago, the crane population has risen to around 50 now, thanks to the involvement of wildlife conservationists. So ardently does the region work to protect its wildlife that offshore drilling rigs are required to close down during the winter months, interrupting their search for another kind of underwater treasure found throughout the Gulf: oil. It's because of this kind of commitment that the cranes have been able to multiply; although it's feared that a shipping accident on the Gulf Intracoastal Waterway, which runs through their refuge, could spell disaster if it released oil or chemicals and killed the crustaceans on which the birds feed.

A harbinger of this was the huge fire on a Mexican rig in 1979, resulting in one of the biggest oil spills in history; fortunately, weather and the barrier islands protected the refuge for the most part.

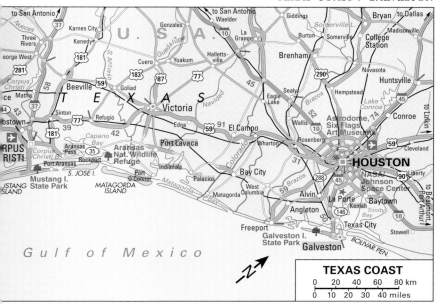

Gulf of Mexico

TEXAS COAST

0	20	40	60	80 km
0	10	20	30	40 miles

Since then, all has gone well; moreover, the cranes, as well as the refuge's ten other endangered species (including sea turtles, alligators and brown pelicans) have adapted well to maritime traffic.

Such juxtapositions of man and nature serve as reminders that there is more to the Gulf Coast than merely tourist pleasures or wildlife refuges. In addition to the forest of offshore drilling rigs that rise up from the waters, the strip of water between the coast and the barrier islands is actually part of the **Gulf Intracoastal Waterway**, which links the Texas ports with New Orleans.

This working aquatic highway runs for a length of about 1,200 miles, from Brownsville all the way to Florida. Completed in 1949, the waterway is continually dredged to assure boats of a channel never less than twelve feet deep and 125 feet wide. The protective islands play a role for these boats too; shielded from the full fury of Gulf storms, they carry about 100 million tons of cargo from port to port every year.

HISTORIC GALVESTON

While you can't drive along the waterway, Route 35 follows the coastline a little way inland, leading to many smaller waterside towns that are part historical port, part fishing village. North of the Aransas Refuge, off Matagorda Bay, **Port O'Connor** and **Port Lavaca** attract sport fishermen, hunters, and, of course, beachgoers.

Many towns haven't managed to withstand the force of the hurricanes which have created trenches in the dunes of Padre and other islands; **Indianola**, for example, was flattened by a storm in the 19th century. **Palacios**, across the bay, was luckier, and has managed to preserve its charm.

Hurricanes have left their mark on more than one of the towns along this coast. **Galveston**, southeast of Houston, was one of the region's leading commercial centers in the 19th century, until September 8 and 9, 1900. The hurricane that struck on that date was so ferocious that it

69

remains one of the worst natural disasters in U.S. history. It killed an estimated 6,000 people, and wiped out the town to such an extent that it was questionable as to whether it should be rebuilt at all.

Fortunately, enough of the beautiful old houses, such as the 1859 **Ashton Villa**, survived, so that Galveston is still an attraction for enthusiasts of Victorian homes – even if, since the hurricane, the town has more or less become a satellite, at best a country retreat, of Houston. A huge sea wall, 17 feet high, has been constructed to prevent similar damage from ever happening again.

Despite the storm, Galveston has more historic charm than Texas's other Gulf cities. One example is the **Strand Historic District**, where Victorian-style warehouse buildings with cast iron façades have been converted into a lively shopping neighborhood. Another relic of

Above: Shrimp cutter in Port Ysabel on the Texas Gulf Coast. Right: Houston skyline by night.

Galveston's pre-hurricane past is the **Grand 1894 Opera House**, one of America's finest old theaters.

Galveston Island is connected to the mainland by highway and, with 30 miles of beach, is known as the *Queen of the Texas Coast*. Like so many of the other Gulf towns, it was once a flourishing fishing village. Reminders of this are the annual springtime **Shrimp Festival**, which opens with a blessing of the shrimp fleet at the start of the season, and which includes *square dancing* with hundreds of participants. Because of the 60 plus varieties of oleander that grow here, Galveston is often referred to as *Oleander City*.

The island's maritime past is preserved at the **Texas Seaport Museum** on Pier 21, where the old sailing ship *Elissa* (1877) is a main attraction. You can also take day cruises from Galveston; or hop on the free ferry over to **Bolivar Peninsula**. After the signature lighthouse at Port Bolivar, the peninsula boasts miles of deserted beaches off the beaten and

developed tourist track. But if you'd rather stay ashore at Galveston, then don't miss **Moody Gardens** - contained within this ten storey glass pyramid is an even greater variety of wildlife than you might find outdoors, like the flora and fauna of a tropical rain forest, for instance. There is also a 3D IMAX cinema that will plunge you into even more exotic realms.

HOUSTON

Leading toward Houston, Route 146 leads up to **Clear Lake** and **Kemah**, where you can eat fresh seafood overlooking fine sea views.

On the opposite shore of Clear Lake, the **NASA/Johnson Space Center**, an earthly magnet for the moonstruck, is a treasure trove of information and memorabilia which fascinates. Here, the National Air and Space Administration (NASA) has a museum and souvenir center with everything from early space capsules to a piece of moon rock. The very

first word spoken to Earth from the moon was, as local residents will all try to tell you, "Houston".

Houston is the largest city in the large state of Texas, and, perhaps this makes it a perfect embodiment of its state. It is named after Sam Houston, a freedom fighter for the liberty of the Texan state. Houston is rich in cultural and ethnic diversity: Latin-, African- and Asian-American communities celebrate their traditions with a host of festivals and holiday.

The arts scene also has contrasts to offer: From the **Houston Opera's** glittering performances to the clubs in the **Richmond Entertainment District**. The latter is near the **Galleria**, an exclusive mall which presents *haute couture* – at equally haute prices.

But Houston also has areas with slightly rough, down-to-earth charm like the fishing district of **Kemah**.

Southwest of downtown are three interesting museums: the **Contemporary Arts Museum**, with changing exhibi-

Above: The Nasa Space Center presents the past and the future of space travel.

tions of modern art, the **Museum of Fine Arts**, with works from all over the world, and the **Menil Museum**, containing, amongst other things, the collection of the de Menil couple, who also commissioned painter Mark Rothko to create the shimmering, luminous canvases which adorn the **Rothko Chapel** down the street.

There's live – or livelier – entertainment in the **Montrose** neighborhood in the west of the city, a diverting and hip region which includes Texas's largest *gay community*. Sidewalk cafés and second-hand boutiques are characteristic of this area, while **Westheimer Street**, which intersects Montrose, adds spice with a number of Tex-Mex restaurants.

Houston's downtown area has an extensive underground tunnel system, which makes it easier to get around. But a car is just as necessary to many residents as a pair of legs. The grid of downtown is the base for a thicket of skyscrapers that provide the only topography in this flat city. Architects who have left their mark here include such American masters as Philip Johnson and I.M. Pei (whose **Texas Commerce Bank Building** has been dubbed "the Texas tombstone").

The **Houston Civic Center** is considered to be the heart of the city's cultural life. The conference and sports center also contains concert halls. South of the Sam Houston Coliseum is **Sam Houston Park**, where the annual *International Festival* takes place. The **Astrodome**, Houston's sports arena (sometimes called the "eighth wonder of the world"), offers football, baseball, motorcycle races, concerts and rodeos.

Further attractions include the **San Jacinto Battleground State Historic Park**, where the battleship *Texas* is anchored, and the combined **Six Flags Astroworld/Waterworld** theme parks.

To the east of Houston is **Port Arthu**r, with its **Pleasure Island** resort complex and the Sea Rim State Park.

CORPUS CHRISTI AND SURROUNDINGS
Area code 361
Accommodation

LUXURY: **Ocean House**, 3275 Ocean Dr., Corpus Christi, Tel: 882-9500, very nice B & B with pool and sauna, owned by a fisherman who can give you some useful tips. *MODERATE:* **Holiday Inn Emerald Beach**, 1102 South Shoreline Blvd., Corpus Christi, Tel: 883-5731. Large house right on the beach, with pool, ideal for families. **Comfort Suites**, 3925 S Padre Island Dr., Corpus Christi, Tel: 225-2500. Located close to all attractions. *BUDGET:* **Drury Inn**, 2021 N. Padre Island Dr., Corpus Christi, Tel: 289-8200.

Sights, Museums and Parks

Aransas National Wildlife Refuge, 35 miles northeast of Rockport, north via TX 35, Information Tel: 286-3559. **Art Museum of South Texas**, 1902 N Shoreline Blvd., Tel: 884-3844. **Bensten-Rio Grande State Park**, 3 miles west on US 83, FM 2062 south, Tel: (956) 585-1107. **Corpus Christi Museum of Science and History**, 1900 N Chaparral St., Tel: 883-2862. **Gladys Porter Zoo**, 500 Ringgold St., Brownsville, Tel: (956) 546-7187. **Heritage Park**, 1581 N Chaparral St. **King Ranch**, west of Kingsville, Tel: 592-8055. **Museum of Asian Cultures**, 418 Peoples St., Suite 200, Tel: 882-2641. **Mustang Island State Park**, 14 miles south of Corpus Christi on TX 361. **Padre Island National Seashore** (accessible from Corpus Christi via the John F. Kennedy Causeway), Information Tel: 937-2621. **Texas State Aquarium**, Corpus Christi Beach, Tel: 881-1200. **USS Lexington**, Corpus Christi Bay, Tel: 888-4873.

Excursions and Sports

Captain Clark's Flagship, Corpus Christi Bayfront, Tel: 884-8306. Steamboat excursions are available daily. **World Winds Windsurfing**, Padre Island National Seashore, Tel: 949-7472.

Tourist Information

Corpus Christi C & V Bureau, 1201 N Shoreline Dr., PO Box 2664, Corpus Christi, TX 78403, Tel: 881-1888. **Port Aransas Chamber of Commerce**, 421 W Cotter, PO Box 356, Port Aransas, TX 78373, Tel: 749-5919.

GALVESTON AND THE TEXAS COAST
Area code 409
Accommodation

LUXURY: **Tremont House**, 2300 Ship's Mechanic Row, Galveston, Tel: 763-0300. An elegant historic hotel. **San Luis**, 5222 Seawall Blvd., Tel: 744-8452. A smart resort situated on Galveston beach,

with spa and superb steakhouse. *MODERATE:* **Holiday Inn on the Beach**, 5002 Seawall Blvd., Tel: 740-3581. Situated directly on Galveston beach with a breathtakingly beautiful view over the Gulf of Mexico, chidren under 19 years are accommodated free of charge.

Sights, Museums and Parks

Ashton Villa, 2328 Broadway (at 24th St.), Tel: 762-3933. **Galveston Island State Park**, 11 miles southwest on FM 3005, Tel: 737-1222. Large recreational area, which incorporates camping and picnicking areas. **Grand 1894 Opera House**, 2020 Post Office St., Tel: 763-7173. **Moody Gardens**, 1 Hope Blvd., Tel: 744-1745. **Strand National Historic Landmark**, between 20th Street and 25th Street. **Texas Seaport Museum**, Pier 21, Tel: 763-1877.

Tourist Information

Galveston Island C & V Bureau, (Visitor Center in Moody Civic Center) 2106 Seawall Blvd. (by 21st St.), Galveston, TX 77550, Tel: 763-4311.
Port Lavaca-Calhoun County Chamber of Commerce, 2300 TX 35 Bypass, PO Box 528, Port Lavaca, TX 77979, Tel: (361) 552-2959.

HOUSTON AND SURROUNDINGS
Area code 713
Accommodation

LUXURY: **La Colombe d'Or,** 3410 Montrose Blvd., Houston, Tel: 524-7999. A very elegant boarding house dating back to the 1920s. **Doubletree Guest Suites**, 5353 Westheimer Rd., Houston, Tel: 961-9000. Large 4-star hotel with suites, in close proximity to the Galleria mall. *MODERATE:* **Lexington Hotel Suites**, 16410 I-45N, Houston, Tel: 821-1000. Suites with kitchenette. *BUDGET:* **Sara's**, 941 Heights Blvd., Houston, Tel: 868-1130, small, relatively simple B & B north of the city center.

Sights, Museums and Parks

Houston Grand Opera, Wortham Theater Center, 510 Preston St., Tel: 546-0200. **Menil Collection**, 1515 Sul Ross, Tel: 525-9400. **Museum of Fine Arts**, 1001 Bissonnet, Tel: 639-7300. **Rothko Chapel**, 3900 Yupon St., Tel: 524-9839. **Sam Houston Historical Park**, 1100 Bagby, opposite Texaco Heritage Plaza. **Space Center Houston**, 35 miles south on I-45, exit 2351, Tel: 244-2100. **Six Flags Astroworld/Waterworld**, 9001 Kirkby Drive, Houston, Tel: 794-3291.

Tourist Information

Visitor Center, 3300 Main St. Further information available at: **Greater Houston C & V Bureau**, 801 Congress, Houston, TX 77002, Tel: 227-3100.

FROM
LOS ANGELES
TO LAS VEGAS

MOJAVE DESERT
DEATH VALLEY
NEVADA
LAS VEGAS

Gray and monolithic, the sprawling city of Los Angeles rests under its own blanket of smog and fumes. Yet leaving town, the sky over the highway up ahead is brilliant blue, the hues of the land become earthier and browner as you go along, and the landscape more monotonous and barren. Every mile is one step further from the metropolis of millions and one step closer to the desert landscapes of California and Nevada.

The road is lined with dried-up salt lakes, abandoned ghost towns and bizarre rock formations that rise high into the sky. And, finally, there is the desert itself, Death Valley and the Mojave Desert, at first glance dead lunar landscapes, yet so full of hidden life. At the end of this 450 mile journey, there's Las Vegas, a glistening and seductive world of roulette, blackjack and one-armed bandits, rising like a mirage from the midst of the desert.

THE MOJAVE DESERT

The eastward route from sprawling Los Angeles to California's desert wilderness leads first to **Barstow** on Interstate 15. This modest town, originally established

Previous pages: Do the neon signs deliver what they promise? Left: View of Death Valley from Zabriskie Point.

tablished as a railway junction, has few if any sights to capture one's attention. Still, a visit to the information center **California Welcome Center** and a tour of the **Mojave River Valley Museum** is worth the effort. Both give information on life in the desert and advice that every tourist should read and heed. A major attraction here are the outlet centers, with their bargain factory prices.

A few miles beyond Barstow is **Calico**, whose silver deposits attracted over 3,500 prospectors in the 1880s. But as the market price for silver dropped after 1896, so did the population of Calico. In the end, all that remained was a ghost town, which has since been carefully restored. Tours through the 30 mile **Silver King Mine** are a must for anyone curious about silver mining or eager to try out panning, have a drink at the saloon, or a ride on an old-time train. If absolutely intent on spending the night in a ghost town, try the nearby camp grounds.

To the north of Barstow is a historic attraction of a different kind: the fossilized remains of insects and animals incrusted in the rocks of **Rainbow Basin** and **Owl Canyon** prove once again that at some time millions of years ago this desert, which seems lifeless today, was a lively and fertile place.

The road into the Mojave Desert passes by numerous dried up salt ponds before entering **Soda Springs**, which lies on the banks of the eponymous (and dry) lake. Once upon a time the town served as a military outpost; then cowboys used it to water their horses and rest their bones; finally, it became a spa of sorts with the odd name of **Zzyzx**. How this moniker should be pronounced remains debatable amongst locals to this day but, at any rate, the days of healing waters are long gone.

Excursions southward into the eastern **Mojave Desert** can be started from **Baker**. At first glance this high altitude plateau, which lies between 3,000 and 5,000 feet above sea level, appears entirely devoid of life. However, in addition to a fauna of desert rabbits, turtles and coyotes, the desert explodes with color in the springtime with a proud variety of flora. Most impressive of all are the high

cactus trees which produce large flowers. Otherwise, the only major sight in the midst of this aridity is south of **Kelso**. Spelunkers in particular will enjoy the **Mitchell Caverns Natural Preserve**, an extensive system of sandstone caves. Highway 127 heads back north into famous **Death Valley**.

DEATH VALLEY

Death Valley covers an enormous 1,500 square miles and is one of the hottest places on earth (the second highest temperature ever recorded was measured here in 1913 at 134° F). Native Americans called it "burning earth", but the white man's awe-inspiring name is the one that stuck. For many, the road of life ended torturously in this inferno, particularly during the gold rush of 1849. Travelers nowadays survive the summer temperatures of up to 110° F – and sometimes more – with air conditioning, but step out of the car and you will be struck by the sheer force of the elements.

Above: Badwater in Death Valley is the lowest point in the Western Hemisphere.

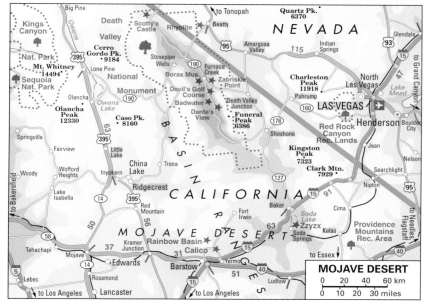

Death Valley is indeed a valley of extremes. **Badwater**, at the lowest point in the Western Hemisphere (282 feet below sea level), is only 80 miles away from the highest mountain of the Sierra Nevada, **Mt. Whitney**, at 14,494 feet. The Valley consists of sand dunes, stretches of salt, canyons and bizarrely formed mountain ranges. The daytime heat is in sharp contrast to the cold at night. And in the midst of this apparently lifeless landscape nearly 40 species of animals (lizards and snakes, of course) thrive, as do unique plants that exist nowhere else on the entire planet.

Canyons and Ghost Towns

Anyone driving through Death Valley should make sure their car is in good working order, and should carry enough drinking water, sufficient paraphernalia for emergencies and also water for the car radiator.

The best place to begin crossing the valley is **Death Valley Junction** on Route 190. At **Furnace Creek Oasis**, the **visitor center** provides maps and informative brochures on the geological history of the desert: During the last Ice Age, the valley was covered by a saltwater lake that gradually dried up. This dried-up lake bed became the desert, with its patches of salt. The Panamint and Sierra Nevada mountain ranges at the end of the valley form a natural barrier against any humidity from the Pacific Ocean, as precipitation occurs over the ranges themselves, hence annual rainfall in the desert amounts to no more than two inches.

Some of the most fascinating panoramas are on the way to the visitor center on Route 190. The most famous, and therefore unfortunately most overrun, is **Zabriskie Point**, which opens up on a lunar scene of jagged rocks and resembles a landscape painting in reds and browns. Sunrise and sunset add an almost unearthly golden sheen to this wild tableau. To the south, a side road leads to **Golden Canyon** (beneath Zabriskie Point), the **Devil's Golf Course**, and finally

79

Dante's View, from where one can get a fine view of Badwater.

Heading back north on Route 178 you bypass **Devil's Cornfield** and **Mosaic Canyon** before reaching the old ghost town of **Skidoo**. This old relic from the history of the Wild West tells the story of the frenzied mining era around 1890. Thousands of adventurers were lured to this place by the dream that the nation's biggest gold stores were lying below the surface of Death Valley.

In actual fact, only a handful of industrialists hit the jackpot in the 1880s, and that by mining not gold but natural deposits of borax, a mineral used in glass-making, ceramics and agriculture, among other things. A few miles north of the visitor center lie the ruins of the **Harmony Borax Works**, one of the first borax processing plants to be established in the region, which is open for viewing.

Above: The Hoover Dam, a masterpiece of American engineering. Right: Las Vegas – den of iniquity and family resort town.

If you are in no hurry to reach Las Vegas, then drive further north to **Scotty's Castle**, which has become something of a legend. Scotty, an adventurer, gold prospector and a star of Buffalo Bill's Wild West Show, got together with a Chicago businessman named Albert M. Johnson and built a playful, castle-like hotel. The building is supposed to be at the entrance of a large gold mine but, in fact, this bit of news was nothing more than an ingenious public relations device to attract guests to the hotel.

CROSSING NEVADA

The 140 mile drive southeast to **Las Vegas** leads over Highway 95 and takes you straight through what is known as Nevada's "Pioneer Territory." Stretches of stark and uninviting desert alternate with extensive mountain ranges.

Some of the most interesting and best-kept ghost towns can be found on this route, all of them petrified testimonies to the gold fever that once upon a time gripped the entire nation, sending herds of hopeful prospectors westward. One of the most picturesque of these old gold mining camps is **Rhyolite** near **Beatty**. At the climax of silver mining era, in 1907, over 6,000 people lived here in the midst of the desert. What is left comprises a few buildings, such as the Vegas & Tonopah Railroad Depot, the **Porter Store** and the **Rhyolite Bottle House**. Lately, a few people have even moved back: no doubt reclusive types. Therefore, as a partly inhabited *ghost town*, Rhyolite is certainly one of a kind.

On the way to Las Vegas another interesting stop is **Amargosa Valley**, a little town with a few motels, gas stations and fast food establishments. The Amargosa sand dunes nearby were created millions of years ago when a lake dried up leaving the sandy bottom exposed.

The ride southeastward can be continued either on rather dull Highway 95 or on the slightly longer Route 160 to the south. The latter is of particular interest to wine connoisseurs, as in **Pahrump**, Nevada's only winery offers tours of its facilities and samplings. The **Pahrump Valley Winery**, with its brilliant white Mediterranean-type buildings, might just as well be in Italy, except from the fact that it sits on the barren soil of the Nevada desert. Some of the wines made here have earned international prizes.

When neon signs begin lighting up the horizon, promising instant fortunes at the gambling table, you know where you're headed: *Las Vegas - here I come!*

LAS VEGAS

It's one of history's ironies that **Las Vegas**, considered by many Americans to be the most sinful of Babylons on the continent, should have started its life as a pious Mormon settlement in the 1850s. The founding fathers of the sect are surely turning in their graves in light of the gambling that has taken over the ci-

ty's economy. Yet Las Vegas (which means "meadows" in Spanish) didn't become a wild den of sin until the 1930s, when Nevada became the only state to legalize gambling. Coincidentally, work on the nearby Hoover Dam began at the same time, and suddenly the little community experienced a boom as thousands of construction workers flocked to the town to spend their hard-earned money and their free time. The somewhat unruly atmosphere of those early days no longer exists, as Las Vegas, in fact, projects an image of clean fun; those in search of topless waitresses, off-color nightclub shows or daring stripteases will be disappointed here.

This demimonde does continue to exist but it is limited in scope, and the average tourist will hardly encounter any of it anywhere. The only halfway decent striptease show you can still find is beyond the city limits, at the *Palomino*. Since the beginning of the 1990s, the town fathers have been trying to clean up Las Vegas' reputation. Prostitution and other forms

81

of dubious entertainment were banned from the theaters and big hotels. Prostitutes nowadays can only be found at the edge of town or on the surrounding highways. A whole slew of gigantic new hotels, sporting adventure and theme parks have helped turn Las Vegas into a place where the whole family can engage in good, clean, traditional American fun, perhaps in the sense of what Republicans refer to as family values. The bottom line is impressive: in 1999, the city entertained a record 33 million guests (over one-third of them under 30 years of age).

Nothing Ventured, Nothing Gained?

Most hotels and casinos are lined up cheek by jowl in **downtown Las Vegas** along the so-called **Las Vegas Strip**, which lies parallel to Interstate 15. In the past few years, the Strip, as well as *Las*

Above and right: Gambling cathedral – respectable couples succumb to the magic of gambling (Luxor Casino).

Vegas Boulevard measuring almost 4 miles in length, has exploded into a massive entertainment district.

To get a feeling of the *genius loci*, visitors should by all means try a few rounds of roulette, blackjack, bingo or craps at one of the leading casinos, the Golden Nugget or Lady Luck, for example. At night, along Fremont Street and along the Strip, huge ornate neon signs illuminate the desert sky like a glittering, shimmering artificial fire, inviting people from far and wide to come and try their luck.

Las Vegas continues to thrive from gambling, even though in the meantime many other states in the country have legalized casinos. Everything in town is aimed at pulling money from the tourist's wallet. Friendly ladies in very tight tops make sure that gambling guests are well supplied with free drinks (including alcoholic ones). Various entertainment programs and theme-based architecture are designed to divert attention from the fact that gambling can get extremely dull after a while. Anyone trying his or her

luck with a few dollars in hand should keep this in mind. Visitors are already greeted by the first seductively blinking slot machines at the airport.

Prices in hotels and in restaurants are almost absurdly low. Cheap weekend flights ship large groups of tourists to Las Vegas from every corner of the U.S. So-called *fun books* offer free coupons for almost every need – from cheap restaurants to discount roulette chips to souvenirs. These coupons can be found at hotels, casinos and, of course, at the tourist information center.

Waterfalls and Mini Volcanoes

In recent years several large hotels were erected in Las Vegas that have helped to give the town its new, cleaner image. These establishments are worth a visit, even if you're not staying in one of them.

The first of these is the **MGM Grand Hotel**, whose 5,005 rooms and suites make it the largest accommodations factory in the world. Construction of this huge building, with an entrance shaped like the MGM lion, cost over a billion dollars. MGM has tried to revive some of the flair of the good old days with a great deal of elegance and select show programming. The newly-sprouted casinos now also emphasize a more family-friendly atmosphere. The idea behind these neat arrangements in hotels and parks is to keep the kiddies happily busy while their parents blow their savings at the casino's gaming tables.

The city's attempt to be family-friendly is also visible in the massive pyramidal **Luxor Hotel**, whose interior is made up to look Egyptian with an artificial river and Nile boats. This hotel even has an entertainment park.

The acme of adventure parks is to be found at the **Treasure Island Hotel**. The very name reveals the subject of its theme park, namely pirates and treasures. Every 90 minutes, 20 actors go about performing an extravagant spectacle involving lots of powder and smoke.

You should plan in a visit to the **Mirage** to see the German-born illusionists Siegfried and Roy. Their perfectly staged performance (with white tigers and a host of other wild animals) is worth the visit, as is the artificial volcano in front of the hotel, which erupts every twenty minutes.

Other places to see are **Caesar's Palace**, for its pseudo-Roman architecture, the **Excalibur**, for its medieval ambiance and **Circus-Circus**, for - you guessed it - its circus performances. Should you want a closer look at, perhaps, New York, Paris or Venice, simply visit one of the newer casinos designed as replicas of these metropolises.

The restaurant scene in Las Vegas is just as exciting. Once upon a time this town was known for its cheap 'all you can eat' buffet and best-known among these are *Bally's Big Kitchen* in the Bally

Above: The pirate plays in the Treasure Island Hotel are one of the new types of attractions in Las Vegas.

84

and *The Carnival World Buffet* in the Rio Suites Hotel. But nowadays top-class restaurants have joined the line-up, attracting even gourmets to the casinos. The best-loved among these excellent casino restaurants are *Picasso* in the Bellagio, *Babbo* in the New York and *Renoir* in the Mirage.

Las Vegas Weddings

Wedding Chapels, or rather, privately-run marriage bureaus which can marry or divorce people in record time and can even provide the witnesses, are abundant in Vegas and in most casinos. Ever since the state of Nevada loosened marriage laws in 1931, any couple can get married here in an express procedure. The responsible state body, the Clark County Marriage License Bureau, is open at weekends and round the clock, and only requires proof of age (18 years minimum), identification and 35 dollars (Clark County Courthouse, 200 S Third St., Tel:(702) 455-4415).

MOJAVE DESERT AND
DEATH VALLEY
Area code 760

Accommodation
LUXURY: **Furnace Creek Inn & Ranch**, Box 1, Death Valley, CA 92328 (1 mile from the Visitor Info), Tel: 786-2361. An extremely luxurious oasis with pool, golf and tennis in the midst of Death Valley. *MODERATE*: **Furnace Creek Ranch**, see above address. The usual motel layout, restaurant, shops (by Visitor Info). **Best Western Desert Villa**, 1984 E Main St., Barstow, Tel: 256-1781. 95 rooms, 9 of them with whirlpool. **Saddle West Hotel & Casino**, Hwy. 160, Pahrump, Tel: 775/7275953. Good value casino complex with 110 rooms. *BUDGET:* **Stove Pipe Wells Village**, CA 190, Death Valley, Tel: 786-2387. No extra conveniences available here.

Guest Ranch / Camping
Furnace Creek Ranch, see above address.
Camping: Information on camping and the quality and state of roads in Death Valley, Tel: 786-2331.

Sights, Museums
and Parks
Borax Museum and Mining Exhibition, Furnace Creek Ranch, Death Valley, Tel: 786-2345. **Death Valley Visitor Center at Furnace Creek**, Tel: 786-2331. **Calico Early Man Archeological Site**, 150 Coolwater Ln., Barstow, Tel: 256-5102. **Calico Ghost Town Regional Park**, 10 miles east of I-15, close to Barstow, Tel: 254-2122. **Central Nevada Museum**, Logan Field Rd., Tonopah, Tel: (775) 482-9676. Exhibition on the varied history of Nevada and also about the history of mining here. **Death Valley National Monument**, National Park Services, Death Valley, Tel: 786-2345. **East Mojave National Scenic Area**, Needles, Tel: 326-3896. **Factory Merchants**, 2552 Mercantile Way, Barstow, Tel: 253-7342. To the 85 Outlet Stores. **Fossil Falls**, on Hwy. 395, north of Ridgecrest, close to Little Lake. Barren waterfalls and cooled-down lava streams, old Indian village and Indian rock paintings. **Maturango Museum**, 100 E Las Flores Ave., Ridgecrest, Tel: 375-6900. Cultural and natural history exhibition centering around the Mojave desert. **Mitchell Caverns Natural Preserve**, Essex (not far from Kelso), Tel: 389-2281. **Mojave River Valley Museum**, 270 E Virginia Way, Barstow, Tel: 256-5452. **Opal Canyon Mine**, 17 miles south of Ridgecrest, on Hwy. 14. Rare opal mine, tours. **Pahrump Valley Winery**, 3810 Homestead Rd., Pahrump, Tel: (775) 727-6900. **Rainbow Basin/Owl Canyon**, 10 miles north of Barstow, on Fort Irwin Rd., Tel: 256-3591. **Rhyolite State Historic Site**, not far from Beatty,

Tel: (775) 553-2424. **Scotty's Castle**, Death Valley, Tel: 786-2392. **Soda Springs**, exit I-15 on Zzyxx Rd. (6 miles west of Baker), Tel: 256-8617. **Tanger Outlet**, 2796 Tanger Way, Barstow, Tel: 253-4812. Approx. 30 Outlet Shops.

Tourist Information
California Welcome Center, 2796 Tanger Way, Barstow, CA 92311, Tel: (760) 253-4782. **Death Valley Chamber of Commerce**, PO Box 157, Shoshone, CA 92384, Tel: 852-4524.

LAS VEGAS
Area code 702

Accommodation
LUXURY: **Luxor Hotel & Casino**, 3900 Las Vegas Blvd., Tel: 262-4000. Huge pyramid-shaped hotel with 4400 rooms plus 400 suites. **New York-New York**, 3790 Las Vegas Blvd., Tel: 740-6969. This is a mega-resort with a total of 2240 rooms. *MODERATE:* **Caesar's Palace**, 3570 Las Vegas Blvd., Tel: 731-7110. **Circus-Circus**, Box 14967, 2880 Las Vegas Blvd. S, tel: 734-0410. Suitable for families. **Excalibur Hotel & Casino**, 3850 Las Vegas Blvd., Tel: 597-7777. The mere appearance of this establishment will fascinate the kids. **The Mirage**, 3400 Las Vegas Blvd., Tel: 791-7111. Beautiful casino, very pleasant rooms and elegant suites. *BUDGET*: **Westward Ho Hotel & Casino**, 2900 Las Vegas Blvd. S, Tel: 731-2900. 1000 motel rooms and 7 pools.

Sights, Museums
and Parks
Bonnie Springs Old Nevada, 20 miles west, on Charleston Blvd., tel: 875-4191. Historical western town with live shows and zoo. **Imperial Palace Auto Collection**, 3535 Las Vegas Blvd. (5th floor in hotel of the same name), Tel: 731-3311. Bizarre exhibition of vintage cars once belonging to the rich and famous. **Las Vegas Art Museum**, 9600 W Sahara Ave, Tel: 360-8000. **Las Vegas Natural History Museum**, 900 Las Vegas Blvd., N., Tel: 384-3466. Natural science museum on North America. **Liberace Museum**, 1775 E. Tropicana Ave., Tel: 798-5595. An exhibition of Liberace's cars and extravagant costumes. **Red Rock Canyon Recreation Lands**, 18 miles west of W Charleston Blvd., close to Las Vegas, Tel: 363-1921. Stunning views of one of the most beautiful gorges in the area. **Treasure Island Hotel**, 3300 Las Vegas Blvd., large adventure theme park, centered around "Treasure-hunting".

Tourist Information
Las Vegas C & V Authority, 3150 Paradise Rd., Las Vegas, NV 89109, Tel: 892-0711, http://www.lasvegas24hours.com

FROM LAS VEGAS TO THE GRAND CANYON

ZION NATIONAL PARK
BRYCE AND GLEN CANYONS
GRAND CANYON:
NORTH AND SOUTH RIMS

Discovering the Grand Canyon or renewing one's acquaintance with it, is one of the aims of this 500 mile tour, which should last about a week. The route begins in Las Vegas, heads northward to the little-known northern rim of the canyon, veers westward to the national park, and ends at the canyon's popular southern border.

From Las Vegas to Zion National Park

Highway 93 leads eastward out of Las Vegas to the beautiful **Lake Mead National Recreation Area**, an expansive stretch of land where many weary gamblers or visitors come to find relax and recover. The lake itself is 115 miles long and cuts quite a peculiar image in the middle of the Nevada desert, with its sand beaches, bathing resorts and watersports centers. The visitor center in **Boulder City** provides information about the lake and the great **Hoover Dam** that was built nearby. This masterpiece of American engineering is 707 feet high and 1,195 feet long and dams the Colorado River to form **Lake Mead**. It was built in

Previous pages: Overview of the Grand Canyon from Dead Horse Point. Left: Bryce Canyon.

the 1930s as one of the NRA jobs programs designed to help pull America out of the Great Depression. The power plants that feed from Hoover Dam still provide neighboring states with electricity.

Narrow Route 147, called **Northshore Road**, meanders along Lake Mead towards the north, ultimately leading into Overton. Making a stop at one of the resorts along the way, such as **Boulder Beach**, **Callville**, **Echo Bay** or **Overton Beach** – some of which have their own campgrounds – is a pleasant way to take a break. The little community of **Overton** is home to about 3,000 people, and was originally founded by Mormons. But much earlier, between A.D. 500 and 1200, Anasazi Indians lived in the region. The relics of their culture that remain are displayed in the **Lost City Museum of Archeology** in Overton.

Traces of this vanished civilization can also be examined in the wilderness. Drive south from Overton, then join Highway 169 to the **Valley of Fire State Park**: the Anasazi left rock drawings on the almost unbelievably shaped sandstone formations. The rock here shines in every imaginable shade of red and brown and, whether at sunrise or sunset, the Valley of Fire truly deserves its name. Another highly impressive sight is **Rainbow**

89

Vista, appropriately named for its wide palette of colors, and **Silica Dome**, a brilliant white natural creation of quartz. The Indians had good reason to hold this magical place in special reverence.

The itinerary continues along I-15, a course that steers through a steppe-like desert landscape, a veritable portrait of the Wild West in reds, sandstone pinks and brown. **Mesquite** is where you cross over into the neighboring state of Arizona before entering Utah, but looking out the car window you'll hardly notice the difference.

The little town of **St. George** warrants a brief stop, even if merely to discover yet another aspect of Mormon history. The community was founded by Brigham Young in the 1860s, mainly as a place to escape the rather unfriendly climate of Salt Lake City. The main sight in town is the shining white tower of the **Mormon Temple**, the first ever to be built in Utah. The brethren had to move many tons of earth and stone in order to get a solid foundation in the muddy soil. 17,000 tons of sandstone had to be quarried for the temple itself. St. George soon earned the nickname "Dixie," because Brigham Young considered planting cotton in the area. The project failed, but Young, one of the founders of the Church of Latter Day Saints, lived in St. George until his death. His house, the **Brigham Young Winter Home**, is open to the public nowadays.

Not far from St. George, north on Interstate 15, is **Cedar City**, also known as "Festival City" and famous for its *Utah Shakespearean Festival*.

ZION NATIONAL PARK

Brigham Young is credited with having once said: "If there is a place on this earth that nobody else wants, that's the place I'm hunting for." The pious settler making his way west sought and ultimately found what we know today as Salt

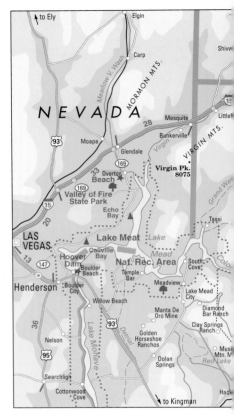

Lake City. His thoughts, however, included the entire state of Utah, which boasts extremely attractive and dramatic landscapes, but is rather poor when it comes to fertile prairies – or gold for that matter. Gold miners and pioneers looking for their respective fortunes tended to shy away from Utah. The state was therefore settled rather late, owing in part to its host of inaccessible canyons, some of which have not been explored to this day. The local tribes of Native Americans, the Utes, Shoshones and Paiutes, had the place to themselves for quite a while.

Zion National Park, with its canyons, caverns, sheer cliffs and deep valleys, is Utah's pride and joy when it comes to natural splendors. Since the Mormons

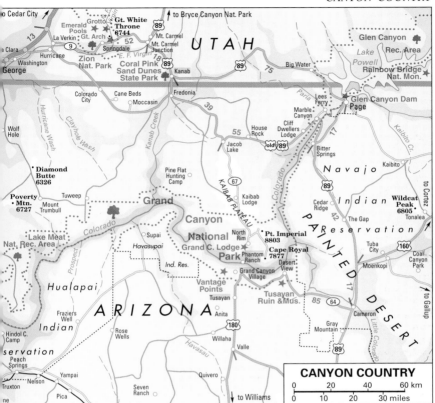

were the first settlers of European descent to leave their traces here, not only the park but many of the names of the natural gloriese here are drawn from the Bible.

The best way to take in some of these sights is by taking I-15 from Las Vegas, and then heading eastward on Route 9. The park's visitor center is located near **Springdale**. There are two possibilities at this point: either the **Zion Canyon Scenic Drive**, which makes a detour in a northerly direction, or catching the eastward extension of Route 9.

The Scenic Drive meanders along the **North Fork Virgin River** on the bed of Zion Canyon. Quite a few hiking paths have been laid out in the wilderness all along the road. Particularly pretty are the climbs up to **Angel's Landing** above the **Grotto** picnic spot, and the path to **Observation Point**. The hikes up to **Emerald Pools** or over to **Hidden Canyon** are somewhat difficult, but the courageous hiker will be rewarded with some especially beautiful panoramic views of the valley. A word of warning: the hikes are long and arduous, so you should be in fit condition and keep an eye on the weather situation.

If you'd rather stay in the car for your tour, your sightseeing will be limited to the fascinating rock formations, among others the famous **Great White Throne**, a white and red monolith, and the **Temple of Sinawava**. The latter is a kind

of semicircle whose two pillars make it strongly resemble an ancient Greek or Roman temple.

The **Gateway to the Narrows Trail** lies at the end of the Scenic Drive, and leads to the famous sandstone formations that appear to touch each other hundreds of feet overhead. The path can only be traversed on foot through the Virgin River, and though relatively short (two miles), it is not easy. The eastward extension of Route 9 leads by the **Great Arch** and on to an extraordinary landscape of rocks and cliffs, whose sense of space and sheer dimensions is second only to the Grand Canyon.

BRYCE AND GLEN CANYONS

Further north from Zion National Park, on Highway 89, Route 12 will take you east to the small but impressive entrance

Above: Hiking in Zion National Park. Right: Lake Powell has developed into a popular watersports center.

to **Bryce Canyon**. It is by definition not really a canyon, but rather the broken-off edge of a plateau.

This is **Paunsaugunt Plateau**, which provides a broad view of a spectacular landscape of red and brown sandstone rocks carved into tall needles, caused by millenia of rain and wind erosion. The Paiute Indians who once lived here had a much more descriptive name for the canyon: "The Place Where Red Rocks Stand Like Men in a Bowl-shaped Canyon."

South of the visitor center there is an impressive view of the **Bryce Amphitheater**. This park, too, has a scenic drive for its visitors. It goes for 18 miles all the way to **Bryce Point**, passing by the most enchanting and peculiar rock formations. Another recommended way to visit the canyon is to walk **Rim Trail**, which, as the name suggests, follows the broken edge of the plateau.

Follow Highway 89 southeastwards to the little town of **Kanab**, which you come to shortly before the Arizona bor-

der. The **Coral Pink Sand Dunes State Park** is just a few miles away. This is an incredibly beautiful nature reserve with endless red-hued desert landscapes, and unfortunately often overrun with tourists. Hollywood discovered the park quite some time ago, and some of the film sets are still in place for visitors to see.

Geographically speaking, the western town of **Kanab** (also known as *Little Hollywood*), lies right in the midst of America's most beautiful collection of canyons. To the south is the all-time favorite Grand Canyon. To the north is Bryce Canyon, and to the east Glen Canyon at Lake Powell.

Staying on Route 89, which heads in an easterly direction, you come to **Glen Canyon Recreation Area**, which sprawls around gigantic **Lake Powell** (186 miles long). The lake is not natural: it came into existence when the Glen Canyon Dam was built on the Colorado River. Lake Powell has long since become a center for aquatic activities, with its almost two thousandmilesofbeachesandnumerous littlebays.

The town of **Page**, to the south of the dam, is a lively holiday resort, and an excellent point of departure for boat tours of the lake. A favorite tour is to the famous **Rainbow Bridge National Monument** to the northeast. This bridge of sandstone, with a span of 260 feet, constitutes the world's largest natural arch.

GRAND CANYON –
THE NORTH RIM

A few hours driving southward from Page along ALT Highway 89 and Route 67 will bring you to the **north rim** of the **Grand Canyon**.

Military intelligence is indeed sometimes a contradiction in terms. About 150 years ago, when American officer Joseph C. Ives led a small force on an exploratory expedition along the Colorado River, he sent back a report on the Grand Canyon that stated: "Altogether value-

less; ours has been the first and will doubtless be the last party of whites to visit this profitless locality." The poor lieutenant made two mistakes in his report. First of all, a Spanish explorer named de Cardenas had already spotted the canyon in 1540. And second, not long after Ives, Americans, white and otherwise, and later droves of tourists from around the world, flocked to the Grand Canyon. In fact, it and the Colorado River here (*colorado* is Spanish for "colored") have become one of the world's favorite destinations, attracting an annual five million visitors.

One attraction of this canyon is undoubtedly its unfathomable proportions. It is the largest in the world: 280 miles long, from half a mile to 18 miles wide and up to one mile deep. Face to face with this superlative natural wonder, even the most hard-boiled tourists fall si-

Above: Young Indian boys sell waterskins for the descent into the Grand Canyon.
Right: Ascent with mules is less strenuous.

lent. The north rim (open from mid-May to October) may be less spectacular than the southern part of the national park, but it suffers far less from overcrowding. Only one tenth of the five million visitors who come here each year actually wander off to the north, and so you have a much greater feeling of being at one with nature here. Whether on the north rim or the south rim, a first-time visitor will be rendered overwhelmed by the beauty and grandeur of the Grand Canyon.

The north rim lies an average of 8,000 feet above sea level, which is between one and two thousand feet higher than the south rim. The bulk of the northern section rests on the **Kaibab Plateau**, an old Paiute Indian word meaning "mountain lying down."

Although the two rims are only ten miles apart from one another, the drive from one to the other on the highway connecting them is 215 miles long.

The best observation points on the north rim are easily accessible by good roads. Cape Royal Road runs southeast to

Walhalla Overlook, **Cape Royal**, and **Angel's Window**. One of the finest lookout points of the entire Grand Canyon area is **Point Imperial**, which at 8,803 feet is the highest spot in the Grand Canyon National Park. It offers not only a broad panorama of the entire canyon, but a breathtaking view of **Marble Gorge** and the **Painted Desert** as well.

The road leads back westwards to the **Supai Tunnel**, the **Grand Canyon Lodge**, where tour information can be obtained, and **Bright Angel Point**, the site of the visitor center. If you register early enough and have no fear of heights, you may want to try hiking one of the trails down to the bottom of the Grand Canyon. These hikes, on foot or mule-back, are guided. The mule alternative is only recommendable for people with a sense of adventure and a resilient back-side, as the trips generally last one or two days and can be quite exhausting. Both the North and the South Kaibab Trails take you all the way down to **Phantom Ranch**, at an altitude of 2,600 feet on the

canyon bed, where beds and also a camp site are available. There are some shorter hikes down the canyon to the west: **Widforss** and **Tiyo Point** trails.

A ride through the canyon is like time travel through the geological history of Planet Earth. Four million years ago, the Colorado River dug its way down into the soft sandstone. From top to bottom you can see the layers of sedimentary stone (sandstone and chalk) from the Paleozoic Era: the Permian period (230 million years ago), the Carboniferous (330 million years), Devonian (370 million), and Cambrian (550 million). Hard and shimmering black, the Vishnu shale and Zoroaster granite at the foot of the canyon date from the Precambrian era, making them about two billion years old; among the oldest stone visible on the surface of the earth.

The geologically newer layers contain fossils of animals, insects and plants, mutely narrating stories about the flora and fauna of long-past epochs of our planet's history.

GRAND CANYON –
THE SOUTH RIM

The **south rim** of the canyon, accessible from Page via highways 89 and 64, also provides visitors with spectacular views and fascinating insights. Route 64, called **East Rim Drive** here, has its fair share of grandiose lookout points between **Cameron** and **Tusayan**. One of the favorites (which means that in summer it is overrun with fellow tourists) is **Desert View**. Information on the Native American cultures that once inhabited this area is documented nearby at the **Tusayan Ruins and Museum**. Before reaching the visitor center in **Grand Canyon Village**, other highlights of this trip are the observation spots of **Grandview Point** and **Yavapai Point**, the latter of which provides a good rundown of the geological history of the canyon in its **Yavapai Museum**.

Above: Wet and wild adventure – rafting on the Colorado River.

Private cars are not allowed along **West Rim Drive** from May to the end of September. This does, however, have the best lookout points, so it is advisable to catch the shuttle bus in Grand Canyon Village, which ferries visitors to the best spots, including **Hopi , Pima** and **Mojave Points**.

Two trails lead from the south rim down into the canyon. Sloping continuously downward, **Bright Angel Trail** is hard on the knees and is a favorite with mule tours – so walkers have to watch out for fresh manure. **South Kaibab Trail** is more beautiful, more solitary, and steeper, with some great views. You can descend both trails in about four hours; the ascent takes seven to eight hours.

You can also view the canyon's grandeur from a birds-eye perspective on ten-seater airplanes, and there are even helicopter tours that can be made from Las Vegas. But only those whose motto is "some like it wet" should attempt the ever popular rubber-raft trip down the **Colorado River**.

UTAH AND THE CANYONS

Accommodation

MODERATE: **Bryce Canyon Lodge**, on UT 63, Cedar City, Tel: (435) 834-5361. Here the accommodation is rustical and comfortable. **Greene Gate Village**, 76 W Tabernacle St., St. George, Tel: (435) 628-6999. This is an authentically-decorated Victorian-style villa with charming rooms. **Zion Lodge**, on UT 9; five miles from the park entrance, Springdale, Tel: (435) 772-3213. Catch some fantastic views of Zion National Park.

BUDGET: **Gold Strike Inn & Casino**, east of US 93; three miles to the west of the Hoover Dam, Boulder City, Tel: (702) 293-5000. Stunning views of Lake Mead.

Camping

Echo Bay Resort, Via Star Route, Overton, Tel: (702) 394-4000. **Overton Beach Resort**, Boulder City, Tel: (702) 394-4040. Situated directly on the banks of Lake Mead.

Sights, Museums
and Parks

Brigham Young Winter Home, 200 North/100 West Sts., St. George, Tel: (435) 673-2517. **Bryce Canyon N.P.**, Information Tel: (435) 834-5322. **Coral Pink Sand Dunes State Park**, 14 miles northwest on route US 89, then 12 miles south on the country road, near Kanab. **Glen Canyon Recreation Area and Lake Powell**, 68 miles in an easterly direction, over US 89, Visitor center on UT 276, near Bullfrog. Park Headquarters in Page, AZ, Tel: (520) 608-6404. **Hoover Dam**, Hwy. 93, situated near Boulder City, Tel: (702) 293-8367. **Hoover Dam Museum**, 444 Hotel Plaza, Boulder City, Tel: (702) 294-1988. **Lake Mead National Recreation Area**, Information: 601 Nevada Hwy., Boulder City, Tel: (702) 293-8907. **Lost City Museum**, 721 So. Hwy. 169, Overton, Tel: (702) 397-2193. **Rainbow Bridge National Monument**, Information Tel: (602) 645-8200. **Temple Visitor Center in St. George**, 440 S/300 East, St. George, Tel: (435) 673-5181. **Valley of Fire State Park**, 18 miles southeast on NV 169, situated near Overton, Tel: 702/397-2088. **Zion National Park**, Springdale, Information Tel: (435) 772-3256.

Sports and Recreation

Black Canyon River Raft Tours, 1297 Nevada Hwy., Boulder City, Tel: (702) 293-3776, for river rafting. **Boat trips on Lake Powell**, on UT 276, exit at Halls Crossing and Bullfrog, Tel: (520) 278-8888. **Lake Mead Cruises**, Boulder City, Tel: (702) 293-6180. For traditional steamboat rides on Lake Mead. **River Mountain Hiking Trail**, c/o Boulder City Visitors Center, see below for address. A hiking trail 5 miles in length, providing beautiful

views over Lake Mead. **Scenic Flights over Glen Canyon**, Page Airport, on US 89, Tel: (520) 645-2494. **Zion National Park Horseback Trips**, rides down into the canyon begin at Zion Lodge, Tel: (435) 772-3967.

Tourist Information

Boulder City Visitors Center, 100 Nevada Hwy., Boulder City, NV 89005, Tel: (702) 294-1220. **Page/Lake Powell Chamber of Commerce**, 644 N Navajo Dr, Box 727, Page, AZ 86040, Tel: (520) 645-2741.

GRAND CANYON

Accommodation

Due to extremely popular demand, accommodation at El Tovar, Grand Canyon Lodge and Phantom Ranch should really be reserved several months in advance: AMFAC Parks & Resorts, 14001 E. Iliff, Aurora, Colorado 80014, Tel: (303) 297-2757, Fax (303) 297-3175, http:// www. grandcanyon.com

LUXURY: **El Tovar**, South Rim, on US 180 (AZ 64). A very elegant lodge with breathtaking views over the canyon.

MODERATE: **Best Western Grand Canyon Squire Inn**, South Rim, 7 miles south, on US 180. Tel: (520) 638-2681, Fax 638-0162, bestwestern@ thecanyon.com **Grand Canyon Lodge**, Canyon North Rim, south of AZ 67. Choice of motel rooms or cabins.

BUDGET: **Phantom Ranch**. Plenty of group accommodation in bottom of the canyon, with good catering.

Camping

Campsites at the **North Rim**, **South Rim** and at **Mather Campsite**, Tel: (301) 722-1257.

Sights, Museums
and Parks

Grand Canyon N. P., P.O.Box 129 Grand Canyon, AZ 86023, Tel: 520/638-7888. **Tusayan Museum**, East Rim Dr., 20 miles east of Grand Canyon Village, no telephone.

Recreation and Sports

Mule Trips, 1-2 day trips on muleback into the canyone, including overnight stays in Phantom Ranch. Bookings under Grand Canyon National Park Lodges (303) 297-2757.

Hiking in the Grand Canyon Area, Back Country Reservation Office, PO Box 126, Grand Canyon, AZ 86023. For a hiking permit to the bed of the canyon, contact the Back Country office of the Camper Service.

Tourist Information

Grand Canyon Chamber of Commerce, PO Box 3007, Grand Canyon, AZ 86023, Tel: 520/638-2901.

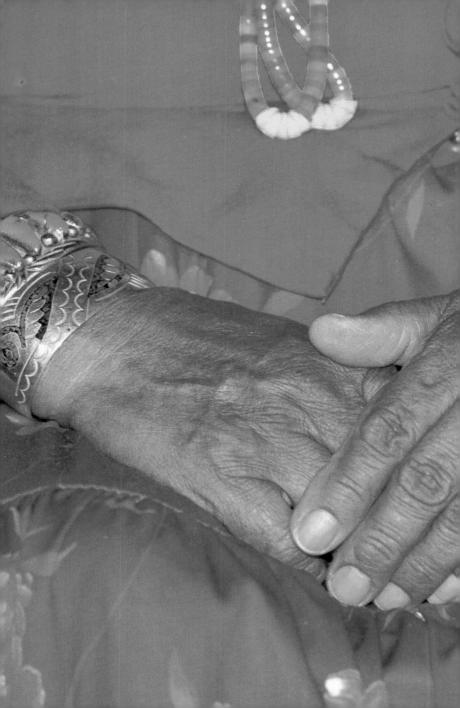

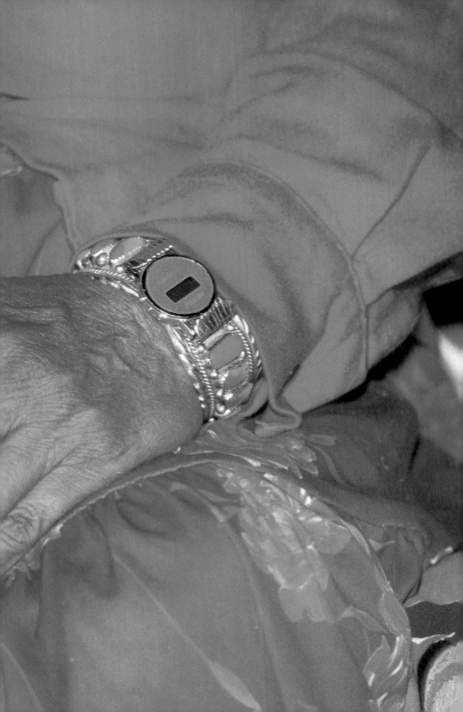

THROUGH NAVAJO AND HOPI COUNTRY

NAVAJO RESERVATION
HOPI RESERVATION
CANYON DE CHELLY
MONUMENT VALLEY
MESA VERDE

A journey through Arizona is a journey through Indian territory. For centuries, well before America was "discovered" by European settlers, highly civilized tribes lived in this region, squeezing every drop of water they could out of the desert. Nowadays, the entire northeastern section of the state is one huge reservation, the land of the Hopi and Navajo tribes.

Old women sell silver jewelry and pottery on the reservations, while young men lounge around the streets and while away the harsh realities of life with the assistance of alcohol. The proud history of this once mighty Indian culture is visible wherever you may care to look, but ironically, bleak proof of their present seemingly hopeless situation is also glaringly obvious; deep lines etched into the older Indian visages tell a thousand dark and wordless stories about the miseries of a single tribe, when entire populations were brutally expelled from their homelands and simply herded onto reservations.

This itinerary leads from the southern end of the Grand Canyon toward the east through the Navajo and Hopi reserva-

Previous pages: Colorful costume and jewelry of a Navajo woman. Left: Monument Valley

tions. The final destination is Mesa Verde, where you can see pre-Columbian cliff dwellings of ancient Indian tribes.

About a week will be needed to cover this approximately 750 mile journey.

THROUGH THE NAVAJO RESERVATION

Highway 64 leads from the southern end of the Grand Canyon to **Cameron** in the **Painted Desert**. The Indian reservations are easily accessible thanks to the highway system. This is both a blessing and a curse. On the one hand, it allows tourists into the land of the Native Americans; on the other hand it also allows for the lifestyle of the whites to penetrate the largest Indian reservation in the United States, making it virtually impossible to preserve old traditions, or retain the Native American languages.

Two hundred thousand Navajos live on this reservation, which was established in 1878. Today, the Navajo are the largest single Indian tribe on the American continent. They are closely related to the Apache tribes (they are in the same linguistic family), and until the settling of the West, they lived quite peacefully in what is today Arizona and New Mexico. Their only competitors, as it were, were the Hopi Indians.

Above: Classroom in a Navajo Reservation school (Chinle).

The Navajo had a semi-nomadic lifestyle, surviving on rudimentary agriculture and from raising sheep. As white settlers increasingly invaded their tribal grounds in the mid-19th century, they started defending themselves with some vehemence. In spite of the fine leadership of the Apache chief Geronimo, the war fought by the Navajo and Apache was a vain enterprise from the beginning.

In the long run, these proud warriors could not hold out against the overwhelming military power of the white man, even using guerilla tactics. With the surrender of Geronimo in 1886, the Indian Wars in the southwestern United States came to an end. Later, the Navajo were permitted to settle a reservation that was on their original tribal grounds. But to this day, the Navajo, like many other Native American tribes, suffer the social plagues of unemployment, alcoholism and general alienation.

On the other hand, the reservation has been fairly well off ever since oil was discovered here. Gambling halls are another major source of income. Nevertheless the brutal reality of cultural uprooting and disorientation has led to the fact that the traditional lifestyle of the Navajo simply cannot be kept alive.

Yet, even today, many ritual dances have survived, and they are not performed solely for the benefit of curious tourists. Among them are the Navajo Fire Dance, the *Yei-bi-chei* Dance (in winter) and, finally, the so-called Enemy Way Dance in summer. If you want to attend, you'll have to arrange for a permit first. Note, too, that photography and sound recording are not allowed.

Anyone exploring Navajo territory should treat the land and its people with respect. Land is something holy to the Indians, which is why you should never camp out in the wild. You might fulfill your wishes to photograph "real Indians," but don't forget to always ask permission first.

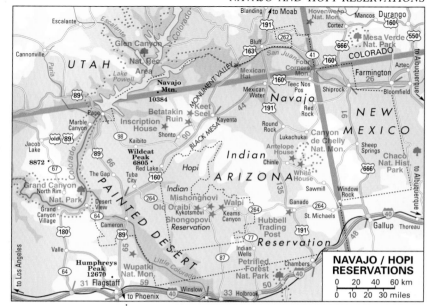

THE HOPI:
THE PEACEFUL PEOPLE

The word *koyaanisqatsi* in the language of the Hopi means something like "self-induced chaos and uncertain future." It seems as if this old word holds true for their present situation, which is more difficult now than ever before.

The small Hopi reservation, founded in 1882, lies in the middle of the Navajo reservation. It is home to 6,000 tribespeople who struggle in vain to save their old traditions from succumbing to outside (white) influences, and to solve old enmities with the Navajos.

The Hopi Indians (the name means "peaceful people") are believed to be descendents of the pre-Columbian Anasazi tribes. Nowadays, they live in independent communities which are spread out over three 600 foot high mesas, or plateaus. On the first mesa is **Walpi**, one of the prettiest Hopi pueblos. Also worth seeing are the three villages on the second mesa, **Mishongnovi**, **Shipaulovi**,

and **Shongopovi**, where (near Hwy. 264) you will find the Hopi cultural center and simple camping sites. The oldest of the villages, **Old Oraibi**, on the third mesa, has been inhabited since 1150. The **Black Mesa**, another plateau that is somewhat to the north, was mined for coal and was almost totally destroyed by the 1960s.

How the Hopi arrived in this area remains a mystery. At any rate, the tribe was able to ward off the Navajos thanks to the excellent natural protection afforded by the mesas. Legend has it that the Hopi, in their efforts to avoid the jealousy of others, toured North America searching for the most barren and infertile land. Rock drawings of their ancestors are visible to this day on the mesas, in caves and in gorges. These cubic drawings, often hundreds of them squeezed onto a tiny area in no particular order, relate the history of the tribe. The mesas had always provided them with good protection, as they could only be occupied with the greatest difficulty. As for the Navajo Indians, they arrived in the region

during the 16th century and gradually invaded larger sections of Hopi territory. But coexistence between the two tribes – on one side settled Hopi corn farmers, on the other nomadic Navajo hunters – was not always simple. Even today border conflicts continue to irritate relationships between the two, and some Navajo families categorically refuse to relinquish Hopi land. As long as anyone can remember the Hopis have looked down on the Navajos, considering them aggressive and dishonest. They call them *tasavuh*, which means something like "killers."

The Hopi Indians are famous for their *kachinas*, sacred figurines carved of wood and used in religious ceremonies. Ceramics and silver jewelry also comprise a significant element of Hopi handicrafts.

Ceramic-making especially is regarded as an almost holy pursuit by the

Above: Petrified tree trunk in Petrified Forest National Park. Right: A place for sunbathing for lizards.

Hopi, as it is with almost all Indian cultures of the Southwest. A potter's wheel is not used in the manufacture of these ceramics, rather, they are made from thick strands of rolled clay which are formed by hand into vases and bowls. The pottery is decorated with symbols handed down from ancient times. Typical of these decorations are the angular drawings of animals and people; from eagles to ants, all forms of life are immortalized on Hopi pottery.

After visiting the mesas you can drive on Route 264 to Ganado. Nearby is the **Hubbell Trading Post**, an old fort dating back to 1878. It is the oldest trading post on Navajo territory, and nowadays serves as a museum. Here, Indians sell their handwoven carpets and silver jewelry, and demonstrate the production of their crafts.

Farther east is the town of **Window Rock**, which is the capital of the Navajo Nation. The democratically elected tribal council, 88 members strong, meets here regularly. The history of the tribe is re-

counted in the **Navajo Nation Museum**. In the immediate proximity is the **Navajo Nation Zoological and Botanical Park**, exhibiting the fauna and flora that enabled the tribe to survive in the desert. The name Window Rock, by the way, refers to the 50 foot natural rock bridge that lies in the midst of a forest of sandstone rock formations.

If you have time, try to make a detour to the **Petrified Forest National Park**, 26 miles east of **Holbrook** on Hwy.180. It consists of a forest of fossilized tree trunks, some of which are up to 225 million years old. Back in the days when these trees were growing and green, the area was a fertile region of swamps and marshes, not a desert. Over the course of millions of years, the dead trunks gradually became covered with sediments, mainly silicate-rich volcanic ash. Because of their state of preservation, every annual ring can still be clearly identified.

Highway 191 heads back northward to one of the most fascinating testimonials to the great Indian culture.

CANYON DE CHELLY: PURE HISTORY

Canyon de Chelly (pronounced *de-shay*) has long been a holy place for the Navajo tribes, who for centuries have lived and sought refuge here. Even today, tourists can only explore a small part of the canyon on their own, namely the **White House Trail**, 2.5 miles in length. For all other trails in the canyon an Indian guide is obligatory, if for no other reason than out of respect for the religious significance of the area. These tours start out from the Thunderbird Lodge in **Chinle**.

Unfortunately, even with a guide, most of the cliff caves, many of which once served as dwellings, are not accessible. The 16 mile **Rim Drive** along the edge of the canyon allows visitors to see the most important sights from their cars.

The Navajos settled the canyon around 1700, but research indicates that tribes had been living here for centuries before that, attracted to the area because of its fertility. Farming is, to this date, one of

the regional mainstays. Around 60 dwellings are still in existence, the oldest ones being approximately 2,000 years old. The most interesting of these are the **White House**, the **Antelope House** and the **Mummy Cave**.

Canyon de Chelly did achieve rather sorry fame in 1864, when the legendary Christopher "Kit" Carson trapped the last Navajo warriors in the valley and forced them to either surrender or die of hunger. During the previous five months he had conducted a war of attrition, destroying fields, capturing herds, and stalking the Navajos across more than 300 miles of prairie. The Indians fled into the Canyon de Chelly, assuming it to be impregnable. But Carson ordered his troops to the other end of the canyon, and after only two weeks the war was over. The Navajos had no choice but to let themselves

Above: Shepherds in Monument Valley.
Right: Young American of Indian descent.
Far right: Ascent to the Balcony House in Mesa Verde National Park.

be herded onto the reservation - the one they still inhabit to this day.

Highways 191, 160 and 163 continue through old Navajo country and as far as Monument Valley.

MONUMENT VALLEY: FIT FOR THE MOVIES

Hardly any other set of cliffs has served as a backdrop for so many films (*Stagecoach*, among others) and advertisements. But it's not for its otherworldly qualities that **Monument Valley** is famous to most people; but rather, for its qualities as an epitome of the unique landscape and character of the Wild West.

Route 163 takes you directly into the valley, past imposing, individual rock giants. Cowboys and Indians never had to bother about dealing with road conditions here, but the modern traveler should keep in mind what kind of weather there's been over the last few days before embarking into the park. Access roads are not paved, and after heavy rainfall or

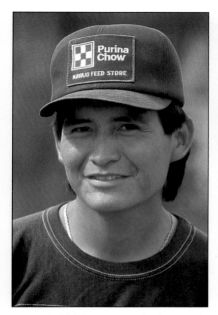

a storm (which happens rarely, however), they are not usable. If you are the kind of person who worries about the paint on your car, you should simply leave it at the visitor center and board the shuttle bus there, which will ferry you off for a closer look at Monument Valley. As an additional note: the valley is not administered by the National Parks Service of the United States, but rather by the Navajo Nation.

Given some extra time, a nice detour awaits in the southwest: About ten miles beyond **Kayenta** road 564 forks off Highway 160 and leads to the **Navajo National Monument**. The three cliff villages here were once inhabited by Kayenta-Anasazi Indians, not Navajos, and are about 800 years old. Of the three dwellings, **Betatakin**, **Keet Seel**, and **Inscription House**, only the first is accessible – albeit from a distance – inasmuch as it can be viewed from a viewing platform. The two other caverns can only be reached after a long hike or on horseback, and Inscription House is closed to the public. Tours lasting many exhausting hours are available for Betatakin and Keet Seel.

Highway 163 continues northward into Utah, allowing you a glance at one of the area's more famous rock formations, **Mexican Hat**, thus named because it looks like an upside-down sombrero. It looks as if a small push might just upset its balance enough to tip it over.

The trip then continues eastward toward Colorado and on to **Four Corners Monument**, on US 160, the only spot in the United States where the borders of four states meet (Arizona, Colorado, New Mexico and Utah). Highway 160 ultimately leads to the last great sight of this trip, **Mesa Verde National Park**.

MESA VERDE:
A JOURNEY INTO THE PAST

A visit to Mesa Verde, northeast of Four Corners, means plunging into the centuries-old historical culture of the Anasazi Indians. Highway 160 takes you

to the Mesa Verde National Park, which in terms of history and culture is probably the most important park in the U.S. Here, as well as in Canyon de Chelly, Hovenweep and Chaco Canyon, pre-Columbian Anasazi tribes lived until around the 13th century. In Mesa Verde, a relatively fertile plateau (its well-earned Spanish name means "Green Table"), they left numerous cliff dwellings; stone houses nestling in the huge yellow and brown sandstone cliffs.

The **Far View Visitor Center** is located a short distance beyond the entrance to the park. Together with the **museum** and the park headquarters a little to the south, it presents information on the various findings that have been made within the park. The cultural Golden Age of this people ended in the early 14th century, long before the European "discovery" of America. At that point they left Mesa Verde. The reason might have

Above: Cliff Palace, the largest stone dwelling of the Anasazi at Mesa Verde N. P.

been an extensive drought that seems to have afflicted the entire Southwest at the time. Another reason might have been overpopulation.

The finest cliff dwelling is **Spruce Tree House**, which stands right behind the museum. This superbly preserved complex boasts over a hundred rooms (all with altars). Behind this house, the road forks into the East Loop and West Loop. The West Loop passes by the **Square Tower House** and the **Sun Temple**, as well as **Sun Point**. The eastern route is even more spectacular, and takes you to **Cliff Palace** and **Balcony House**. With its 200 rooms, Cliff Palace is the largest and most famous dwelling in Mesa Verde. Balcony House is only accessible by climbing a 32 foot ladder and is crisscrossed by a tunnel network.

On the way back, halfway between the *Headquarters* and the park entrance, you should keep an eye out for **Park Point Fire Lookout**. From its altitude of 8,572 feet there is an extraordinary view over the entire Four Corners region.

NAVAJO AND HOPI INDIAN RESERVATIONS, CANYON DE CHELLY AND MONUMENT VALLEY
Area code 520

Accommodation
MODERATE: **Best Western Adobe Inn**, 1701 N Park Dr., Winslow, Tel: 289-4883. **Best Western Canyon de Chelly Inn**, Chinle, three blocks east on AZ 191, Tel: 674-5875. Best Western motel with restaurant. **Goulding's Monument Valley Lodge**, Monument Valley, 21 miles north, then west on US 163, Tel: (801) 727-3231. Best Western with pool and campsite, daily tours to Monument Valley. **Little America Hotel**, 2515 E Butler Ave., Flagstaff, Tel: 779-7900. Well-kept complex with restaurant, children's playground, all rooms with refrigerator, iron, coffee-maker. **Thunderbird Lodge**, Chinle, 3 miles southeast of AZ 191, Tel: (602) 674-5841. In Canyon de Chelly, partly with small rooms within the original old stone structures.
BUDGET: **Best Western Arizonian Inn**, 2508 E Navajo Blvd., Holbrook, Tel: 524-2611. Nice motel with pool and restaurant nearby which is open round the clock. **Econo Lodge East**, 3601 E Lockitt Rd., Flagstaff, Tel: 572-1477. **Super 8**, 3725 Kasper Ave., Flagstaff, Tel: 526-0818, US 66, 89 on Business Rte. 40.
CAMPING: Information on camping possibilities in Arizona's state parks is available at: **Arizona State Parks**, 1300 W Washington, Phoenix, AZ 85007, Tel: (602) 542-4174. For information about campsites within the Indian reservations you should contact the relevant reservation bureau. Random camping within the reservations is not recommended!

Sights, Museums and Parks
Canyon de Chelly N. M., Chinle, Tel: 674-5500. **Hopi Cultural Center** (with restaurant and motel), Tel: 734-2421 (reservations urgently recommended). **Hubbell Trading Post National Historic Site**, 1 mile west on AZ 264, tel: 755-3475. Oldest trading post in Navajo country. **Navajo County Historical Museum**, 100 E Arizona, Holbrook, Tel: 524-6558. Exhibition centered around the culture of the Apache, Navajo and Hopi Indians (in the old courthouse building). **Navajo Indian Reservation**, Information Tel: 871-6659. **Navajo N. M.**, 20 miles southwest of Kayenta, on AZ 564, Information Tel: 672-2366. **Navajo Nation Museum**, Tse Bonito Park (easterly junction of AZ 264/Indian Rte. 12), Window Rock, Tel: 871-6673. **Navajo Nation Zoological and Botanical Park**, Tse Bonito Park (easterly junction of AZ 264/Indian Rte. 12), in the Navajo Arts and Crafts Enterprise Center, Tel: 871-6573. **Old Trails Museum**, 212 N Kinsley Ave., Winslow, Tel: 289-5861. Exhibition centering around Indian art and handicrafts. **Petrified Forest National Park**, 26 miles east of Holbrook, off Interstate 40, Information Tel: 524-6228. Countless colored fossilized tree trunks.

Sightseeing Tours
Crawley's Monument Valley Tours Inc., Tel: 697-3734/3463. There are daily tours through Monument Valley, Mystery Valley and Hunt's Mesa. **Thunderbird Lodge Canyon Tours**, Tel: 602-5841, daily jeep rides into the canyons available.

Tourist Information
Hopi Tribe, PO Box 123, Kykotsmovi, AZ 86039, Tel: 734-2441, Ext. 190 (Tel. 734-6648 for information about current events taking place on the Mesas). **Monument Valley Navajo Tribal Park**, Box 360289, Monument Valley, UT 84536, Tel: 435/727-3287. **Navajoland Tourism Department**, Box 663, Window Rock, AZ 85615, Tel: (871) 6436-7371.

MESA VERDE NATIONAL PARK AND SURROUNDING AREA
Area code 970
Accommodation
MODERATE: **Fair View Lodge**, Mancos, (by Navajo Hill, in the Park, 15 miles away from Mesa Verde Park entrance), Tel: 529-4421.
BUDGET: **Anasazi**, 666 S Broadway, Cortez, Tel: 565-3773. **Holiday Inn Express**, 2121 E Main St., Cortez, Tel: 565-6000.

Sights, Museums and Parks
Anasazi Heritage Center & Escalante Ruins, on CO 184, near Cortez, Tel: 882-4811. Museum based on the now extinct Anasazi culture. **Far View Visitor Center**, 15 miles south of the entrance to Mesa Verde Park. **Far View Museum**, near the park's headquarters, 21 miles south of the park entrance. **Park Point Fire Lookout**, halfway between the entrance to Mesa Verde Park and the Park Headquarters.

Tourist Information
Colorado Welcome Center, 928 E. Main St. Cortez, CO 81321, Tel: 565-4048, Fax 565-4828. **Mesa Verde National Park Superintendent**, PO Box 8, Mesa Verde National Park, CO 81330, Tel: 529-4465.

FROM THE GRAND CANYON TO DENVER

ASPEN AND VAIL
DENVER
ROCKY MOUNTAIN NATIONAL PARK

The snow-capped Rocky Mountains, the highest mountain range on the North American continent, are a constant reminder of what the pioneers were up against as they pushed their way westward. In the last century, the goal was "Pikes Peak or Bust!"– the prospectors' oath that they would reach the site of a gold discovery in the Rockies successfully or go broke in the attempt.

This is a journey of 651 miles, which, allowing for some boating and a detour to a ski resort, should take about four days.

Lake Powell

From the north rim of the Grand Canyon, take Route 67 to Jacob Lake. Turning right on US ALT 89 leads eastward to **Lake Powell** (see map page 103). This lake came into being in 1963, when the U.S. Government built a dam here. It stretches for almost 200 miles from northern Arizona into southern Utah, and has some 2,000 miles of convoluted shoreline. Close to 3.5 million visitors come to Lake Powell each year, some bringing their own boats, and others renting houseboats; motels can be found in nearby Page.

Left: The Maroon Bells, mirrored in Maroon Lake near Aspen, Colorado.

Four Corners and Durango

US 89 heading south leads away from Lake Powell down to the junction with Route 160. Turning left and heading east leads to **Four Corners Monument**. There's a monument at the exact location where the state lines of Arizona, Colorado, New Mexico and Utah intersect, offering an unusual travel opportunity: where else can you visit four states in only a few seconds?

During the summer months in **Mesa Verde National Park**, about 30 miles from Durango, you can take a tour of the Anasazi Indian cliff dwellings, which date all the way back to the 12th century (see page 107).

Back on Route 160, the journey continues on to **Durango**, a charming, historic community which sprang to life in 1880 when the gold rush town of **Silverton**, which is 45 miles to the north, needed a railhead through which to send its ore. The narrow-gauge (light railway) railroad which was responsible for Durango's birth still exists today. Instead of ore, though, the sightseeing train now carries visitors between the two towns.

The **Million Dollar Highway**, US 550, meanders from Durango northwards and leads straight through the very heart of the Rocky Mountains. At the town of

111

Delta, the road becomes Route 50, which brings you to **Grand Junction**.

North of here, and just north of the town of Dinosaur, is **Dinosaur National Monument**. It is world famous as a fossil site, and rafting trips can be made on both rivers running through the park, the Jampa and the Green River.

Near Grand Juntion are a couple of natural wonders: west of I-70 (via Fruita) is **Colorado National Monument** with its bizarre rock formations; south on Highway 50 is the **Black Canyon of the Gunnison National Monument**, named for its dark stone, through which the Gunnison River flows. Heading west on I-70, then south on Route 128 you reach **Moab** in Utah, which is known as the *Mountainbike Capital* for its *Moab Slidrock Bike Trail*. It is also well-known for being the starting point for rafting trips down the Colorado River.

Above: The Rocky Mountains were the most difficult parts of the journey for wagon trains to the West. Right: Skiing in Aspen.

Taking Highway 191 north from Moab brings you to **Arches National Park**, which features impressive natural stone arches, including Landscape Arch and Delicate Arch.

From the Arches Park Visitor Center, taking Highway 191 a few miles north and then Route 313 west will bring you to **Dead Horse Point State Park**, as well as to **Canyonlands National Park**. From **Dead Horse Point Overlook** there is a fantastic view of the Colorado River and the Canyonlands.

The **Island in the Sky Plateau**, a high plateau between the Green and Colorado rivers, can be found inside Canyonland Naitonal Park. To the south of the confluence of these two rivers, the picturesque rock towers of **Needles District** stretch out.

ASPEN AND VAIL

From **Grand Junction**, Highway 6/Interstate 70 is the main thoroughfare crossing the state of Colorado from west

to east. Thanks to their height, the cold winters, and the level of humidity that drifts over from the Pacific, the Rockies here are blessed with a lot of snowfall. Around just about every bend in the road in Colorado there's a ski resort – old, new, or just being built and soon to be opened. Some of the most famous of these are either on I-70 or not too many miles away from it.

The most prestigious ski resort in the western United States is, without a doubt, **Aspen**, which is reached by turning right off Interstate 70 onto Route 82 at Glenwood Springs, and driving a further 42 miles. It's not unusual to run into a few Hollywood stars or other celebrities during an Aspen visit. In summer, Aspen offers the usual array of mountain activities: biking, hiking, climbing and fishing. A challenging river for rafting and canoeing fans is the **Fork River**, which roars out of the Sawatch Range.

Visually, Aspen is delightful, as its governing body energetically controls construction and signage, thus avoiding

that well-known junky look that too many resorts suffer from.

Another famous resort is **Vail**, lying further east on I-70. An alternative route for the daring driver- but only in summer - is from Aspen over **Independence Pass** (12,095 feet), a stunning mountain drive past Mt. Elbert, at 14,433 feet, which is the highest point in Colorado.

Vail is a fairly new resort, having only taken shape in 1952. Its architecture is borrowed from the Austrian Alps, and it somehow gives the impression of having been tucked away in the Rockies for ages. Vail stretches for almost ten miles along the narrow Rocky Mountain Valley; many parts of town are closed to traffic, so that skiers get around via (free) shuttle buses.

There are six skiing pistes in this area: **Mongolia**, **Siberia**, **China**, **Teacup**, **Sunup** and **Sundown**, which cover some ten square miles, making Vail and adjacent Beaver Creek the largest skiing area in the United States. The skiing season runs from December to April.

Copper Mountain and Breckenridge

Just a few miles southeast of Vail along I-70 is **Copper Mountain**, which is both a ski resort and a convention center. Golf is also very popular at Copper Mountain, not least because in the thin air, 9,600 feet above sea level, the ball seems to fly for miles if it is well struck. The resort's 18 hole course, designed by Pete and Perry Dye, is considered to be the highest 18 hole golf course in North America.

East of Copper Mountain and accessible via I-70 and then south on Route 9, is **Breckenridge**, yet another much-loved Colorado resort. One of its main attractions is the **Breckenridge Brewery & Pub**; often, the beer you're served here has just been brewed minutes before in the micro-brewery on the premises.

With more than 350 historic builings listed on the National Historic Register, one could say that Breckenridge is the most historic of all the Colorado ski resorts. The town enjoyed three mining booms and is now raking in its current wealth from skiers. Gold was first discovered here in 1859. Silver was mined here twenty years later, and made the town a second fortune. Then another generation of pioneers came to pan and mine gold here in the 1930s.

Many old homes of previous miners and their bosses are now B&Bs, restaurants or chic boutiques.

DENVER

The city of **Denver** is popularly known as "*Mile High City*," as the 13th step of the State Capitol Building lies at an altitude of precisely 5,280 feet above sea level. This is a remarkably neat state capital, in contrast to most big cities in the American West, boasting more than 200 parks and dozens of attractive, tree-lined boulevards. While most Western cities spread out over many square miles, Denver has a dense, central downtown area that can easily be explored on foot.

At dawn and at dusk, the city is beautifully backdropped by the the silhouette of the sunkissed Rocky Mountains, some 30 miles to the west. To the south, on a clear day, you can see **Pike's Peak** (14,108 feet), where a gold strike in the mid-1800s started a worldwide rush of miners and fortune hunters to the area. There is a toll road to the mountaintop.

From Denver, it is also possible to make a day trip to Pike's Peak by cog railway. This is the highest railway of its kind in the world, and it takes passengers from Manitou Springs right up to the peak. At the beginning of July each year, an exciting mountain rally takes place in Pikes Peak.

Larimer Street is a good place to strike up a walking acquaintance with *LoDo* (lower downtown) Denver. This street is Denver's oldest and, once upon a time, wildest. That Wild West feeling has been rekindled with gas lamps, arcades, fine Victorian woodwork, and there are also coaches on hand to take visitors around in traditional style. Bat Masterson once tended bar here, and Soapy Smith ran the West's largest gang of crooks, thieves and conmen. In recent times, LoDo has developed into a real tourist magnet, attracting people to its 70 new restaurants and brew pubs (including the famous Wynkoop Brewery). Connecting with it is 16th Street and its **Pavilions Complex** - a blend of hotels, restaurants and shops which are open til midnight during the week. About two miles northwest of here is the **Colorado's Ocean Journey** aquarium and the **Six Flags Elitch Gardens** amusement park, with its breathtaking rollercoaster ride.

In downtown Denver you'll find carefully restored old buildings from the city's colorful past on practically every

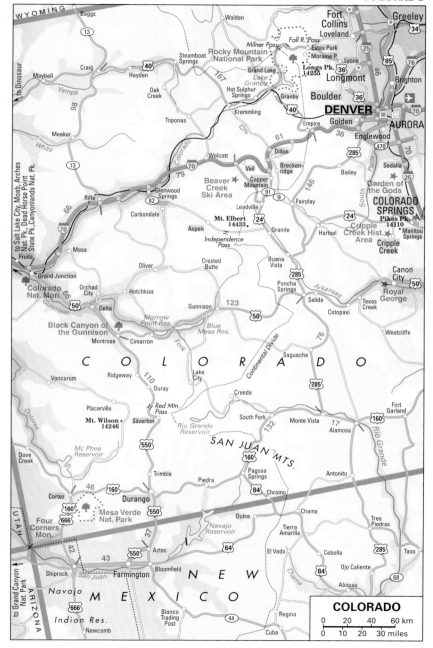

WYOMING
Baggs
13
Walden
Fort Collins
Loveland
Greeley
34

Maybell
Craig
40
Hayden
Steamboat Springs
Oak Creek
to Dinosaur
Milner Pass
Fall R. Pass
Rocky Mountain National Park
Estes Park
Moraine P.
Lyons
25
85
76
Brighton
70
Grand Lake
Lake Granby
Longs Pk. 14255
Longmont
98
Yampa
167
Hot Sulphur Springs
Granby
Boulder
36

Meeker
White
13
Toponas
Kremmling
40
Empire
Golden
DENVER
AURORA
61
36
Englewood
470
70

Rifle
66
70
Glenwood Springs
82
79
70
Wolcott
Vail
Beaver Creek Ski Area
Copper Mountain
91
9
Dillon
Breckenridge
146
Bailey
285
Sedalia
25

Carbondale
Leadville
Mt. Elbert 14433
24
Fairplay
Hartsel
24
Garden of the Gods
COLORADO SPRINGS
Pikes Pk. 14110
Manitou Springs
Cripple Creek Hist. Area
Cripple Creek

Mesa
Aspen
Granite
South Platte
to Salt Lake City, Moab, Arches Nat. Pk, Dead Horse Point State Pk., Canyonlands Nat. Pk.
Fruita
Grand Junction
Colorado Nat. Mon.
66
50
Orchad City
Hotchkiss
Oliver
Crested Butte
Independence Pass
Buena Vista
285
Poncha Springs
Arkansas
Salida
Texas Creek
Canon City
50
Royal George
Westcliffe

Gunnison
Delta
Gunnison
123
50
Morrow Point Res.
Blue Mesa Res.
Fork
Saguache
76

Black Canyon of the Gunnison
Montrose
Cimarron
COLORADO
Continental Divide
285

Vancorum
Ridgeway
110
Ouray
Lake City
Creede
Fort Garland
160

Placerville
Red Mtn. Pass
Silverton
Rio Grande Reservoir
South Fork
132
Monte Vista
17
Alamosa

Dove Creek
Dolores
Mt. Wilson 14246
550
Mc Phee Reservoir
SAN JUAN MTS.
160
Rio Grande

Cortez
46
160
Trimble
Piedra
Pagosa Springs
84
Chromo
Antonito
Tres Piedras
285
Taos

UTAH
Four Corners Mon.
160
666
Mesa Verde Nat. Park
550
Durango
Dulce
Chama
Tierra Amarilla
Cebolla
68

42
43
550
Aztec
37
64
El Vado
84
Ojo Caliente

to Grand Canyon Nat. Park
ARIZONA
Shiprock
666
San Juan
Farmington
Bloomfield
Navajo Reservoir
Chama

Navajo
Indian Res.
Newcomb
NEW
Blanco Trading Post
44
Regina
Cuba
MEXICO
Abiquiu

COLORADO			
0	20	40	60 km
0	10	20	30 miles

street corner: the **Molly Brown House** on Pennyslvania Avenue, for instance. "Unsinkable Molly" entered Denver folklore in 1912 when she booked passage on the ill-fated *Titanic*. She was the wealthy but not very well educated wife of a Denver gold miner, returning from a European jaunt. Wearing her $60,000 chinchilla cape (and very little else), she calmed passengers aboard the sinking ship, led them to lifeboats and, waving the pistol she always carried, ordered the crew to keep rowing until rescue arrived. Her house is open to visitors and contains original furnishings and mementos of her remarkable life.

The **State Capitol Building** on Colfax Avenue is another one of Denver's more impressive sights. If the 13th step of the building's west side seems especially worn, it is: that's because standing on this step puts you at exactly

Above: Denver against the backdrop of the Rocky Mountains. Right: The area around Moffat is ideal for horse ranching.

5,280 feet – one mile – above sea level. The capitol was modeled after the U.S. Capitol in Washington, D.C., and its dome positively glows at sunrise and sunset because it is covered with 200 ounces of 24 karat gold leaf.

There is a lot of money being made in Denver – literally: 40 million coins a day to be precise, which are minted, bagged and shipped by the **U.S. Mint**, also located on Colfax Avenue, and which is a tourist attraction in itself. You can stand and watch 800 coins a minute being stamped and shot from each of 60 punch presses into growing piles that give the Mint the appearance of a slot machine gone crazy.

The **Denver Art Museum**, just a block south of the Mint on 14th Avenue, is a 28 sided, ten storey structure, which is in itself a piece of sculpture. Over one million special gray glass tiles are wrapped around the building like a second skin, each tile reflecting light in a different way. Inside are more than 35,000 works just waiting to be admired - works of art

from Europe, Asia and the U.S.; probably the most famous being the collection of totem poles in the **American Indian Hall**.

The **Museum of Western Art** on Tremont Place is much more traditional looking and has a typical Western appearance. It is home to paintings and sculptures, including a number of Western classics by Remington, Russell and Georgia O'Keeffe. West of here you'll find Denver's Performing Arts Complex, comprising 8 theaters and enough room for 10,000 visitors. Here, you can enjoy plays, operas and symphonic concerts. Visitors coming here in the wintertime will have the opportunity to admire a completely different attraction: Every year, in January, during the *National Western Stock Show*, one of the largest rodeos in the world takes place right here in Denver.

If you haven't yet taken the opportunity to sample some of the freshly brewed beer in Lower Downtown, then perhaps you should pay a visit to **Coor's**, America's largest beer brewery, which offers daily tours of its huge plant in suburban Golden. These tours naturally end with a free product sampling. While out in Golden inspecting the brewery, you ought to take in the **Colorado Railroad Museum** with over 80 vintage steam locomotives and carriages on display. The grave of **Buffalo Bill** and its small museum is also well worth visiting.

Colorado Springs and Boulder

South of Denver and accessible by heading down I-25, is **Colorado Springs**. The area has been revitalized in recent years by the building of the ultramodern **U.S. Air Force Academy** in the community. A favorite daily event, for visitors and locals alike, is the 11 a.m. formation, when all 4,000 cadets march to the mess hall for lunch.

Just a few miles west is the **Garden of the Gods**, a geological wonder where massive, bright-red sandstone formations rise up to 600 feet into the blue Colorado

sky. **Cripple Creek** is a restored gold-mining town 48 miles west of Colorado Springs along Route 67 (via US 24). An hour's drive southwast of Colorado Springs, via Routes 115 and 50, is **Royal Gorge**, with one of the world's highest suspension bridges (1,053 feet).

Northwest of Denver on US 36 is another college town, **Boulder**, home of the **University of Colorado**. The first white settlers came to the area in 1858, and they left behind them a large number of attractive Victorian buildings. The restored downtown **Historic District** is well worth strolling through. **Pearl Street** was once a mining service center lined with log cabins. Today, it is an award-winning, open-air pedestrian mall, listed on the National Register of Historic Places, famous for its late 19th and early 20th century superbly preserved commercial buildings.

Above: Phosphorescent lichens in the forests of the Rocky Mountains. Right: Bighorn sheep in Rocky Mountain National Park.

ROCKY MOUNTAIN NATIONAL PARK

It is little wonder that the **Rocky Mountain National Park** is Colorado's most popular single attraction, and it draws over 3 million visitors annually.

The entrance to the park is about 40 miles from Denver, following US 36 in a northeasterly direction. The road leads directly to the park via the spectacular **Estes Valley** to **Estes Park**. A mountain tramway leads from Estes Park to a lookout platform on **Prospect Mountain** allowing a spectacular view of the other mountains in the park.

The little town of Estes Park, by the way, was named after Joel Estes, one of the first people to explore this region. In the mid-19th century he set out on several reconnaisance missions to this part of the Rocky Mountains, and kept returning. In 1915, the Rocky Mountains National Park was officially established. This was partly thanks to the American writer Enos Mills, who described the

mountains as follows: "He who feels the spell of the wild, the rhythmic melody of falling water, the echoes among the crags, the bird songs, the wind in the pines, is in tune with the universe."

Today, the park preserves 412 square miles of rugged and untouched nature, punctuated by 78 peaks, each of which is over 12,000 feet high. The area is also known as the **Front Range** of the Rockies, the initial wave of mountains rising out of America's central plains. They are part of a long chain of high peaks which stretches all the way from 300 miles above the Canadian border to northern New Mexico.

The Rocky Mountains, belonging to the world's highest mountain ranges, were formed by tectonic shifts about 70 million years ago. They owe their current wild beauty to the natural forces of fire, ice, water and wind. Over millions of years these young mountains were further shaped by tectonic and volcanic activity, and during the past two million years the mighty glaciers resulting from

four Ice Ages forced their way through the mountains. Some ranges were flattened, others were heaved up by the incredible pressure of the ice. As the glaciers dwindled, they left clear lakes in their wake.

A drive through Rocky Mountain National Park allows visitors to experience a variety of climatic zones in just a few hours; the higher you climb, the more dramatically the weather can change. In the lower valleys, the weather is relatively warm and dry. Blue spruce and red cedar line the gently curving highway. Trapped between the peaks are crystal-clear lakes, the residue of the five separate glaciers that still exist. As the car climbs up the mountain slopes, along twisting and turning roads, the trees change to dense pines and aspens. Above 9,000 feet the trees are twisted and bent by the fierce, buffeting winds.

Because the park is so close to Denver (only a two hour drive from the city), this section of the Rocky Mountains is usually hopelessly overrun by people

during summer weekends. If in search of solitude, either avoid these rush days or else drive to the more remote western part of the park.

The 50 mile long **Trail Ridge Road**, the highest in the world (open only from late May to October) and **Fall River Road** are the two interlinked roads which cross the park and eventually climb well above the timberline into a tundra that covers more than a third of the park area. Colorado's state flower, the blue columbine, can be spotted at nearly every elevation. In the tundra are alpine buttercups and forget-me-nots, and dwarf clovers, all with a brief blooming season of about six weeks in June and July. The park's symbol is the bighorn sheep, and visitors with strong binoculars might be lucky enough to spot one or two of them.

The high point – literally – of Trail Ridge Road is **Milner Pass**, which is precisely at the Continental Divide. From this point, all the streams flowing down the western slopes of the Rockies end up in the Pacific Ocean, while all those on the eastern slopes eventually spill into the Atlantic Ocean or the Gulf of Mexico.

Photographers will love **Many Parks Curve** and **Rainbow Curve** along Trail Ridge Road; both are exceptional spots with breathtaking views.

The park has 355 miles of hiking trails. Several self-guiding nature trails begin directly off the main park roads. These include the **Colorado River Trail** and the **Tundra Trail**. The former begins a few miles southwest of Milner Pass, while the latter begins a few miles to the east of it. In **Moraine Park** and **Glacier Creek** horses can be hired. Hikers in need of a serious challenge can try the 16 mile trail up to **Longs Peak**, the highest mountain in the park at 14,256 feet. It is covered in snow all year. One recommended stop is at **Fall River Pass**, where the **Alpine Visitor Center** has exhibits on the ecology of the tundra and the world of the park.

Above: The gold mine in Idaho Springs is today a mining museum.

DURANGO, ASPEN, VAIL
Area code 970

Accommodation
LUXURY: **Vail Athletic Club**, 352 E Meadow Dr., Vail, Tel: 476-0700. Top-class hotel with spa, also open to visitors who not residing in the hotel, for a small fee.
MODERATE: **General Palmer Hotel**, 567 Main Ave., Durango, Tel: 247-4747. Victorian B & B. **River Mountain Lodge**, 100 S Park St./Ski Hill Rd., Breckenridge, Tel: 453-4711. In close proximity to ski lifts, health club and parking.

Sights and Parks
Breckenridge Ski Area, Ski Hill Rd. (one mile westwards, via CO 9), Breckenridge, Tel: 1-800-221-1091. **Copper Mt. Resort Ski Area**, 12 miles southwest, junction of I-70 and CO 91, close to Dillon, Tel: 968-2882. **Mesa Verde N. P.**, 8 miles east of Cortez, on US 160, Information Tel: 529-4465. **Durango-Silverton Narrow Gauge Railroad**, Depot, 479 Main St., Durango, Tel: 247-2733. **Vail Ski Resort**, off I-70, take exit 176, Tel: 476-5601. **Dinosaur N. M.**, Superintendent, 4545 Hwy. 40, Dinosaur, CO., 81610, Tel: (970) 374-3000. **Arches N. P.**, Superintendent, P.O. Box 907, Moab, UT, 84532, Tel: (435) 259-8161. **Canyonlands**, UT, Tel: (435) 259-7164.

Sports and Recreation
Colorado Riff Raft, 555 East Durant Ave., Tel: 1-800-7593939. Whitewater rafting available on the Roaring Fork, Colorado and also on other rivers. **Outlaw Jeep Tours**, Durango, Tel: (877) 259-1800. **Skiing in Aspen**, Aspen Cross-Country Center, Tel: 925-2145 or the Snowmass Club, Tel: 923-3148.

Tourist Information
Aspen Chamber Resort Assn., 425 Rio Grande Pl., Aspen, CO 81611, Tel: 925-1940. **Lake Powell Chamber of Commerce**, PO Box 727, Page, AZ 86040, Tel: (520) 645-2741. **Grand Junction V&C Bureau**, 740, Horizon Dr., CO 81506, Tel: (970) 244-1480.

DENVER, COLORADO SPRINGS AND BOULDER
Area code 303

Accommodation
LUXURY: **The Brown Palace,** 321 17th St., Denver, Tel: 297-3111. This is a traditional yet luxurious first-class hotel. *MODERATE:* **Holiday Chalet**, 1820 E Colfax Ave, Denver, Tel: 321-9975. Good hotel, all rooms are equipped with a kitchenette. **Lost Valley Guest Ranch**, Rte. 2, Sedalia, Tel: (303) 647-2311. Ranch with cabins.

Sights and Museums
Center for the Performing Arts, 1245 Champa St, Tel: 572-4462. **Colorado's Ocean Journey**, 700 Water St, Tel: 561-4450. Aquarium. **Colorado Railroad Museum**, 17155 W 44th Ave. Golden, Tel: 279-4591. **Coors Tour**, 13th/Ford Sts., Golden, Tel: 277-BEER. **Denver Art Museum**, 100 W 14th Ave. Pwy., Tel: 640-2793.

Garden of the Gods, Visitor Center, 1805 N. 30th St. off Gateway Rd., Tel: (719) 685-5401. **Molly Brown House**, 1340 Pennsylvania St., Tel: 832-4092. **Museum of Western Art**, 1727 Tremont Pl., Tel: 296-1880. **Pavilions**, 16th St., Entertainment complex with shops. **Pikes Peak Railway**, 515 Ruxtun Ave., Manitou Springs, Tel: 719/634-6666.

Six Flags Elitch Gardens, Elitch Circle, Tel: 5954386. Amusement park. **State Capitol**, E Colfax Ave./Sherman St., Tel: 866-2604. **United States Mint**, 320 W Colfax Ave., Tel: 844-3582.

Tourist Information
Boulder C & V Bureau, 2440 Pearl St., Boulder, CO 80302, Tel: 442-2911. **Colorado Springs C & V Bureau**, 104 S Cascade, Suite 104, Colorado Springs, CO 80903, Tel: (719) 635-7506. **Denver Metro C&V Bureau**, 225 W Colfax Ave, Denver CO 80202, Tel: 892-1112.

ROCKY MOUNTAIN NATIONAL PARK
Area code 970

Accommodation
MODERATE: **Elkhorn Lodge & Guest Ranch**, Estes Park, Tel: 586-4416. Traditional working and guest ranch with riding stables. **Peaceful Valley Lodge & Guest Ranch**, Star Rte., Lyons, Tel: (303) 747-2881. Dude ranch with various cabins, activities for kids. *BUDGET:* **Alpine Trail Ridge Inn**, 927 Moraine Ave., Estes Park, Tel: 586-4585. Good value motel close to the National Paerk, rewsetaurant with Mexican/German cuisine.

Museums and Parks
Estes Park Area Historical Museum, 200 Fourth St., Estes Park, Tel: 586-6256. **Rocky Mountain National Park**, Park Headquarters 3 miles west of Estes Park, on US 36, Tel: 586-1206.

Sports and Recreation
Aerial Tramway, 420 Riverside Dr., Estes Park, Cable car up to Prospect Mt., Tel: 586-3675. **Silver Creek Ski Area**, 3 miles southeast on US 40, near Granby, Tel: 887-3384.

Tourist Information
Estes Park Information Center at the Chamber of Commerce, 500 Big Thompson Ave., PO Box 3050, Estes Park, CO 80517, Tel: 586-4431.

FROM
LOS ANGELES TO
SAN FRANCISCO

SANTA BARBARA
BIG SUR / CARMEL
MONTEREY BAY
SALINAS AND SANTA CRUZ
SAN JOSE

California's beautiful coastline has made the state one of the world's most popular tourist destinations. It is rugged and unspoiled, with deep blue Pacific waves crashing onto sandy beaches and rocky shores that rise steeply toward snow-capped mountains and tall forests of sequoias.

The famous **Pacific Coast Highway** (State Highway 1) narrowly meanders directly beside the coastline, affording the visitor some of the most spectacular views in the entire U.S. There are indeed quicker ways of getting to San Francisco, but this is by far the most beautiful. Allowing for overnight stops at Santa Barbara and near San Simeon, plus two nights in Monterey, this can be a very leisurely five-day trip. And the breathtaking scenes along the way may encourage you to take even more time to cover this tour of 380 miles.

SANTA BARBARA

The city of **Santa Barbara**, just under 70 miles north of downtown Los Angeles, is a Spanish-looking, white-washed, red-tile-roofed community smug

Previous pages: The coast north of L.A. is an El Dorado for surfers and windsurfers. Left: Sun protection American style.

in its wealth, conservative in its politics and blessed with a temperate Southern Californian climate. Santa Barbara was established by Spanish missionaries, followers of Father Junipero Serra, in the 18th century. Among the genuinely old buildings is **Mission Santa Barbara**, one of 21 of Serra's missions. In the buildings adjacent to it are replicas of a Spanish padre's cell, and a 19th century kitchen.

Santa Barbara can best be explored by foot on the **Red Tile Route**: red sidewalk markers leading visitors on a building-by-building stroll around twelve square blocks of the city center.

Just off State Street is **El Paseo**, a Spanish-style shopping arcade constructed alongside the **Casa de la Guerra**, an 1829 adobe structure built for the Spanish commanding officer of the tiny garrison which once guarded the entrance to this important port. Several blocks northeast is the parade ground where Spanish troops once marched. Facing this is the **Santa Barbara Historical Society**, containing a fascinating range of exhibits detailing the city's Spanish, Mexican, Indian and American heritage.

The hills above Santa Barbara have become increasingly profitable to their owners, thanks to the introduction of

many fine wineries into the area. There are close to 30 of them in the nearby **Santa Maria** and **Santa Ynez** valleys at the present time and many of them can be toured. The 30 miles or so of beaches around Santa Barbara offer swimming, surfing, diving and sailing opportunities.

San Luis Obispo and Morro Bay

Beyond the **San Ysidro Ranch** is a breathtaking drive along US 101, switching to State Highway 1, which leads to the historic town of **San Luis Obispo**. This town at the foot of the Santa Lucia Mountains, founded as a Spanish mission in 1772 and today a commercial and university city, is precisely halfway between Los Angeles and San Francisco. The **Mission Station** and the kitschy **Madonna Inn** are two of the town's tourist magnets.

Pismo Beach, due south, the only California beach where cars can be driven on the sand, is California's clamming headquarters; its chowder attracts visitors from miles around.

Nudists who normally have a hard time in prudish America can head for nearby **Pirate's Cove** at **Avila**, a few miles north along the coast, where it's safe to take a daring dive. A coastal town, it lies in the shadow of giant, 576 foot high **Morro Rock**, on a bay where visitors flock for bird watching, beachcombing, picnicking, sailing, swimming and fishing. Trails for hiking lead out into dunes where 250 species of birds wheel and swoop. The **Embarcadero**, where the fishing fleet ties up, is a lively area with restaurants, bars and cafés.

North of San Luis Obispo, on the Pacific Coast Highway, is an amazing mansion, **Hearst Castle** near **San Simeon**. Those who have seen Orson Welles' classic film *Citizen Kane* have already had a preview of San Simeon. The fictional character of Kane was patterned after American publisher William Ran-

dolph Hearst, a 20th century press baron. In the film, Kane's mansion was furnished with valuable European and Asian art was called "Xanadu." Hearst's home at San Simeon is even more sensational than that created on celluloid by Welles. More than ten million dollars, an unimaginable fortune in those days, was expended to construct the museum-like building. Gardens and reflecting pools link the main house to a trio of so-called guest "cottages." Within, the baronial walls are cluttered with antique, medieval and Renaissance art, sculptures, tapestries and other artifacts. The main building alone has 38 bedrooms and 41 bathrooms, a dining room of Arthurian dimensions with a 30 foot round table, a plush cinema where first-run Hollywood films were shown, often with their stars in attendance, and an indoor swimming pool so vast that there is room on its roof for two full-sized tennis courts!

Above: Luxurious Renaissance-style swimming pool in Hearst Castle.

Cars can't get much closer than five miles to San Simeon; after parking, tourists are taken by shuttle bus on a drive through Hearst's forests to the dwellings. There are five different narrated tours, each about an hour and a quarter long. One tour, staged only in the summer months, takes place only in the evenings, with the gardens and sculpture splendidly spotlit. Actors and staff dress up in 1930's garb, and it's almost like being back in the era of F. Scott Fitzgerald and *The Great Gatsby.*

After a day at San Simeon, northbound travelers rejoin Highway 1 for the 60 mile drive along the Pacific to Big Sur.

EXPLORING THE PACIFIC COAST HIGHWAY TO BIG SUR

This rugged coastline is everyone's image of California. For almost 90 miles, from San Simeon to Monterey, the Pacific crashes into the base of the Santa Lucia mountain range with so spectacular an impact that writers, artists and photog-

raphers (along with millions of tourists a year) have flocked to the area to be inspired by the beauty of it all.

Until 1937, when bridges went up over many of the jags along the coastline, allowing motorists to access the area more easily, this part of California was isolated from the rest of the state. Poets, such as Robinson Jeffers, novelists, such as Henry Miller, and photographers, such as Anselm Adams, came here to appreciate the solitude and beauty.

The wildlife around **Big Sur** is truly awesome. Gray whales can be seen spouting in the pacific twice a year; once while heading south to Mexican waters in the fall, and once again in the springtime when swimming north to Alaskan waters with their young. Hunting hawks circle over the canyons, coyotes howl loudly at night - particularly when the moon is full.

Above: The Pacific Coast Highway is one of the most beautiful coastal roads in the world. Right: Sea lions on the cliffs near Monterey.

But this stunning coastline also has its perils: So many ships have hit rocks off **Point Sur** over the decades that the authorities installed a lighthouse atop the point to warn sailors of the dangers ahead. The lighthouse is open for guided tours most weekends, with a park ranger outlining the light's history and answering questions.

The perfect place to eat in Big Sur is the **Nepenthe Restaurant**, some three miles south of the **Pfeiffer Big Sur State Park**. Literally hanging on a hillside over the edge of the ocean, many food critics insist this restauran has the most magnificent view of any dining spot in the world.

ON TO CARMEL

Some visitors still arrive at this northern exit from Big Sur expecting to see "Dirty Harry," Clint Eastwood, in the Mayor's office of this tiny coastal village. For several years, this Hollywood megastar did indeed govern Carmel. But Eastwood declined to run for re-election, and now confines his Carmel activities primarily to improving his **Mission Ranch Inn**, a sprawling, 20 acre property. Father Junipero Serra, who established most of the missions of southern California, is buried here.

Around Carmel and Monterey Bay are brilliant green forests of Monterey cypress, many of the trees gnarled, twisted and wind-bent in eerie, unearthly shapes. Beyond is the bay, its waters reflecting the distinctive azure blue of the California sky, a deep ocean trench filled with exotic marine wildlife.

Carmel River State Park covers more than 100 acres along the bay, an area of dunes as fine and white as icing sugar, which form a nesting area for sandpipers, hawks and full-bellied pelicans that occasionally plummet into the sea and rise up again successfully with wildly flapping fish in their beaks.

Just south of Carmel is **Point Lobos State Reserve**, best accessed on foot. **Sea Lion Point Trail** is a fascinating walk, leading to rocky coves where otters, harbor seals and California sea lions bask in the sun or cavort in the sea.

The city of Carmel has long considered itself to be a tidy, tiny, English-style village which just happens to have found itself, miraculously, cast up on a Pacific shoreline. "Ye Olde" type tearooms are on several shopping streets. Don't look for house numbers here; Carmel's homes are known by their names: "Dove House," "The Kestrels" or even "Mon Repos." Don't look for sidewalks either; there aren't any, except for the streets around **Ocean Avenue**.

The **Hog's Breath Inn** downtown is owned by Clint Eastwood and, naturally, the menu features items like a *"Dirty Harry Hamburger"* and a *"Dirty Harry Dinner."* Surprisingly, the decor isn't Dirty Harry at all, no sawdust on the floor or spilled beer on the bar; instead, it's candlelit and romantic. Poetry lovers simply must visit **Tor House**, a unique

stone cottage high on a bluff over the Pacific built by American poet Robinson Jeffers in 1918.

17 Mile Drive

This last private toll road in the U.S. west of the Mississippi, encircles four of the world's most famous golf courses at **Pebble Beach** on the southern shore of Monterey Bay. Along **17 Mile Drive**, as the stretch of road from Pacific Grove to Carmel is known, there are great views of **Seal Rock** and **Cypress Point**.

Scottish novelist Robert Louis Stevenson wrote of the area: "On no other coast that I know shall you enjoy in calm, sunny weather such a spectacle of ocean's greatness, such beauty of changing color or such degrees of thunder in the sound."

Todays residents, too, know the value of this stretch of coastline, for along this part of the Moneterey peninsula stand some of the most expensive mansions in the world, each trying to outdo the other

in opulence and splendor. All enjoy perfect views of the ocean, the pine and cypress forests and the fairways of the classic golf courses. Also visible is a bizarrely-decorated tree close to one of the club houses. Whenever a member dies, his golfing mates conduct a ceremony of hanging the deceased's golf bag on a branch of the tree, which is by now quite laden down.

MONTEREY

Monterey is surely the most interesting community between Los Angeles and San Francisco, and is well worth an extended visit.

Initially an ancient Indian settlement, it later served as Spain's colonial headquarters. The United States claimed the region in 1846, at the beginning of the Mexican-American War.

Above: Monterey Bay Aquarium. Right: John Steinbeck discovered many characters for his stories in Monterey.

The town's tourist office has compressed a good deal of Monterey's early history into a self-guided, two-and-a-half-mile walk around Monterey - the **Path of History** tour. This leads you mostly through the **Monterey State Historic Park**, where the earlier buildings, all lovingly preserved, are grouped.

Custom House Plaza is the logical starting point, facing as it does the two-story adobe **Custom House** through which the Spaniards cleared goods beginning in 1827.

A new building, the nearby **Monterey Maritime Museum**, contains many artifacts: sailors' scrimshaw, prints and maps, weapons, uniforms, and photos. Also on Custom House Plaza is **Pacific House**, built around the time that gold was discovered at Sutter's Mill and now a museum. It used to be a saloon where forty-niners lost their gold nuggets over the bar and across the poker tables.

All of these buildings overlook **Fisherman's Wharf**, which juts out into the bay, flanked with piers for daily excursion boats, slips for yachts and moorings for the local fishing fleet. It's where visitors usually have lunch, very often selecting a local fish soup which is served in a bowl made of a hollowed-out loaf of bread.

Life on the wharf has the atmosphere of an ongoing carnival: artists sketch you in just a few minutes for a small fee; a monkey and an organ grinder amuse the throngs; tourists come ashore from fishing expeditions to have their photos proudly taken next to their catch.

Walking westwards from the wharf, you enter the **Cannery Row** world of author John Steinbeck. The world he described was harsh, with a Chinese merchant selling groceries to workers and hosting illegal gambling games out back, with saloons where hookers were busy dusk-till-dawn every payday. The old buildings still stand, but when the schools of sardines mysteriously disappeared in 1945, the old life of Monterey petered out as well.

Inside the refurbished shell of one of the largest canneries is the remarkable **Monterey Bay Aquarium**. More than $50 million was spent to allow visitors an underwater look at the complex and fascinating marine life offshore. Some of the aquarium's display tanks are three stories high, filled with long tendrils of transplanted kelp. Several times a day, a divers enter the pool to feed the fish, and lecture the spectators at the same time via a radio/PA link. The range of jellyfish here are also worth a closer look.

SALINAS AND SANTA CRUZ

John Steinbeck was born in **Salinas**, and his home, **Steinbeck House**, at 132 Central Avenue, has been restored as a restaurant-cum-museum to his memory. Nearby, a house on West San Luis serves as the **Steinbeck Library** and contains his works and his private correspondence. The area around Salinas has some

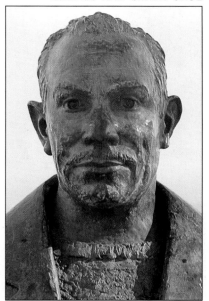

of the richest farmland in America, supplying the entire region with produce.

Santa Cruz, on the north side of Monterey Bay, retains some of the hippie feeling of the 1960s. The **University of California** has an attractive campus, and the college kids prefer to bike instead of drive, the restaurants feature *tofu*, and the cry *"Surf's up!"* is enough to get everyone down to the beach to take on the waves. It's a town still rebuilding after being hit by an earthquake in 1989, whose noisiest citizens are the barking sea lions who congregate by the **Municipal Wharf** and beg for table scraps. **Natural Bridges State Park**, at the end of **West Cliff Drive**, is famous for its admiral butterflies and tidal pools filled with crabs and lobster.

THE WAY TO SAN JOSE

San Jose, today one of the state's biggest cities was, in 1777, the first pueblo built by the Spaniards in Northern California. Until 40 years ago, the plum or-

chards surrounding the city supplied half the country with their fruit. Now it's the home of the micro-electronics industry.

After driving northeast from Santa Cruz, you enter the world-famous **Silicon Valley**, that remarkable complex of high-tech laboratories and factories which, since World War II, have catapulted the world into the electronic era. It's only natural that this should be home to the **Tech Museum of Innovation.**

A visit back to the age when the Spaniards ruled begins in the city center at the **Peralta Adobe**. Across the street is **Fallon House**, the home of a U.S. Army captain who galloped into this tiny town in 1846 at the head of a column of armed volunteers to raise the Stars and Stripes for the first time.

There are two bizarrely vintage tourist attractions from that era that continue to appeal to visitors: **Winchester House** is a remarkable Victorian structure which comprised eight rooms when Sarah Winchester, the heiress to the repeating rifle fortune, bought it in 1884. A fortune teller warned her that the ghosts of all those killed with her family's rifles would haunt her unless she built new rooms where she could hide if they came after her. By 1922, when she finally passed away, she had had 160 rooms added, and hundreds of tourists visit them daily. There are doors that open onto blank walls, staircases that don't go anywhere, and corridors that are mazes.

The Brotherhood of the Rosicrucians, at Park and Naglee Avenues, has built an interesting **Egyptian Museum** with a planetarium, which is one of the area's largest attractions. It is crammed with the Pacific Coast's largest collection of Babylonian, Assyrian and Egyptian artifacts and mummies.

Leaving San Jose on Route 280 and heading north through **Palo Alto**, with prestigious **Stanford University**, the trip continues on to San Francisco.

Above: Dramatic coastline ensures Pacific Coast Highway drivers an adventure.

SANTA BARBARA AND
SURROUNDING AREA
Area code 805
Accommodation

LUXURY: **Mission Ranch Inn**, 26270 Dolores St., Carmel, Tel: (831) 624-6436. Farm converted by Clint Eastwood, now a luxury hotel. **Madonna Inn**, 100 Madonna Rd, San Luis Obispo, Tel: 543-3000, http://www.madonnainn.com/. Interesting place - rooms partly with cliff showers. *MODERATE:* **Blue Sail Inn**, 851 Market St., Morro Bay, Tel: 772-2766, view of the bay. *BUDGET:* **Sea Gypsy**, 1020 Cypress, on Wadsworth St., Pismo Beach, Tel: 773-1801. On the beach, view of bay.

Sights, Museums
and Parks

Hearst San Simeon State Historical Monument, 750 Hearst Castle Rd., San Simeon, Tel: 927-2020. **Mission San Luis Obispo de Tolosa**, 782 Monterey St., San Luis Obispo, Tel: 543-6850. **Mission Santa Barbara**, Laguna and Los Olivos Sts., Santa Barbara, Tel: 682-4726. **Morro Bay Embarcadero**, 893 Napa St., # A-1, Morro Bay, Tel: 772-2694. **Morro Bay State Park**, south of town, Tel: 772-2560. **Morro Rock**, 895 Napa St., # A-1, Morro Bay, Tel: 772-4467. **Oceano Dunes State Vehicular Recreation Area**, Grover City, Tel: 473-7220. Dune beach south of Pismo Beach on which you can drive. **Pfeiffer Big Sur State Park**, Information Tel: (831) 667-2315. **Point Lobos State Reserve**, Rte. 1, Carmel, Tel: (831) 624-4909. **San Luis Obispo County Historical Museum**, 969 Monterey St., San Luis Obispo, Tel: 543-0638. **Santa Barbara Historical Society Museum**, 136 E. De La Guerra St., Tel: 966-1601. **Tor House**, Carmel Point, Carmel, Tel: (831) 624-1813.

Sports and Recreation

Morro Bay Harbor Cruises, 1205 Embarcadero, Morro Bay, Tel: 772-2257. **Sea Landing & Condor**, Cabrillo at Bath, Santa Barbara. Tel: 963-3564. Whale-watching, diving.

Tourist Information

Carmel Business Assn., San Carlos (between 5th/6th Sts., PO Box 4444, Carmel, CA 93921, Tel: (831) 624-2522.**Santa Barbara C & V Bureau**, 12 East Carrillo St., Santa Barbara, CA 93101, Tel: 966-9222.

MONTEREY BAY AND
SURROUNDING AREA
Area code 831
Accommodation

MODERATE: **Merritt House**, 386 Pacific St., Monterey, Tel: 646-9686. B&B in adobe house from 1830. **Spindrift**, 652 Cannery Row, Monterey, Tel: 646-8900. Private beach, lovely view of the Bay.

BUDGET: **Padre Oaks**, 1278 Munras Ave., Monterey, Tel: 373-3741.

Sights, Museums
and Parks

Cannery Row, 765 Wave St., Monterey, Tel: 649-6690. **Custom House**, Custom House Plaza, Monterey, no phone. **Fisherman's Wharf**, Monterey, Information Tel: 373-0600. **Monterey Bay Aquarium**, 886 Cannery Row, Monterey, Tel: 648-4888. **Maritime Museum of Monterey**, Stanton Center, #5 Custom House Plaza, Monterey, Tel: 373-2469. **Monterey State Historic Park**, 20 Custom House Plaza, Monterey, Tel: 649-7118. 8 historic 19th century houses. **Presidio of Monterey**, Pacific St., north of Scott St., Monterey, Tel: 372-2074. Large fort, open to visitors.

Tourist Information

Monterey Peninsula Chamber of Commerce und V & C Bureau, 380 Alvarado St., PO Box 1770, Monterey, CA 93940, Tel: 649-1770. A Visitor Center is located on Camino El Estero/Franklin Sts.

SALINAS, SANTA CRUZ AND
SAN JOSE
Area code 408
Accommodation

MODERATE: **Briar Rose**, 897 E Jackson St., San Jose, Tel: 279-5999. B&B in previous victorian farmhouse. **Dream Inn**, 175 West Cliff Dr., Santa Cruz, Tel: 426-4330. Directly on the beach. *BUDGET:* **Inncal**, 320 Ocean St., Santa Cruz, Tel: 831/458-9220. Close to the beach. **Vagabond**, 1488 N First St, San Jose, Tel: 453-8822.

Sights, Museums
and Parks

National Steinbeck Center Museum, 371 Main St., Salinas, Tel: (831) 796-3833. **Natural Bridges State Park and Beach**, Santa Cruz, Tel: 423-4609. **Peralta Adobe and Fallon House**, 175-186 W St./John St., San Jose, Tel: 287-2290. **Rosicrucian Park**, Park/Naglee Aves., San Jose, with **Planetarium** and **Egyptian Museum** Tel: 947-3636. **Steinbeck House**, 132 Central Ave., Salinas, Tel: (831) 424-2735. **Tech Museum of Innovation**, 145 W San Carlos St, San Jose, Tel: 279-7150. **Winchester Mystery House**, 525 S Winchester Blvd., San Jose, Tel: 247-2101.

Tourist Information

Salinas Chamber of Commerce, 119 E Alisal St., PO Box 1170, Salinas, CA 93902, Tel: (831) 424-7611. **San Jose Visitors Bureau**, 333 W San Carlos St, San Jose, CA 95110, Tel: 295-9600. **Santa Cruz County Conference & Visitors Council**, 701 Front St., Santa Cruz, CA 95060, Tel: (831) 425-1234.

FROM LOS ANGELES TO YOSEMITE NATIONAL PARK

PASADENA
SEQUOIA AND KING'S CANYON NATIONAL PARKS
YOSEMITE NATIONAL PARK

The inland road, an alternative way to bridge the miles between the two great cities on the West Coast, is one of the finest drives in the U.S. It begins in Pasadena, that Los Angeles suburb where so many of America's sports megastars have performed. It is a lively and sophisticated place bathed in the neon and floodlights of show biz. Just a few hundred miles to the north another fabulous stretch of California landscape begins - the national parks of the Sierra Nevada. Here, the stars are the world's largest and oldest trees, thundering waterfalls, glacial valleys, snow-capped mountain ranges, lumbering black bears and soaring eagles. It's an area that also recalls the great pioneering days of the 19th century, when thousands risked everything to find, if not an earthly fortune, then at least an earthly paradise.

The drive straight through from Los Angeles to San Francisco, a distance of about 400 miles, can be made in around seven hours. But to enjoy the remarkable display of wilderness along the way, sample the hiking and riding, and observe the flora and fauna of this pristine area, it is best to plan about a week on the road.

Left: Bridal Veil Falls in Yosemite National Park.

PASADENA

In July 1994, more than a billion of the world's soccer fans learned precisely where in California **Pasadena** is situated. The final game of the World Cup took place in front of hundreds of television cameras in the community's famous **Rose Bowl**. This huge oval stadium, which can hold more than 100,000 spectators, has been in use since the 1920s. It hosts an annual football festival at the beginning of every year that has become one of America's most popular and important sporting events.

There is an old quip about Los Angeles: "L.A. is a dozen suburbs in search of a city." Pasadena is one of the earliest of these suburbs to have been incorporated and the first you will come across when heading from L.A. to San Francisco along the inland route. It's a community where modern technology and turn-of-the-century architecture combine with typical California charm and traditional lifestyle. It is also home to three institutions of higher learning, the **California Institute of Technology** (founded in 1891), **City College**, and **Pacific Oaks College**. For decades, its main claim to fame was that its 2,000 citrus trees produced more than a million oranges a year.

Today, Pasadena is a city of more than 132,000 residents, boasting a long list of arts and cultural centers, in particular theaters where many of Hollywood's rising stars hone their talents in the early stages of their careers.

Pasadena also has a great deal of art and culture to explore, thanks, indirectly, to the climate: many millionaires used to spend their winters in this town, and they ultimately left their collections to local institutions. The **Huntington Complex**, consisting of a library, museum and botanical gardens, has even achieved international renown. Its collections were once the pride and joy of railroad and real estate magnate Henry E. Huntington.

A more recent millionaire – Norton Simon – has also turned over his art collection to Pasadena. The **Norton Simon Museum of Art** is filled with a remarkable array of masterpieces, including works by Rembrandt, Rafael, Goya, Monet, Renoir, Degas, van Gogh, Cezanne, Picasso, Braque, Kandinsky and Klee. Complementing the displays of Western art is an outstanding sculpture collection from India and Southeast Asia.

A popular hobby of millionaires has long been horse racing. In addition to helping to tap into the kind of aristocratic image usually associated with the British Isles, keeping thoroughbreds also has certain tax advantages. Furthermore, horse racing and betting is a nerve-wracking and fun way of risking one's own fortune.

The wealthy families who came to Pasadena in the past brought their equestrian interests with them. Horse racing began here at the end of the 19th century, when one Lucky Baldwin, a colorful desperado on his way to California, built a race course in **Santa Anita**, near Pasadena. It has been functioning without interruption ever since. The current track, far more

Right: Exploring the giant sequoias in Sequoia National Park.

luxurious in its appointments than the original, was opened on Christmas Day in 1934.

Exploring the High Sierra

I-5 on the way to the **Sierra Nevada** is not without its own special sights. **Bakersfield**, the largest town in famous **Kern County** in the south of the San Joaquin Valley, provides a comprehensive look at the toils and troubles of California history. Great derricks, their pumps serenely swinging, stand out in the landscape of expansive wheat and cotton fields. The oil boom, which still governs the regional economy, replaced the gold rush at the end of the 19th century. Bakersfield was founded as a gold-mining town in 1885. Its history is highlighted in the **Kern County Museum** and the **Pioneer Village**, as well as in the **West Kern Oil Museum**.

A trip east along the Kern River on Route 178 is perhaps the best way to experience the region's idyllic landscape.

To prepare for a trip through the Sierra Nevada with its wild animals and abundant variety of flora, spend some time exploring these natural treasures at the **California Living Museum**. In this combination of zoo and botanical gardens, you can see all the plants and animals you might come across later in their natural habitats.

SEQUOIA AND KING'S CANYON NATIONAL PARKS

After leaving Bakersfield, the drive northward on Route 99 heads towards the Californian equivalent of the Alps, through one of America's most bountiful farming areas.

At the junction with Route 198, head east along the latter, passing through Visalia and into **Sequoia National Park** through its Ash Mountain Entrance. Be sure to pick up the most recent issue of

The Sequoia Park at the entrance gate; this is a free newspaper which lists all local activities by day, week and month.

Although they're technically two separate national parks, Sequoia and **King's Canyon National Park** are really one contiguous mountain area covering more than 1,300 square miles of gorgeous California countryside, crowned by Mount Whitney, at 14,495 feet the highest peak in the continental United States.

Both national parks are part of the Sierra Nevada, a plateau that was created by tectonic shifts in the earth's crust about 150 million years ago. About two million years ago, i.e., relatively recently, geologically speaking, glaciers planed down these piled-up layers and exposed the great granite formations that can be seen today.

The Sierra Nevada is, without doubt or exaggeration, a unique natural paradise. In addition to alpine lakes, virtually untouched forests and wildlife ranging from mule deer to coyotes, this area also boasts the fantastic **sequoias** – gigantic evergreens which, at up to 2,500 years of age, are older than any other living thing on this planet. Though not quite as tall as their twins, the giant redwoods (see page 177), which grow further north, the sequoias are also hardier than anything else alive. They are so strong, indeed, that they never die: at some point they just topple over, uprooting themselves, and it's this, not age, which kills them. Around the world there are just 75 remaining groves of these mammoth trees, 30 of which are in the Sequoia and King's Canyon National Parks.

In and out of these groves and the parks' almost 864,000 acres, there are some 800 miles of mountain walking and hiking trails, but not a single paved road crosses the park from east to west.

Not far from the main gate is a perfect point to grasp the grandeur all around. It's called **Moro Rock**, a high point more than 6,500 feet above sea level overlook-

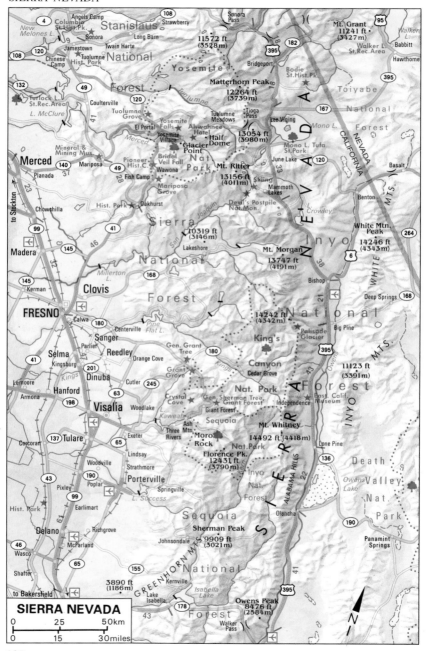

SIERRA NEVADA

| 0 | 25 | 50km |
| 0 | 15 | 30miles |

ing the **Giant Forest**. The 400-stepped staircase to the top of the rock and the crowning platform was, by the way, built by the young, unemployed men of the *Civilian Conservation Corps (CCC)* during the Great Depression. The view from the platform is one of the most spectacular in all of California. Far, far below you can spot white-flecked, briskly flowing rivers, like the **Kaweah River**, and to the east you'll see the Great Western Divide.

Just a short ride away is **Tharp's Log**, a giant, fallen sequoia which was hollowed out into a rustic cabin in the late 19th century by a plucky cattleman named Hale Tharp.

Connecting the Sequoia and King's Canyon National Parks is the **General's Highway**, running from the Ash Mountain entrance gate through Giant Forest and **Grant Grove** with its **General Grant Tree** (265 feet tall) – passing **Boyden Cave** - and leading into **Kings Canyon**, where it ends at **Cedar Grove**. This is a wonderfully scenic road which links all four of the major visitor areas of both parks by a single ribbon of asphalt. Almost everywhere else in these parks visitors have to make their way on foot, on horseback, or in tour buses.

General Sherman, of American Civil War fame, is very prominent in these national parks because the highest tree in Sequoia was named after him. It is estimated to be over 2,500 years old, is close to 276 feet tall and weighs about 1,400 tons. With its base girth of well over 100 feet, the **General Sherman Tree** is frustrating to photograph because it is impossible to get it all into a single frame.

All around are other incredible giant sequoias: one is called the **Auto Log**, a fallen tree wide enough to drive a car along. Another is the **Tunnel Log**, which has been hollowed out at its base so that cars can pass through it. These are indeed remarkable trees, indeed: trees that were alive at the height of the Roman Empire; trees as high

as the dome of the U.S. Capitol Building in Washington, D.C.

But these trees haven't always been respected. Nearby is the **Big Stump Area**, the sad remains of a massive logging effort which took place in these forests during the 1880s. The sea of stumps remaining from these once-beautiful forests is a powerful indictment of those timber interests, which, to this day, would like to continue clearing forests away on an unregulated basis.

Not all the greatness of these national parks is above ground. You can also take a look below its surface in **Crystal Cave**, the only one of a total 80 caverns in both parks that is open to visitors. A twisting path leads down to the cave's entrance from the main road, and while the half-mile descent is easy, the 30 minute hike back up can be a little tiring.

After a couple of days of looking at God's handiwork, many visitors either leave the parks via Route 180 and head back to Fresno, or else decide to head north to see yet another one of nature's jewels: Yosemite National Park.

YOSEMITE NATIONAL PARK

The road to **Yosemite National Park** begins in **Fresno**, and, following Route 41 northwards, leads to the southern entrance of Yosemite, the most magnificent national park in California. It's approximately a six-hour drive from Los Angeles, and more than three million visitors make the pilgrimage annually. So expect it to be cramped and crowded during the busiest summer months.

Among the first white men to visit Yosemite was a member of the California militia, and the memorable awe-struck comment he made then sums up the feelings that many visitors have since had when they behold the beauty of the Yosemite wilderness for the first time: "As I looked, a peculiar sensation seemed to fill my whole being, and I found my eyes in tears of emotion."

John Muir, the famed California naturalist, also had words of reverence for Yosemite, which made a profound impression on him as the following comment suggests: "As long as I live, I will hear waterfalls, birds and winds sing."

Native Americans were here first, however, specifically a tribe called the Ahwahneechees. The area which they called Ahwahnee, meaning "deep, grassy valley," was for a long time their home, until Major James Savage and his Mariposa Battalion drove them out in 1851. Even though the white man cut timber from the forests and mined in the hills, some had foresight enough to see that Yosemite's virgin beauty simply had to be preserved, and, in 1864, while the Civil War was raging, President Abraham Lincoln presented the area to California to be a state park. It became a national park in 1890.

Above: Family excursion in Yosemite National Park. Right: The Jeffrey Pine in Yosemite National Park.

Yosemite consists of 1,170 square miles of mountain peaks, deep valleys, soaring granite spires, rushing waterfalls and thick, richly-foliated forests. It takes its name from the Indian word for grizzly bear, *u-zu-ma-te*, which was eventually corrupted into "Yosemite."

Most visitors circle the main valley on a convenient sightseeing bus. Hikers take to the many trails winding their way down the valleys and up the hills. There are rental bikes available, as well as horses. Rock climbers can tackle the many granite faces, accompanied by experienced guides. At **Fish Camp**, just south of the park, there's even an old, narrow-gauge railroad that chugs its way along a four mile track into the piney woods.

Entering the park from the south, via Route 41, the first major stop is the **Mariposa Grove of Giant Trees**. King of this cluster of huge trees is the **Grizzly Giant**, estimated to be almost 3,000 years old. It has a base diameter of about 31 feet, a circumference of almost 100 feet, and reaches over 210 feet into the California skies. Hugging this tree might prove a little challenging - it would take almost two dozen people linking hands to encircle the trunk of the largest of these trees.

Alongside the Wawona River, at **Yosemite Village**, is Yosemite's **Pioneer Center** and the park's visitor center, a collection of transplanted and recreated log cabins designed to take visitors back to the pioneer days of the late 1800s.

The Ahwahnee Hotel

The queen of the valley is undoubtedly the legendary **Ahwahnee Hotel**, for which rooms must often be booked at least a year in advance. The Ahwahnee is located about one mile east of Yosemite Village on Route 140, and was built after a titled Englishwoman visited Yosemite and was inconvenienced by the primitive appointments of the few lodgings in the

area. She made a complaint to the director of the United States National Park Service that local accommodation was a disgrace, and largely because of this complaint plans were drawn up for a luxury hotel.

The Ahwahnee is built of stone and timber. The hotel's huge fireplace usually holds a blazing fire and the restaurant is truly magnificent and worth dining in. It is also open in the winter. Its doors first opened in 1927, and since then an impressive number of VIPs, including England's Queen Elizabeth, Ethiopian emperor Haile Selassie and several American presidents, have enjoyed its warm and elegant hospitality here.

The Ahwahnee is even believed to be home to a famous ghost: in August 1962, President John F. Kennedy stayed at the hotel, and the management thoughtfully had a special rocking chair constructed for him because rocking soothed his war-injured back. Guests today swear they can sometimes hear the rocker creaking in the night.

Waterfalls in Yosemite Valley

There is water rushing, surging and falling at almost every turn in the Yosemite Valley. The valley's highest single waterfall is **Ribbon Falls**, where water cascades down 1,612 feet in a blur of spray and mist.

The highest waterfall in all of North America is **Yosemite Falls**, but it comes in three parts. This is the fifth highest water drop in the world, with the **Upper Falls** tumbling 1,430 feet, **Middle Spill** 675 feet, and **Lower Cascade** 320 feet. It is a quarter mile walk from the always crowded parking lot to see the water as it hits bottom. Alternatively, you can climb a posted three and a half mile path, rising almost a half a mile, to see the magnificent spill from the top.

Another favorite is **Bridal Veil Falls**, which is fed by melting snows from the Sierra Range.

The most famous rock formation in Yosemite is **El Capitan** (7,569 feet), which rises about 3,000 feet above the

valley floor and is twice the height of the Rock of Gibraltar. Visitors examining El Capitan through their binoculars will usually be able to discern the tiny figures of climbers, clambering about on the rock, who come from around the world to ascend its face – for it is here that *"free climbing"* came into existence. Photographer Ansel Adams shot this rock climbers' paradise time and time again, and with each occasion found a different angle and a brand new image.

Another memorable rock formation is **Half Dome**, which stands almost 4,600 feet over the valley floor at an altitude of 8,842 feet above sea level. Tectonic forces allegedly split Half Dome away from North Dome, an adjacent peak. But native Americans tell a more romantic tale; they have a legend about a lovers' quarrel which ended by two sweethearts being turned into two stone peaks, facing each other forever.

Above: Bizarre limestone towers on the South Bank of Mono Lake.

For truly the most spectacular panoramic view in of Yosemite Valley, take the time to travel the 32 miles up to **Glacier Point** at the top of a 3,200 foot cliff. From this point you can see all the way across to Nevada over the entire Sierra Nevada Range.

Route 120 is the only road that crosses Yosemite from east to west. The main reason to take this route is because it leads to **Tuolumne**, an expansive alpine meadow, which is ideal for picnics and short hikes. Farther east, and outside the park boundaries, is extremely photogenic **Mono Lake** (6,200 feet above sea level), with its limestone formations on the southern shore. This is an unusual sight, as the rocks appear to be growing directly out of the water.

To get to San Francisco from Yosemite National Park, take the western exit out of the park: Route 140 east leads to Interstate 5 north. From I-5, take the turnoff for I-580, which later merges into I-80. After crossing the Bay Bridge, you will have arrived in the San Francisco.

PASADENA AND SURROUNDING AREA
Area code 624

Accommodation
LUXURY: **The Ritz-Carlton Huntington**, 1401 Oak Knoll Ave., Pasadena, Tel: 568-3900. Restored and elegant hotel, dating from 1900. *MODERATE:* **Holiday Inn**, 303 E. Cordova St., Pasadena, Tel: 449-4000.

Sights, Museums and Parks
Fenyes Estate, 470 W Walnut, Tel: 577-1660. Villa dating back to 1905, a fine example of the wealth of Pasadena millionaires. **Huntington Library, Art Collections and Botanical Gardens**, 1151 Oxford Rd., San Marino, Tel: 405-2141. **Los Angeles State and County Arboretum**, 301 North Balwin Ave., Arcadia, Tel: 821-3222. Artificial plant paradise with species from all over the world. **Mission San Gabriel**, 537 W Mission Dr., San Gabriel, Tel: 282-5191. One of the most beautiful examples of the architectural beauty of the early Spanish missions. (The chapel and museum date back to the early 18th century). **Norton Simon Museum of Art**, 411 W. Colorado Blvd., Tel: 449-6840. **Rose Bowl**, Rose Bowl Dr. (accessible from Arroyo Blvd.) Tel: 577-3100. **Santa Anita Park**, 285 W Huntington Dr., Arcadia, Tel: 574-7223. Structure belonging to the historical horse racing track. **The Gamble House**, 4 Westmoreland Pl., Pasadena, Tel: 793-3334. One of the most beautiful American villas, fully furnished in wood. Wonderful wood carvings (1908). **Wrigley Gardens**, 391 S Orange Grove Blvd., Tel. 449-4100. The estate of the inventor of chewing gum.

Tourist Information
Pasadena C & V Bureau, 171 S. Los Robles Ave., Pasadena, CA 91101, Tel: 795-9311.

SIERRA NEVADA, SEQUOIA AND KINGS CANYON N.P.

Accommodation
MODERATE: **Wuksachi Village & Lodge**, Sequoia N.P., Tel: (559) 565-4070, Tax 565-0103. New lodge with 102 rooms, 2 miles from Lodgepole Visitor Center. **Buckeye Tree Lodge**, 46000 Sierra Dr, Three Rivers, Tel: (559) 561-4119. Best Western just before Sequoia N.P. **Rankin Ranch**, three miles east of Caliente, near Bakersfield, Tel: (661) 867-2511. Expansive working ranch, in the Tehachapi Mountains. **Spalding House**, 631 N Encina, Visalia, Tel: (209) 739-7877. Restored hotel in pseudo-colonial style. *BUDGET:* **Parkway Inn**, 3535 Rosedale Hwy, Bakersfield, Tel: (661) 327-0681. Good value motel with restaurant.
CAMPING: **Lodgepole Campground**, Atwill Mill, Grant Cove. Reservations Tel: 1-800-365 CAMP or Tel. (301) 722-1257.

Sights, Museums and Parks
California Living Museum, 14000 Alfred Harrell Hwy., Bakersfield, Tel: (661) 872-2256. **Kern County Museum**, 3801 Chester Ave., Bakersfield, Tel: (661) 852-5000. **Sequoia und King's Canyon National Parks**, Information Tel: (559) 565-3341. With the Visitor Centers of **Foothills**, Tel: (559) 565-3134, **Lodgepole**, Tel: (559) 565-3782, **Grant Grove** Tel: (559) 335-2856, and **Wuksachi Village**, Tel. (559) 565-3351. **West Kern Oil Museum**, 184 Wood St./Hwy. 33, Taft (near Bakersfield), no telephone.

Tourist Information
Bakersfield C & V Bureau, 1033 Truxturn Ave., Bakersfield, CA 93301, Tel: (661) 325-5051. **Sequoia and King's Canyon National Parks**, Three Rivers, CA 93271, Tel: (559) 565-3341.

YOSEMITE NATIONAL PARK
Area code 559

Accommodation
LUXURY: **Ahwahnee**, Yosemite Village, 14 miles east of park entrance, on CA 140, Tel: 252-4848. Lodge from 1927, pleasant ambiance. **Tenaya Lodge**, Fishing camp, Tel: 683-6555. 4-star lodge with 2 restaurants, 2 miles from southern park entrance. *MODERATE:* **Pines Resorts**, Bass Lake, Tel: 642-3121. Chalets with kitchens. *BUDGET:* **Mariposa Lodge**, 5052 CA 140, Mariposa, Kreuzung CA 140/49, Tel: (209) 966-3607, 45 rooms.
CAMPING: For reservations and information: Tel: 1-800-4367275 or (301) 722-1257.

Sights and Museums
Mono Lake, east of Lee Vining, in Mono Lake Basin National Forest, Tel: (760) 647-3044. One of the oldest saltwater lakes in the world, unusual tufastone and sandstone formations. **Pioneer Yosemite History Center**, a few miles from Mariposa Grove, in Wawona. Open-air museum with live events. **Yosemite Mountain-Sugar Pine Railroad**, 4 miles south of the southern park gate on CA 41, Tel: 683-7273. **Yosemite National Park**, Yosemite, Tel: (209) 372-0265, Recorded weather and road reports - Information Tel: (209) 372-0200. Visitor Center in Yosemite Village.

FROM
SAN FRANCISCO TO
SALT LAKE CITY

**SAN FRANCISCO
SACRAMENTO
LAKE TAHOE
NEVADA DESERT
SALT LAKE CITY**

San Francisco, it has been said, is the most European city in the United States. Salt Lake City, a town originally founded and developed by a ragged group of religious breakaways, the Mormons, is probably the most mainstream of American communities. Parts of the route are known as "the loneliest road in America." While there may not be towns and crowds to amuse the traveler, there is still magnificent scenery to enjoy: huge woods of ancient trees, craggy mountains topped with snow and striated with ski lifts, broad blue mountain lakes and shimmering desert wastes. This 850 mile trip should take at least nine days, if done at a leisurely pace.

SAN FRANCISCO - THE CITY BY THE BAY

San Francisco was founded in 1776, when Juan Bautista de Anza established a Spanish stronghold on this strategically important bay now bearing the city's name. It was merely a backwater of Spanish colonialism until the year 1848, when James Marshall, while building a

Previous pages: Heavy traffic at an altitude of 220 feet on the 1.7 mile long Golden Gate Bridge. Left: Christopher Street Day – here celebrated with a creative hairdo.

mill for John Sutter on the Indian River about 100 miles northeast of the city, found some nuggets of gold. Once news of his find leaked out, San Francisco's fortunes grew. In just four years, the community blossomed into a city of a quarter of a million miners, victuallers, barkeepers, saloon girls, day laborers and desperados, many culled from the fresh waves of immigrants disembarking in the east.

The town needed that rousing spirit to recover from the 1906 earthquake and subsequent fire that destroyed 464 city blocks – in other words nearly half of the city's dwellings. San Francisco, now covering 46.6 square miles on a peninsula jutting into the Pacific, was built on shaky ground, namely the **San Andreas Fault**. In 1989, the city rocked again, killing nearly 100 people and leaving a trail of destruction. It has once again recovered from the trauma, but each time Mother Earth shivers, all America wonders "Is this the Big One that will heave San Francisco into the ocean?"

The best way to get an impression of town before honing in on some of its special sights is to take the 49 mile scenic drive that is plainly signposted by blue and white signs. What strikes everyone first are the hills. If you get tired of climbing one, so a local saying goes, just lean up against it. Some of these hills have achieved high ranking in the city's social structure. **Nob Hill**, for instance, soaring over Union Square, was where four wealthy San Francisco families – the "Big Four" of the Central Pacific Railroad – built their mansions; and today the hill is capped by the homes of prominent locals, as well as by luxury hotels.

Further south is lively **Market Street**, with the **Civic Center**, a huge administrative complex. Southwest of here are the **Twin Peaks**, which offer a good view of the city, and northeast is the **Embarcadero Center**, with impressive highrises, shops and restaurants.

Telegraph Hill is where the harbormaster used to signal incoming ships to detect their provenance and cargos. Today, it is topped by **Coit Tower**, a construction built as a tribute to the city's firemen by a wealthy dowager who had been an enthusiastic fire buff since she was a teenager. A platform at the top, accessible by elevator, provides one of the most breathtaking views of the city, its two great bridges, the sea of houses, and the glittering bay with Alcatraz Island.

A hill which simply must be ascended (and the city has 42 of them!) is **Russian Hill**, not so much for its summit, but rather to experience the nine dizzying hairpin bends of **Lombard Street**, the most winding street in San Francisco.

The city's hills caused the deaths of many a horse in the era before gasoline engines. In 1873, Andrew Hallidie saw a horse-drawn carriage sliding backwards down a San Francisco hill, dragging its horses behind it, and decided that the town needed a **cable car** system to get passengers up and over the peaks without killing animals in the process. Today, this system comprises 39 cars on three lines in a network covering twelve miles. The cars travel at 9.5 mph and can overcome the 21 percent gradient of some streets. Many of the cars operating today were built around the turn of the century.

Exploring the City's Neighborhoods

San Francisco boasts many distinct neighborhoods, and each differs from the others: Italian North Beach, the Latino Mission District, elegant Pacific Heights, stoned-out Haight and the gay Castro.

The Italian-influenced section spreads out from **Washington Square**, which is a popular spot for office workers to spend their lunch hours, especially when the sun is out.

Haight-Ashbury used to be home to Janis Joplin, Jefferson Airplane and the Grateful Dead. The hippies of the Sixties are long gone, and this is now largely a yuppified neighborhood with trendy clothing stores, busy restaurants and lively entertainment.

The heart of San Francisco's downtown is **Union Square**. The name goes back to pre-Civil War days, when anti-Secessionists successfully demonstrated to convince the state's government to stand by the Union. The square itself consists of pleasant greenery. Unfortunately, on some days, it tends to become a haven for a rather aggressive community of panhandlers, and cannot be recommended as a place to stroll or take a lunch break. In typical American contrast, the immediate area boasts luxury hotels and a long list of America's finest department stores.

The heavily Latino **Mission District** has developed around **Mission Dolores**, the Franciscan church built with Indian labor in 1791. Its elaborate altar is a beautiful example of Mexican naive artistry. The adjacent museum has a range of exhibits. The simple pioneer cemetery is the final resting place for many of San Francisco's earliest residents.

Chinatown – The Gateway to Asia

Exotic **Chinatown** stands out from all the other quarters and is a remarkable area which was established in 1847,

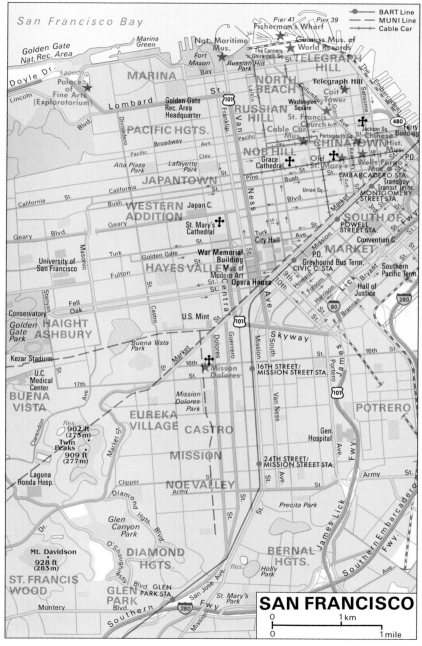

San Francisco Bay

Golden Gate
Nat. Rec. Area

Doyle Dr.

Lincoln

Marina
Green

Golden Gate
Nat. Rec. Area

Lagoon

Palace
of
Fine Arts
(Exploratorium)

Blvd.

Divisadero

Lombard

Fort
Mason

MARINA

Russian
Hill
Park

Nat. Maritime
Mus.

Fisherman's Wharf

Pier 41   Pier 39

Guiness Mus. of
World Records

The Cannery
Ghirardelli Sq.

Russian Hill
Bay

St.

Franklin

Van

Ness

Larkin

NORTH
BEACH

Columbus

TELEGRAPH
HILL

The Embarcadero

BART Line
MUNI Line
Cable Car

Golden Gate
Rec. Area
Headquarter

Pacific

Broadway

PACIFIC HGTS.

Alta Plaza
Park

Clay

Ave.

Lafayette
Park

Telegraph Hill

Coit
Tower

RUSSIAN
HILL

Washington
Square

St. Francis
Church

Cable Car
Mus.

Grant

Portsmouth Sq.

Jackson Sq.

Ferry
Building

480

Ave.

Sansome

Chinese
Hist.
Mus.

CHINATOWN

P.O.

Wells Fargo

3rd

St.

California

St.

JAPANTOWN

Bush

St.

NOB HILL

Grace
Cathedral

St.

Pine

Old
St. Mary's
Church

Keary

Union Sq.

California

St.

Masonic

Geary

WESTERN
ADDITION

Japan C.

Geary

St. Mary's
Cathedral

Market

St.

EMBARCADERO STA.

Transbay
Transit Term.

MONTGOMERY
STREET STA.

University of
San Francisco

Turk

Golden Gate

Fulton

St.

HAYES VALLEY

St.

War Memorial
Building

Mus. of
Modern Art

Opera House

Turk

City Hall

Blvd.

POWELL
STREET STA.

Convention C.

SOUTH OF

MARKET

Mission

St.

Greyhound Bus Term.

CIVIC C. STA.

Howard

Folsom

Southern
Pacific Term.

Geary

Blvd.

Ave.

St.

9th

10th

St.

Fwy.

Conservatory

Golden
Gate
Park

Kezar Stadium

U.C.
Medical
Center

HAIGHT
ASHBURY

Fell

Oak

Stanyan

Masonic

U.S. Mint

Castro

101

Dolores

Guerrero

Mission

Market

Bryant

Lick

Harrison

Brannan

80

Hall of
Justice

280

St.

St.

St.

17th

BUENA
VISTA

Clarendon

Res.

902 ft
(275 m)

Twin
Peaks

909 ft
(277 m)

Buena Vista
Park

Market

16th

St.

Mission
Dolores

Mission
Dolores
Park

EUREKA
VILLAGE

CASTRO

St.

16th

St.

Skyway

South

St.

Van Ness

Potrero

16th STREET/
MISSION STREET STA.

16th

St.

POTRERO

Southern Embarcadero Fwy.

101

Laguna
Honda Hosp.

Mt. Davidson

928 ft
(283 m)

ST. FRANCIS
WOOD

Montery

Diamond Hgts. Blvd.

O'Shaughnessy

Glen
Canyon
Park

DIAMOND
HGTS.

GLEN
PARK

Blvd.

Blvd.

Clipper

Army

MISSION

NOE VALLEY

Army

St.

St.

24TH STREET/
MISSION STREET STA.

Gen.
Hospital

Ave.

Precita Park

St.

Res.

Holly
Park

BERNAL
HGTS.

James Lick

Fwy.

Army

St.

Ave.

GLEN
PARK STA.

San Jose Ave.

St. Mary's
Park

280

Mission

Southern

Fwy.

SAN FRANCISCO

0   1 km

0   1 mile

when Chinese laborers began arriving in San Francisco. They had originally come to work in the mines, but they were soon heavily involved in the building of the transcontinental railway. This is thought to be the largest single Chinese community outside Asia.

Walking through the green-tiled dragon-topped Chinatown gate at **Bush Street** and **Grant Avenue**, you will soon realize that you have entered a totally different world. Men in loose-fitting clothes do slow and concentrated *tai chi* exercises in the early morning mists to the steady clicking of mah-jongg tiles.

Grant Avenue is the main street to visit in Chinatown. It leads through brightly-colored ethnic markets, shops and restaurants with displays of orange Peking ducks dangling in the windows, paper-thin dried fish as well as green and white *bok choi*.

Above: A cable car climbs steep Hyde Street; Alcatraz Island in the background. Right: Mural in Chinatown.

Strolling along Fisherman's Wharf

The fishermen themselves may have long since gone, but **Fisherman's Wharf** has turned into a bustling, lively and profitable place to shop and eat. Today it attracts large crowds of tourists with its bright palette of shops, galleries and seafood restaurants. Many have spilled over from nearby **Ghirardelli Square**, where an erstwhile chocolate factory was turned into a trendy and profitable shopping and entertainment complex.

From nearby **Pier 41**, curious visitors can sail off on the two and a half hour cruise around **Alcatraz Island** and hear the gruesome stories of America's public enemies who were once incarcerated there.

The most unusual residents of **Pier 39**, a two storey bayfront tourist attraction, are more than 600 sea lions who have completely taken over certain areas of the marina. They lie around on the docks all day, barking at the tourists or merely sunning themselves.

The Golden Gate Bridge

There are two breathtaking avenues that lead out of San Francisco. One of these crosses the world famous **Golden Gate Bridge**. 8,981 feet long and swaying 220 feet above the bay, this bridge carries about three million vehicles a month to and from neighboring **Marin County**.

The Bayside villages of **Sausalito** and **Tiburon** offer spectacular views back across the bay to San Francisco – well, if the fog has lifted, that is. Both of these towns are artists' colonies, harboring exquisite restaurants with balconies overlooking the bay, and both can also be reached by ferry boat. A drive to some of the wineries in the **Napa** and **Sonoma** areas is well recommended; wine tastings and tours are extremely popular diversions here.

About seventeen miles northwest of San Francisco is the 580 acre **Muir Woods National Monument**, an impressive and majestic grove of red-woods, some of which are close to 1,000 years old and almost 250 feet tall.

The other famous bridge is the 8.25 mile long **Bay Bridge**. Completed in 1936, this is the longest suspension bridge in the entire world. It leads travelers to **Oakland**, a cosmopolitan city and seaport where more than 80 different languages are spoken. The city is well worth a visit, even if only for **Preservation Park**, a complex of 16 restored Victorian houses, and the **Jack London Waterfront Area**, with its old saloons and houses – including the author's Yukon cabin, which was transported south. These are both among the major tourist attractions here.

In the city of **Berkeley**, just north of Oakland, a stroll around the campus of the famous **University of California** is well worth taking. Also worth a visit here are the **Museum of Anthropology** and the **University Art Museum**, which houses an impressive collection of modern art.

SACRAMENTO

Four important freeways intersect at **Sacramento**, the capital of California and one of its oldest and most popular communities. I-580 is probably the most modern road leading from San Francisco into the broad and fertile San Joaquin Valley. Mile after mile of agricultural landscape unfolds as you move northwest on I-5 towards the signature **Capitol Dome**, which stands out in Sacramento's skyline.

This area began to boom as early as 1839, when Swiss immigrant John Augustus Sutter arrived on the banks of the American River and built a fort and trading post he called New Helvetia.

By 1848, Sutter's community was prosperous enough for him to start a mill in the nearby foothills. When a certain John Marshall commenced the construction of Sutter's mill, he chanced upon a

Above: A little confusing for the mailman? – Mailboxes in Sausalito.

gold nugget in the river. This discovery changed the face of western America forever. Within months, most of Sutter's employees and neighbors were chasing lodes of gold up in the hills, and the population of nearby Sacramento and its adjoining areas multiplied exponentially as gold fever spread nationwide. Sutter himself was ruined as a result of land claim disputes.

The **Old Sacramento Historic District** today is very much a replica of the city as it was when it prospered in the era from 1850 until the turn of the century. **Sutter's Fort** has been completely reconstructed, and there are self-guided tours with explanations of the exhibits, which include a blacksmith's shop, a prison, a bakery, living quarters and a corral.

Sacramento was so important as a communications hub in its early days that the famous Pony Express had its western terminus here. Just before the telegraph came west, California was linked to St. Joseph, Missouri and the rest of the East

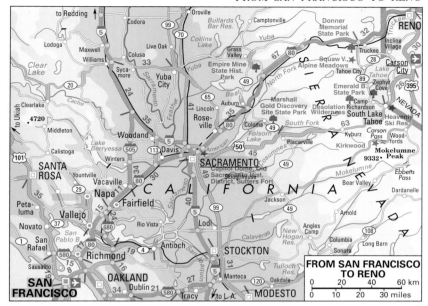

by a network of 80 riders who galloped their small but swift ponies over the 1,966 mile route in under ten days. This epic era in American history is marked by a monument at Second and J Streets.

Sacramento's major business, besides tourism, is government. The **State Capitol Building** is a massive, domed, marble- encrusted affair, where the business of leading America's most populous state and deciding the administrative fate of its 30 million inhabitants is conducted. The building boasts seven historic rooms, plus a theater and some exhibits. Visitors can join tours through the State Capitol twice a day. Nearby is the **Governor's Mansion**, a Victorian residence with 30 rooms.

After the demise of the Pony Express, the railroad became a vital link between Sacramento and the eastern United States. The heyday of rail travel is lavishly documented at the **California State Railroad Museum**, a huge complex exhibiting over 21 restored locomotives and railroad cars.

With Sacramento bounded by two rivers, the **American River** and the **Sacramento River**, water recreation tops the list of outdoor activities. There are plenty of fishing boats eager to take interested parties out after salmon and steelhead trout. River rafting along some of the upland streams is very popular. Houseboating is a favorite pastime in the area as well. With over 1,000 miles of navigable waterways, there's plenty of room to find solitude on the rivers.

Gold Fever

Just about everyone who originally came to Sacramento was after gold, so you should plan to visit the **Mother Lode** as well. This gold vein stretches over 120 miles along Highway 49. North on Route 49 is the **Empire Mine State Historic Park** in Grass Valley. This was the largest, richest and deepest of the California mines, and there are still visible traces of the digging and dredging that frantically went on in the area.

North of Placerville along 49 is the **James Marshall State Historic Monument** and **Gold Discovery Site State Park**. Here is where it all began: a statue of John Marshall stands on a hilltop, gesturing and pointing dramatically to the spot where he allegedly made his historic discovery of gold.

Further south on Route 49 is **Columbia**, a fully restored Gold Rush town, where visitors can actually pan for gold themselves, climb aboard stagecoaches, drink and dine in Wild West style saloons, and relive the past. Like most of the *forty-niners* (gold-seekers of the previous century), few visitors today leave Sacramento and Gold Country with nuggets in their pockets. They do depart, however, with golden memories of what California used to be like in the bad old days. Heading East on US 50, the journey continues to Lake Tahoe.

LAKE TAHOE

Mark Twain said it all when he described **Lake Tahoe**, sitting high in the Sierras astride the California-Nevada border, as "the fairest picture the whole earth affords."

Its brilliant blue surface reflects its stunning surroundings and it is indeed a spectacular oasis of color, 22 miles long and eight miles wide, and has been attracting vacationers and settlers since the 1800s. The 72 mile drive around the lake on routes 28, 50 and 89 is a tour leading to one of the best skiing areas in North America, and through some of its most exciting casinos.

Steamboats were the preferred mode of transport around the lake in early days, and two paddlewheelers still chug tourists along the shoreline. The newest is the 151 foot *MS Dixie II*, which takes passengers over to **Emerald Bay**. For

Right: Reno, not nearly as glitzy by day as by night.

those who prefer to propel themselves using their own steam, there are kayaks available for rent at the **Camp Richardson Resort** on the south shore.

Captain Kirk's Beach Club at **Zephyr Cove** has an enormous fleet of jet skis, waterskiing equipment, pedalos and fishing boats for rent. Even parasailing is available for those who prefer a more elevated view of the lake.

Fishing has no special season on the lake. Anglers will find Mackinaw trout biting twelve months out of the year. Hikers are everywhere around Tahoe, and with a little luck they'll spot the odd coyote, a couple of mule deer and perhaps even a black bear or two.

Adventurous mountain bikers can strap on their helmets and chance the exhilarating ride down the breathtaking **Flume Trail**, which was once a logging route.

Another place to take chances is at Tahoe's gambling tables. Lady Luck arrived at the lake and unpacked her bags in 1944, when **Harvey's Wagonwheel** opened the area's first gaming establishment. This occurred just across the California line in Nevada, where gambling has been legal since 1931. The border between California and Nevada runs right through the town of **South Lake Tahoe**. In the Nevada section, eight casnos with wedding chapels have been established, where one-armed bandits, roulette, craps and blackjack tables rake in the cash. Most of the large casinos in Nevada offer massive buffets at bargain prices, designed to lure customers in so that they might become inspired by the jingling sound of jackpots being won.

The best overall views of the Tahoe region are from the basket of one or another of the various hot air balloons which take passengers aloft at dawn and at dusk when the weather is good. Or, there's the option of going to the **Heavenly Ski Resort**, with its 50-passenger tram which carries its human

load 2,000 feet up the slopes, where they can enjoy a breathtaking view of the countryside.

Some of the attractions to be seen in this region include **Vikingsholm**, a 38-roomed mansion completed in 1929, which is based on an 8th century Viking fortress.

East of **Incline Village**, on Route 28, is **Ponderosa Ranch**, instantly recognizable to anyone who has seen the television series *Bonanza*, which was shot here. On display for visitors are the Cartwright Ranch, a complete Western town and a saloon.

In winter, Tahoe is difficult to reach because at over 6,000 feet there's a lot of snow. Then again, it is an ideal area for skiing, with 19 resorts located within a 45 minute drive of the lake. The most famous resort is **Squaw Valley**, host to the 1960 Winter Olympics.

Alpine Meadows is usually the first of Tahoe's ski resorts to open in the fall, thanks to an extensive number of snow-making machines. Insiders report that the pistes leading into Nevada are less crowded than those into California. **Kirkwood**, at 7,800 feet, is the highest of the Tahoe resorts, making for lighter, drier powder than the heavier snows which local skiers describe as "Sierra cement." It takes its name from Zachary Kirkwood, a pioneer who established an inn here in 1874 to service silver miners.

A few miles north of Lake Tahoe, off I-80, is the most historic monument in the area. It is a tribute to the so-called Donner Party, a group of 89 pioneers who headed west in late 1846 and early 1847, and got trapped in the Sierras by snowdrifts 22 feet high. The 47 who survived admitted that they had eaten the remains of some of their fellow travelers. A 22 foot high monument commemorates the tragedy.

Also worth visiting is **Desolation Wilderness**, 64,000 acres at the southwest corner of the lake, which consists of a jungle of granite peaks, heavy forests, glacier-carved valleys, and more than 50 smaller lakes ideal for fishing in and hiking around.

THE NEVADA DESERT

Reno, which bills itself as "the biggest little city in the world," is just a few miles northeast of Lake Tahoe along I-80. This neon-lit town has recently invested in an enjoyable **River Walk** along the banks of the **Truckee River**, and it stages a year-long calendar of events, ranging from rodeos and logger jamborees to wine-tastings and ethnic events, in an effort to attract clients to its gaudy casinos and drive-through wedding chapels.

Reno is the last outpost of civilization for a while on the way east. South of it is Nevada's capital, Carson City, which bathes in the tourism of Lake Tahoe. But the eastward drive ending in Salt Lake City goes through the **Great Basin** of the Nevada Desert.

There are two major east-west arteries across this wasteland. Travelers heading for Salt Lake City usually take I-80, which, with its parallel highway I-50, shares the nickname of "the loneliest road in America." In earlier days the route was called the *Humboldt Trail*, and was trod by thousands of forty-niners headed for the gold fields of Sacramento.

This route crosses a land virtually void of water, a barren waste of alkaline sand. The saying here is that the topography is so harsh, it takes 40 acres to feed a single cow, several square miles to support a human, and a ton of stone to get an ounce of gold.

You can travel for dozens of miles without seeing much more than sage-brush or creosote bushes, the only sign of civilization being an occasional ranch house amidst a cooling cluster of cotton-wood trees.

Here and there you'll see isolated houses without cattle, often surrounded by sleek limousines from Vegas or Reno. These are some of Nevada's legal brothels or out-of-the-way gambling

Right: Too much salt can sometimes be de-sirable – salt production on Great Salt Lake.

houses, which do a lively business, often hosting busloads of visiting Japanese tourists or delegates escaping a boring trade show. Stopping in for just a drink is not discouraged.

Few towns have even the barest of tourist facilities, **Winnemucca** is one of these towns but is worth a stopover, and is perhaps the logical place to spend a night. In 1850, it was known as Frenchman's Ford and had a toll booth that charged those crossing the Humboldt River on their way to California. The town takes its name from the Indian chief who used to hold sway in the area.

The most famous (apocryphal) event in Winnamucca's history is the bank robbery staged here by Butch Cassidy and the Sundance Kid. They allegedly rode off with almost $33,000. Winna-mucca still runs its annual **Butch Cassidy Days Fiesta**, and hopes in vain that Paul Newman and Robert Redford will show up. To ward off boredom in the evening, the town has four casinos designed to separate travelers from their funds in an entertaining fashion.

Closer to the Utah border is **Elko**, the hub of northeastern Nevada, and with 14,700 residents the largest town between Reno and Salt Lake City. Chances of getting authentic French-Spanish food in town are quite good due to the large number of Basque shepherds who once settled nearby to tend their flocks of sheep.

SALT LAKE CITY

Salt Lake City is unique, perhaps the only theocratically run city in the U.S. Clean, honest, forthright, it also tries to be cosmopolitan, with modern high-rise commercial centers, some interesting sights and a lot of history.

The first white settlers to arrive in large numbers in this region were pioneers of a brand new sect, the Church of *Jesus Christ of Latter-Day Saints* – more com-

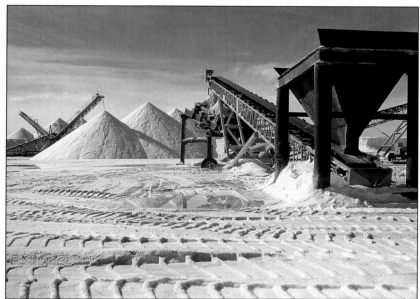

monly known as Mormons. They were led into the valley in 1847 by Brigham Young, a church patriarch who was looking for a place where they could practice their religion – which included polygamy – without persecution. Young uttered the immortal and prosaic phrase when he saw the valley: "This is the right place!" And the Mormons have been ensconced here ever since.

Their pioneer town was planted alongside the enormous **Great Salt Lake**, 50 miles wide, 80 miles long and up to 36 feet deep. It is the largest lake in the U.S. west of the Mississippi, a remnant of gigantic Lake Bonneville (which used to cover a massive expanse in Utah) which evaporated over thousands of years. Great Salt Lake's salt content is up to 27 percent. Floating in the lake water is easy and fun; swallowing it is not.

The best place from which to view the lake is the **Saltair Resort**, less than 15 minutes from downtown. This is an amusement park which has had more than its share of bad luck: it has burned down three times since it first opened and was flooded once. At the time it began operating, in 1893, it boasted the world's largest dance pavilion.

Following the Gospel

A tour of Salt Lake City probably should begin at the **State Capitol**, with its granite walls and unique copper dome. Perched majestically on a hillside high above the city, this is one of the first buildings to be sighted by new arrivals. It was too expensive for the state to put up until a local millionaire railway baron passed away, and the tax collectors used the revenue from his estate to erect it.

The **Mormon Tabernacle Headquarters** on historic **Temple Square** should be visited to learn more about Mormon theology. There are docents on hand throughout the day who will explain Mormonism and trace its history through the past 150 years.

Every Tuesday evening, from 8 to 9:30 p.m., the famous **Mormon Tabernacle**

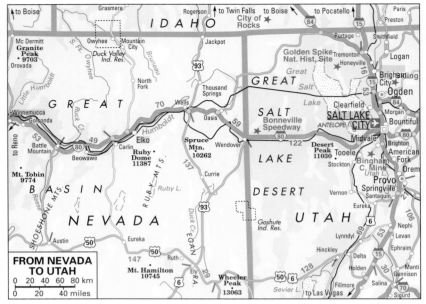

**FROM NEVADA
TO UTAH**

0 20 40 60 80 km

0   20   40 miles

Choir, a choral group of some 320 voices, practices, and visitors are invited to listen. Early risers on Sunday who are in their seats by 9:15 a.m. can catch the choir's weekly radio and television concert.

Next to the King's College Choir in Cambridge, this is probably the best-known religious choral group in the world. They have performed at four presidential inaugurations, have sung with a number of famous symphony orchestras, and have produced more than 150 recordings, several of which have gone gold. Singing is a family tradition, with 20 married couples performing, and a number of families have more than one generation in the choir.

Also on Temple Square is the **Family History Library**, which is a collection of genealogical information totaling 1.9 million rolls of microfilm plus 250,000 books. Given a little time, its staff can trace just about any name genealogically

Right: The Mormon Tabernacle Choir is one of the best-known church choirs in America.

during the period from the mid-1500s up until the present day.

Salt Lake City has for a long time been a transportation hub. The golden spike celebrating the first completed transatlantic railway link between the east and west coasts in the mid 1800s was driven in 90 miles north of the city, an event which is celebrated annually. The **Golden Spike National Historic Site** is located near **Brigham City**.

Trolley cars were once the major form of local transportation, and today **Trolley Square**, located just a few blocks from downtown, is a remodelled complex housing specialty shops, theaters, art galleries and restaurants.

Salt Lake City is very much an outdoors-minded community. Less than 20 minutes from downtown a driver can step out of his car amidst secluded mountain paths of exquisite beauty, flanked by multicolored meadows of wildflowers and clear streams, with the distinct possibility that, with a bit of patience, deer and elk might wander into view.

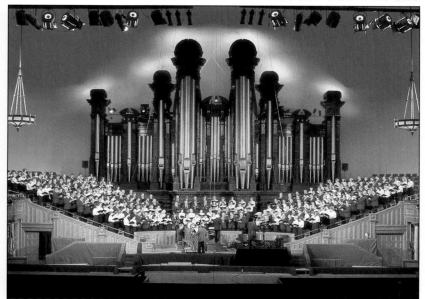

Brighton Resort, at the top of **Big Cottonwood Canyon**, is the start of a 2.5 mile trail to lakes **Mary**, **Martha** and **Catherine**, all fed by a melting mountain glacier. For those who want to go up the hills without too much strain, there's a tram at **Little Cottonwood Canyon** which drops hikers off at 11,000 feet, from where five states can be viewed.

One of the most remarkable events in the U.S. takes place on **Antelope Island** in Salt Lake every November. It's a ten-day affair, as cowboys and helicopters combine to corral one of the largest and oldest buffalo herds in the country. The cowboys move the herd into holding pens for their annual autumn physicals, and to sort out the weak animals.

Since mining has contributed to much of Salt Lake City's more recent wealth, people like to see where the ore comes from. This makes the **Bingham Canyon Copper Mine** a major tourist attraction. It used to be a mountain; now it's a huge bowl covering 1,900 acres. From the rim, trucks and steam shovels below look like toys as they move their loads to the ore crusher. The visitor center, off State Rd. U-48 and I-15, exhibits and presents mining operations. Not far away are the ghost towns of **Leadmine** and **Bingham**, with their **House of Copper Museum** and the rustic **Leadmine Bar**, which still boasts traditional swinging doors.

Skiing has gained in popularity around Salt Lake City in recent years, especially in the areas of Alta, Deer Valley, Snowboard and Park City to the southeast. The **Wasatch Mountains** receive an average of 460 inches of light, fluffy snowfall a year, which has prompted the community to bid for the Winter Olympic Games in 2002. The U.S. Ski Team headquarters is in Utah, putting a lot of top-flight talent on the slopes.

Not far away is **Sundance**, where Robert Redford purchased some land 20 years ago and founded a conservation area on it. In spring the town gears up for the annual Sundance Film Festival, which is known for its alternative air and is rapidly gaining popularity.

159

SAN FRANCISCO AND SURROUNDING AREA
Area code 415

Accommodation
LUXURY: **Four Seasons Clift**, 495 Geary St., Tel: 775-4700. *MODERATE:* **Alamo Square**, 719 Scott St., Tel: 922-2055. Carefully restored pension. **Washington Inn**, 465 10th St., Oakland, Tel: (510) 452-1776. Historic building from 1900. *BUDGET:* **Grant Plaza**, 465 Grant St., Tel: 434-3883. Small hotel in Chinatown. **Sheehan**, 620 Sutter St., Tel: 775-6500. Near Union Square. **San Remo**, 2237 Mason St., Tel: 776-8688, partly with showers on each floor.

Cafés and Restaurants
EXPENSIVE: **Farallon**, 450 Post St, Tel: 956-6969, serves the finest seafood. **Kyo-ya**, 2 New Montgomery St, Tel: 546-5000, all Japanese delights. *GOOD VALUE:* **Yank Sing**, 427 Battery St, Tel: 362-1640, superb Dim-Sum dishes. **The Cheesecake Factory**, in Macy's on Union Square, 251 Geary Blvrd., Tel: 391-4444, dishes from burgers to pizza, for dessert you'll have to make a choice between 40 different kinds of cheesecake!

Sights, Museums and Parks
Alcatraz Island, Tel: 773-1188 (Info), Tel: 705-5555 (Ferry tickets). **Asian Art Museum**, Golden Gate Park, Tel: 379-8800, chinese art. **The Cannery**, 2801 Leavenworth St., Tel: 771-3112. Shopping mall and art galleries. **Chinese Historical Museum**, 650 Commercial St., Tel: 391-1188. Exhibits Chinese-American art. **Coit Tower** on Telegraph Hill, Tel: 362-0808, viewing platform. **Fort Point National Historic Site**, Presidio of San Francisco, Tel: 556-1693. **Ghirardelli Square**, between Beach and Polk St., shopping and restaurant quarter. **Golden Gate National Recreation Area**, Park Headquarters, Fort Mason, Tel: 556-0560. **Golden Gate Park**, McLaren Lodge (Fell/Stanyan Sts.), Tel: 666-7200. **Guinness Museum of World Records**, 235 Jefferson St., San Francisco, Tel: 771-9890. **Jack London Square**, 30 Jack London Square, Oakland, Tel: (510) 814-6000. **Mission Dolores**, 3321 16th St., Tel: 621-8203. **Muir Woods National Monument**, Mill Valley, 12 miles north on Hwy. 101, Tel: 388-2595. **Palace of Fine Arts**, 3601 Lyon St, Tel: 567-6642, Buildings of the Panama-Pacific-Exhibition of 1915 with **Exploratorium**, an interactive experience. **Pier 39**, Tel: 705-5500. **Museum of Modern Art**, 151 Third St, Tel: 357-4000. **Performing Arts Center**, 401 Van Ness Ave., Tel: 552-8338. **San Francisco Zoo**, 1 Zoo Rd., Tel: 753-7080. **SoMa (South of Market)**, south of Market St., culture and entertainment quarter. **Union Square**, 323 Geary St., Tel: 781-7880 (Information). **Wells Fargo Bank History Museum**, 420 Montgomery St., Tel: 396-2619. Exhibition with the original coach, gold coins and gold nuggets.

Tourist Information
Oakland C & V Bureau, 1000 Broadway, Suite 200, Oakland, CA 94607, Tel: (510) 839-9000. **San Francisco V & C Bureau**, 201 Third Street, Ste. 900, San Francisco, CA 94103, Tel: 391-2000. http://www.sfvisitor.org **San Francisco Visitor Center**, Hallidie Plaza, Lower Level, 900 Market St., San Francisco, Tel: 391-2000. **Sausalito Chamber of Commerce**, 333 Caledonia St., PO Box 566, Sausalito, CA 94965, Tel: 332-0505.

SACRAMENTO AND GOLD COUNTRY
Area code 916

Accommodation
MODERATE: **Amber House**, 1315 22nd St., Sacramento, Tel: 444-8085. Historic hotel pension. **Best Western Placerville Inn**, 6850 Greenleaf Dr., Placerville, Tel: (530) 622-9100, also suites with fireplace, restaurant nearby. **Vizcaya**, 2019 21st St., Sacramento, Tel: 455-5243. Small victorian B & B. *BUDGET:* **Holiday Lodge**, 1221 E Main St., Grass Valley, Tel: (530) 273-4406. **La Quinta**, 4604 Madison Ave., Sacramento, Tel: 348-0900.

Sights, Museums and Parks
California State Railroad Museum, 125 I St., Sacramento, Tel: 332-9280. **Columbia State Historic Park**, north of Sonora, Tel: (209) 532-4301. **Crocker Art Museum**, Sacramento, 216 O St, Tel: 264-5423, European and Californian collection. **Discovery Museum**, 101 I St., Sacramento, Tel: 264-7057. Exhibits the gold rush. **Empire Mine State Historic Park**, 10791 E. Empire St., Grass Valley, Tel: (530) 273-8522. **Governor's Mansion State Historic Park**, 1526 H St., Sacramento, Tel: 323-3047. **Marshall Gold Discovery Site State Historic Park**, 310 Back St., Coloma, Tel: (530) 622-3470. **Old Sacramento**, 1104 Front St., Old Sacramento, Tel: 264-7777. Historic old town. **State Capitol Museum**, State Capitol, Room B-27, Sacramento, Tel: 324-0333. **Sutter's Fort State Historic Park**, 2701 L Street, Sacramento, Tel: 445-4422. Open-air museum. **State Indian Museum**, 2618 K Street, Tel: 324-0971. Indian canoes, weapons, ceramics and weaving. **Towe Ford Museum**, 2200 Front St., Sacramento, Tel: 442-6802. Over 180 vintage exhibits.

Tourist Information
Grass Valley/Nevada County Chamber of Commerce, 248 Mill St., Grass Valley, Tel: (530) 273-4667. **Sacramento Visitor Center**, 1102 Second St., Sacramento, Tel: 442-7644.

RENO, LAKE TAHOE, NEVADA DESERT
Accommodation

MODERATE: **Silver Legacy Resort Casino**, 407 N Virginia St, Reno, Tel: (775) 325-7401, new resort with 1720 rooms in Victorian style with spa. **Cal-Neva Lodge Hotel Spa Casino**, 2 Stateline Rd., Crystal Bay, Tel: (775) 832-4000. This hotel once belonged to Frank Sinatra, and is a place in which many famous personalities have spent the night. All rooms have a view of Lake Tahoe. *BUDGET:* **Super 8**, 3600 Lake Tahoe Blvd, South Lake Tahoe, Tel: (530) 544-3476, 110 good motel rooms, 1 suite with fireplace. *CAMPING:* **Keystone R.V. Park**, 1455 W 4th Street, Reno, Tel: (775) 324-5000. **Campground by the Lake**, Hghwy 50 & Rufus Allen Blvd, South Lake Tahoe, Tel: (530) 542-6096.

Sights, Museums and Parks

Emerald Bay State Park, 22 miles south of Tahoe City, on CA 89, Tel: (530) 541-3030. **Lake Tahoe Nevada State Park**, Incline Village, Tel: (775) 831-0494. **Lake Tahoe Historical Society Museum**, 3058 US 50, Tel. (530) 541-5458. Exhibition on local Indian history. **Ponderosa Ranch**, 100 Ponderosa Ranch Rd., Incline Village, Tel: (775) 831-0691. **Tahoe Rim Trail**, 3170 Hwy. 50, Myers, Information Tel: (775) 588-0686. **Toiyabe National Forest**, 10 miles west on I-80, then west on NV 27, extensive forest area, horse trekking, hunting, angling and camping. **Vikingsholm**, Emerald Bay, one mile from Hwy. 89, Tel: (530) 525-7277. **National Automobile Museum**, 10 S Lake St., Reno, Tel: (775) 333-9300. Exhibition on over 200 vintage automobiles, with some live shows and events.

Sports and Recreation, Boat trips

Alpine Meadows, 10 km northwest of Tahoe city, via CA 89, Tel: (530) 538-4232, http:// www.skialpine.com, an excellent and popular region for skiing. **Camp Richardson Corral**, Hwy. 89 So., PO Box 8335, South Lake Tahoe, CA 96158, Tel: (530) 541-1801. **Club Kirkwood**, 30 miles south via CA 88, Tel: 209/258-6000. **Squaw Valley USA**, 8 km northwest of Tahoe City, via CA 89, Tel: (530) 583-6985. **Heavenly Ski Resort**, one mile east of US 50, South Lake Tahoe, Tel: (775) 586-7000. **Dream Weavers Hot Air Balloon Co.**, Tel: 1-800-FUN-ALOFT, balloon flights over the Sierra. **MS Dixie Cruiseship**, 760 Highway 50, Zephyr Cove, Tel: (775) 588-3508. Daily boat trips departing from Zephyr Cove Resort ab. **Northstar-at-Tahoe**, Hwy. 267 on Northstar Dr., Tel: (916) 562-1010. Mountainbike tours.

Tourist Information

Humboldt County Chamber of Commerce (Winnemucca), 30 W Winnemucca, NV 89445, Tel: (775) 623-2225. **North Lake Tahoe Chamber of Commerce**, PO Box 884, Tahoe City, CA 96145, Tel: (530) 581-6900. **Lake Tahoe Visitors Authority**, PO Box 16299, South Lake Tahoe, CA 96151, Tel: 1-800-AT-TAHOE. **Reno/Sparks C & V Authority**, 405 Marsh Ave., Box 3499, Reno, NV 89505, Tel: (775) 686-3030.

SALT LAKE CITY
Area code 801
Accommodation

LUXURY: **Little America Hotel and Towers**, 500 S. Main Street, Tel. 363-6781. Comfortable rooms and a good restaurant. *MODERATE:* **Brigham Street Inn**, 1135 E South Temple St., Salt Lake City, UT 84102, Tel: 364-4461. Beautiful Victorian-style B & B. **Brighton Ski Lodge**, 25 miles north via UT 190, in Big Cottonwood Canyon, Brighton, Tel: 532-4731. *BUDGET:* **Super 8**, 616 S 200 West St., Tel: 534-0808. Centrally situated downtown.

Cafés and Restaurants

The Salt Lake Roasting Co., 320 East 400 South. 40 varieties of coffee, cakes and snacks. **Diamond Lil's at the Old Salt City Jail**, 460 South 1000 East. Enjoy prime rib and steaks in a Wild West ambiance.

Sights, Museums and Parks

Bingham Canyon Mine, 25 miles southwest, on UT 48, Tel: 322-7300. **Family History Library**, 35 N West Temple, Tel: 240-2331. **State Capitol**, Head of State St., Tel: 538-3000. **Lion House/ Beehive House**, 63 & 67 E South Temple, Tel: 240-2571. Family home of Brigham Young. **Pioneer Memorial Museum with Carriage House**, 300 N Main St., Tel: 538-1050. Exhibition on the good old pioneering days and the pony express. **Temple Square with Temple, Tabernacle and Assembly Hall**, Temple/Main Sts., Tel: 240-3221. **Trolley Square**, 500-600 South St./600-700 East St., Tel: 521-9877.

Sports and Recreation

Lots of information on **skiing possibilities** in Salt Lake City: http://goutah.com/utah/ **Moki Mac River Expeditions**, Tel: 268-6667. Whitewater rafting trips on the Green and Colorado Rivers. **Raging Waters**, 1200 West 1700 South, Tel. 972-3300. Water Adventure Park, over 30 attractions.

Tourist Information

Salt Lake C & V Bureau, 90 S West Temple, Salt Lake City, UT 84101-1493, Tel: 521-2822.

FROM SALT LAKE CITY TO YELLOWSTONE NATIONAL PARK

POCATELLO AND IDAHO FALLS
GRAND TETON NATIONAL PARK
YELLOWSTONE NATIONAL PARK

The road winding its way through **Idaho** is long and lonely. Huge areas of the state are still almost uninhabited and population density averages about ten people per square mile. It is spectacularly beautiful country, where drivers are seldom out of sight of snow-capped mountains and are almost always within earshot of frothy, white rivers plunging their way through steep, walled canyons. Idaho calls itself the "Gem State," and nearly all of the souvenir shops feature counters selling attractively polished and displayed semi-precious stones, which are found in abundance here.

The drive north out of Utah from Salt Lake City and on into Idaho and Wyoming, to Grand Teton and Yellowstone National Parks, begins on Interstate 15. This is a drive of well over 500 miles, including detours, which, depending on fishing, hiking and camping diversions, could last a week or more.

POCATELLO AND IDAHO FALLS

Pocatello is the largest industrial city on the road, but it is not much of a tourist attraction. The **Bannock County Historical Museum** and the **Museum of**

Left: One of about 200 geysers in Yellowstone National Park.

Idaho State University display objects from Shoshone Indian culture. The reconstructed **Fort Hall Trading Post**, on the Indian reservation of the same name, tells the history of the *Buffalo Soldiers*, a unique unit of African-American soldiers who, liberated after the Civil War, were sent west by the government to quell Indian rebellions.

The huge **American Falls Reservoir** nearby is a center for boating and fishing activities.

Idaho Falls, to the northeast, is as prosperous, bucolic and seemingly idyllic as Pocatello is industrial and run-down. The Idaho Falls skyline is dominated by a seven storey **Mormon Temple**, which some say resembles a wedding cake. There are no longer any falls at Idaho Falls; the Idaho River has long been tamed by a dam near the town center. Green belts along the banks near the dam lend a peaceful air to the downtown area. **Lindsay Boulevard** is one of the town's most important streets, and along it travelers will discover the new visitor center (don't miss the scale model relief of the entire valley which is on display).

An excursion 90 miles westward on US 20 leads to the **Craters of the Moon**. Halfway, there's an unassuming red brick building concealing a remarkable history; the world's first nuclear reactor was installed here, and it is open for viewing. Behind it lies 800 square miles of wilderness which serve as a national nuclear waste dump.

The **Craters of the Moon National Monument** is composed of 83 square miles of black hell. At midsummer, the surface temperatures here can reach 200° F. This lunar landscape of volcanic basalt was created as molten lava oozed to the earth's surface and crusted over every thousand years or so. A seven circular route leads through cones, lava tunnels, craters and caves, all of which have been sandblasted into eerie shapes by winds whipping across the wasteland.

GRAND TETON
NATIONAL PARK

From Idaho Falls, Route 26, a hilly, winding road, leads east to Wyoming. Near the entrance to **Grand Teton National Park** is the city of Jackson, at the southern edge of the **Jackson Hole** valley.

This area has been inhabited for over 12,000 years, according to archeologists. Blackfoot, Crow, Shoshone and many other Native American tribes used to come down into this valley during the winter months. The first white man to arrive here was John Colter, a pioneer and trapper who hit the jackpot in the area in 1807/08. When word got out of his discovery, hordes of fellow trappers followed, eager for beaver pelts to sell at great profit to the fashionable hatters on the U.S. East Coast and in Europe. When the fashion for beaver petered out in the 1840s, things became quiet in Jackson Hole, until the mid-1880s, when cattle and sheep ranchers began moving their herds in. "Hole" is what these pioneers called any valley in a mountain range.

As 20th century tourism began to take hold, some alert ranchers began to realize that tourists would even pay to visit Jack-

son Hole in the winter. As these ranchers put it, "dudes winter better than cows." (Dudes are city slickers who want to experience the hard life of a real cowboy life for a short time). And so farming and grazing areas began to be converted into *dude ranches* and ski slopes. Since then, big money has flowed into Jackson Hole. Some years ago, billionaire John D. Rockefeller Jr. purchased a huge chunk of the area and gave it as a gift to the U.S. government, demanding, as any good businessman would, that the park concession company which he owned would control all future concession activities in the area. The Grand Teton National Park was established in 1929, and was expanded to include Jackson Hole in 1950.

The park totals about 310,000 acres and is flanked on its west side by the **Teton Range**, jagged, glacially carved peaks from the Ice Age that jut sharply into the skies, some 40 miles of mountains in the Rockies. The highest of these Grand Tetons ascend more than 13,000 feet into the heavens. Earthquakes have in the past 1,000 years or so shaken the valley mightily, and ensuing glaciers have carved and gouged deep valleys between the peaks. The mountains were named by French trappers in the pioneer era, who thought the mountain peaks looked like the snow-white breasts of the women they left behind (*teton* is French for "breast").

Seven sparkling lakes glitter at the feet of these mountains, with shores flanked by colorful wildflowers. Bisecting the valley is **Snake River**, its banks lined by tall cottonwood and spruce. A fascinating array of animals, including beavers, wild geese and white pelicans, live near the river. With a little luck, while on a whitewater rafting expedition you might see an elk or two grazing peacefully along the river bank, while bald eagles let warm air streams carry them along overhead. Anglers will have to apply for a state fishing license before casting their lines,

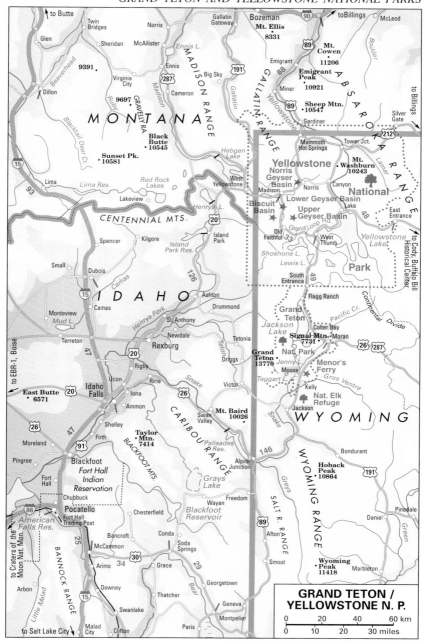

to Butte
Twin
Bridges
Glen
Sheridan
McAllister
Ennis L.
Gallatin
Gateway
Bozeman
Mt. Ellis
8331
to Billings
McLeod
Norris
Virginia
City
9391
Ennis
287
Big Sky
191
Emigrant
89
Mt.
Cowen
11206
Boulder
toBillings
90
Dillon
9697
GRAVELLY RA.
Cameron
Gallatin
88
Emigrant
Peak
• 10921
Miner
MONTANA
Ruby
Madison
MADISON RANGE
Sheep Mtn.
• 10547
89
Gardiner
ABSAROKA RANGE
Silver
Gate
212
to Billings
Black
Butte
• 10545
Hebgen
Lake
Mammoth
Hot Springs
Tower Jct.
15
Lima
Blacktail Deer Cr.
Sunset Pk.
• 10581
West
Yellowstone
Yellowstone
Norris
Geyser
Basin
Mt.
Washburn
10243
National
93
Lima Res.
Red Rock
Lakes
Madison
Canyon
Norris
CENTENNIAL MTS.
Lakeview
Henrys L.
20
Biscuit
Basin
Lower Geyser Basin
Upper
Geyser Basin
Lake
48
East
Entrance
Spencer
Kilgore
Island
Park
Old
Faithful
Grand Loop
Grand
West
Thumb
Yellowstone
Lake
to Cody, Buffalo Bill
Historical Center
Small
Dubois
Island
Park Res.
126
Shoshone L.
Lewis L.
49
Park
Monteview
Mud L.
15
Camas
Camas
Ashton
Drummond
South
Entrance
IDAHO
Henrys Fork
St. Anthony
Newdale
Flagg Ranch
Pacific Cr.
Continental
Divide
Terreton
20
Rexburg
Tetonia
Teton
Driggs
Grand
Teton
Jackson
Lake
Grand
Teton
Nat. Park
Colter Bay
Signal Mtn.
7731
Moran
26
287
Ucon
Rigby
Victor
Grand
Teton
13770
Jenny
Menor's
Ferry
East Butte
• 6571
20
Idaho
Falls
Ammon
Iona
26
Snake
Moose
Taggart L.
Kelly
Gros Ventre
Nat. Elk
Refuge
Shelley
CARIBOU RANGE
Mt. Baird
10026
Swan
Valley
Jackson
WYOMING
26
Moreland
47
Taylor
• Mtn.
7414
Blackfoot MTS.
Palisades
Res.
Bondurant
Pingree
91
Firth
Alpine
Junction
146
Snake
WYOMING RANGE
Hoback
Peak
• 10864
191
Fort
Hall
Blackfoot
Fort Hall
Indian
Reservation
Grays
Lake
Freedom
Grays
SALT R. RANGE
Pinedale
Daniel
Green
to EBR-1, Boise
Chubbuck
86
Pocatello
Fort Hall
Trading Post
25
Chesterfield
Wayan
Blackfoot
Reservoir
89
Conda
Afton
to Craters of the
Moon Nat. Mon.
American
Falls Res.
Bancroft
McCammon
Soda
Springs
Smoot
Wyoming
• Peak
11418
Marbleton
Arbon
BANNOCK RANGE
Arimo
30
34
Grace
29
Georgetown
Bear
Downey
Thatcher
Geneva
Swanlake
Malad
City
Clifton
Paris
Montpelier
to Salt Lake City

GRAND TETON /
YELLOWSTONE N. P.

| 0 | 20 | 40 | 60 km |
| 0 | 10 | 20 | 30 miles |

which is available from just about every business operating in the park. From the ranger station on **Colter Bay** and **Jackson Lake Lodge**, excursions on horseback can be made (after prior booking).

Jackson

Jackson itself is a real Wild West town, with wooden boardwalks and old-fashioned saloons complete with swinging doors and elk heads on the walls. You enter the town's central square through arches fashioned of countless antlers; and Wild West shows are held throughout the summer on the square itself. Yet the atmosphere here also reflects the jet set; almost every other shop is a chic art gallery, designer boutique, or café selling exotic types of coffee.

The **Wildlife of the American West Museum** displays North American land-scape and wildlife painting; the **Teton County Historical Center** documents the development of the fur trade and the history of the local Indians, while the **Jackson Hole Museum** is devoted to the history of the valley's settlement. In winter, the area becomes a luxury ski resort with some of the longest runs in the U.S. It usually has 100 inches of snow before other resorts get their first winter's dusting.

On the northern edge of town is the impressive **National Elk Refuge**, where at the beginning of winter you can see more than 10,000 of these massive animals fleeing the bitter cold of the mountain peaks for the relative warmth of the valley. In the winter season, from mid-December to March, park rangers offer guided tours, hikes, and horse-drawn sleigh tours to observe the wildlife.

Trails and Lakes

There are more than 200 miles of hiking trails within the park, ranging in

Above: In the National Elk Refuge. Right: The 13,000 foot peaks of Grand Teton National Park mirrored in Jackson Lake.

degrees of difficulty from easy walks along the valley slopes to difficult climbs up the steep mountainsides. Rock climbers here should not take to the mountain faces on their own, however; all climbers must register on arrival and departure at the **Jenny Lake Ranger Station**, which also provides hikers with information.

Two of the tougher trails are the **Teton Crest**, which takes hikers to 11,000 feet above sea level, and **Indian Paintbrush Trail**, so named because of its beautiful wildflowers. There are easier, less taxing trails, as well: the **Lunch Tree Hill Trail** is only a half mile walk, starting not far from the **Jackson Lake Lodge**, which is entirely self-explanatory; at intervals along the way there are small signs to tell you about the flora and fauna that can be seen. **Cunningham Cabin Trail** is an interesting three-quarter mile walk that gives visitors some vivid insights into the early ranching days in the Grand Tetons area, as it follows old routes used by cowboys to herd their cattle.

At the **Taggart Lake** parking area the 3.2 mile **Taggart Trail** begins, which leads past many of the area's major historical sites, including the blackened ruins of the 1,028 acre **Beaver Creek Fire**.

Fire is a favorite subject in Grand Teton Park and at the **Cottonwood Creek Picnic** area, **Jackson Lake Overlook**, and at **Flagg Ranch**; there are signs which explain the various ecological consequences of forest fires and the history of previous major forest fires.

Driving north from Jackson on Route 191, early stops are **Menor's Ferry** and the **Chapel of the Transfiguration**. This step into the Grand Tetons of yesteryear is enhanced by a visit to the cabin of pioneer Bill Menor and to inspect the replica of the ferry that used to cross the Snake River a century ago. The adjacent chapel has an altar window which frames the tallest of the Tetons' peaks as beautifully as if it were a painting. Heading north once again, the Teton Park Road winds along the east bank of Jenny Lake.

At the **Cathedral Group Turnout** there is a parking area that commands a spectacular view of **Mount Owen**, **Tweewinot** and **Grand Teton**, three dramatically prominent peaks. There is a six mile walking trail around Jenny Lake, and shuttle boats that take visitors to the west side of the lake in summer.

A little higher up is a fork onto a five mile road leading to the top of **Signal Mountain**, some 8,000 feet above the valley. The vista here is breathtaking, with a panoramic view of the entire Teton Range, Jackson Lake and most of Jackson Hole. Get there early, or plan to arrive late, because parking at the overlook is severely restricted; trailers and large motor homes are discouraged from trying to make it up the road.

Further north on the shores of Jackson Lake are the **Colter Bay Visitor Center** and the **Indian Arts Museum**. The

Above: Ground squirrel. Right: Morning Glory Pool in Yellowstone National Park, an impressive spectacle of color.

museum contains an impressive collection of the arts and crafts of the Shoshone, Blackfoot and Crow tribes to whom this whole area once belonged.

Grand Teton Wildlife

Grand Teton is to America what the *veldt* is to South Africa – an area where an enormous amount of wildlife roams about in its natural habitat. Out in **Cascade Canyon**, west of Jenny Lake, there are golden-colored ground squirrels flitting around **Inspiration Point**, and yellow-bellied woodchucks hide amongst the rocks. Mule deer and moose can be spotted munching contentedly on shrubs growing at the mouth of the canyon.

Jackson Lake was formed from an enormous glacier. Its cool waters provide a habitat for trout and other fish, which in turn become prey to river otters, ospreys, bald eagles, American white pelicans and ducks, all of which can be observed fishing during the day. At dawn and dusk beavers emerge to swim in the lake.

Hiking along the trails gives one ample opportunity to examine the park's flora. June in Jackson Hole is particularly colorful, with clusters of *yellow arrowleaf balsamroot*, a daisy-like flower with arrow-shaped leaves. As the month progresses, spikes of blue-purple lupines appear, as well as yellow mountain sunflowers, pink hollyhock, pink sticky geraniums and purple upland larkspur. In the canyons between the Teton peaks, hikers can stroll through meadows with a rainbow mix of colors: bluebells, yellow columbine, lavender asters, red paintbrush and pink daisies. And the official flower of Grand Teton is the blue alpine forget-me-not found on the slopes.

Surprisingly, forest fires increase the wildflower population in subsequent years because the unexpected sunlight reaching the forest floor enhances the fertilizing effect of the nitrogen-rich ash. Magenta firewood and yellow heartleaf arnica, pink spreading dogbane and snow-brushed ceanothus all flourish around the **Taggart Lake Trail**, which goes through an area that suffered a major forest fire in 1985.

After taking in the Tetons' majesty over several days, the pioneering urge to see what's over the next ridge will take hold. To most visitors, this means heading north to Yellowstone.

YELLOWSTONE NATIONAL PARK

There are five entrances to **Yellowstone National Park**, but most summer guests who have visited Grand Teton National Park go to Yellowstone's southern end via the **John D. Rockefeller, Jr. Memorial Parkway**.

Founded in 1872, Yellowstone is America's oldest National Park and the largest in the lower 48 states. Covering 3,400 square miles, it sits in the northwest corner of Wyoming, also touching on the states of Montana and Idaho. It is also one of America's most popular parks, so do not expect to see it in solitude. There are crowds everywhere, and only the bravest visitor who cuts

through winter's snow and ice can hope to see Yellowstone in its natural, crowd-free state.

But even in summer, Yellowstone is a remarkable experience. Its volcanic origins are still visible in the form of geysers, pools of bubbling mud and steamy thermal springs. The rich soil, another gift from the volcanoes, is a fertile bed for a myriad of wildflowers. Majestic snow-capped peaks rise dramatically along valleys where herds of buffalo and elk graze.

This is not land which has been reclaimed from farmers and herders; Yellowstone is the only large area (2.2 million acres) in the continental United States that has never been farmed, fenced in or developed. It was in 1807 that John Colter wandered across this wilderness and discovered, to his amazement, acres of scalding hot springs, bubbling pools

Above: Limestone terraces in Yellowstone National Park. Right: Old Faithful, the largest geyser, attracts many tourists.

and plumy geysers that squirted boiling water and steam hundreds of feet into the air. A veteran of the Lewis and Clark Expedition, Colter was ridiculed when he returned to the East with his stories of what became laughed at as "Colter's Hell." But others soon confirmed his stories and, in 1870, the U.S. government dispatched survey teams to the area. Their reports urged that the landscape not be exploited by hunters, lumberjacks or miners. In 1872, President Ulysses S. Grant signed the documents which made Yellowstone the first National Park in America, in the words of the document, "...reserved and withdrawn from settlement and dedicated and set apart as a public park or pleasuring ground for the benefit and enjoyment of the people."

In its earliest days there was little funding to protect the park from its visitors – and vice-versa. Jokers were fond of sticking soap down the geyser holes so that bubbles would come up with the steam. Outlaws hid along the first paths and stripped tourists of their wallets and valuables as they came by. The Nez Percé Indians even scalped some of the early visitors. Things got so bad that, in 1886, the U.S. Cavalry was put in charge of policing the park. Mammoth Hot Springs, now Yellowstone's headquarters, is constructed on the site of Fort Yellowstone, built during the era when the army ran things. The **Albright Visitor Center** on the site of the former Army Bachelor Officers' Quarters has slide shows and exhibits exploring the history, fauna and flora of the park, as well as documenting the devastating fire in 1988 which destroyed large areas of forest and killed innumerable animals.

There are other visitor centers about every 20 miles along the 200 mile long figure-of-eight shaped **Grand Loop Road**, which links most of the park's major tourist attractions.

Geyser Country

What sets Yellowstone apart from all other national parks are its approximately 200 active geysers – a world record for density. Most of these geysers are found on the park's west side, along a 50 mile stretch of road between Mammoth Hot Springs in the northwest and the Old Faithful geyser in the southwest. The thermal **Mammoth Hot Springs** are a tremendous natural spectacle; the hot water runs down through ten terrace-like natural pools, one over the other, and on into the depths.

Farther south is the **Norris Geyser Basin**; here, the Echinus Geyser shoots aloft every hour; the Steamboat Geyser, the largest in the world, spouts 425 foot jets of water; and the Norris Museum provides visitors with detailed information about geysers. Southwest of here is the **Lower Geyser Basin**; here you can see the Fountain Paint Pot, which is filled with red mud, and the Great Fountain Geyser, which sends its fountains aloft once a day.

In the **Upper Geyser Basin**, legion geysers show their stuff. One highlight is the **Morning Glory Pool**, shaped like a huge blossom, blue within and gold without. The magma which drives this steam and water to the surface is between two and three miles below the surface. Ground water seeps into the red-hot rocks, which are around 1,000° F. The water then shoots up to the surface.

Supreme among the geysers is **Old Faithful**, discovered by explorers in the 1880s. About every 70 minutes, it fires steam and 8,400 gallons of water almost 200 feet into the air, the jet sometimes continuing for as long as five minutes.

Don't, however, let spectacle distract you from more ordinary, yet no less beautiful, forms of water. Take **Yellowstone Lake**, North America's largest alpine lake, with 110 miles of shoreline, and a favorite with fishermen. At **Roosevelt Lodge**, you can embark on a real stagecoach ride. For more air-conditioned comfort, climb into one of the many luxury buses on hand for a sight-

Above: Caution, do not disturb! Bison are easily excitable.

seeing tour of the park; the bus stops at the most scenic spots.

Yellowstone boasts the greatest concentration of mammals in the lower 48 states: everything from white pelicans to bison, elk, moose, wapiti and mule deer, black bears and grizzlies. The early morning and early evening hours are the best times to see the animals when they flock to the watering holes. Beware of bison: they look big and slow, but they have bad tempers and move very swiftly indeed when provoked. A 2,000 pound bison can charge at speeds of up to 30 mph, three times faster than the average human can run.

Bear attacks are not infrequent. Black bears weigh about 300 pounds and are about three feet high when on all fours. Much more dangerous, though, are the grizzlies, weighing up to 700 pounds, and varying in color from black to blond, depending on the time of year. When they stand on their hind legs, they can be as tall as six feet.

The most important advice about bears is: try not to meet one. They dislike noise, so conversation on the trail, whistling or singing will usually drive the bear away from visitors. Bears, like bison, are fast-moving, running at speeds of around 30 mph, faster than the fastest Olympic sprinter. Faced by a bear, therefore, don't try to run; running can encourage it to attack, and it will be faster than you anyway. Sometimes, a bear bluffs a charge and will pull up at the last minute. Standing still and facing down the bear seems to be the best advice. If it does attack, drop into the fetal position, cover up your head and hope for the best.

Bears have an acute sense of smell, so it's important not to leave food or garbage out under any circumstances. If you want to sleep under the stars, never do so close to food; stash both food and garbage, well covered and weighted-down, at least 100 yards or so away from your campsite.

If you wish to sleep under a roof rather than in a tent, there are a number of hotels within Yellowstone. One stands out because of its long and colorful history: the **Old Faithful Inn**, a huge log hotel constructed in 1904, is a National Historic Landmark. Its rooms are rustic but comfortable, and its lobby is unique; it is seven stories high, and constructed around a 40 foot high fireplace and an 80 foot chimney built of hand-quarried lava blocks. The ghost of the hotel's designer, Robert Reamer, is reportedly sometimes seen worriedly pacing the halls of his old abode, which is the largest log cabin ever built.

The nearby town of Cody, to the east, also thrives from Yellowstone tourist dollars. The **Buffalo Bill Historical Center** located here is an interesting museum complex that not only details the life of the famous Indian scout, but highlights the culture of the Indians as well.

IDAHO FALLS UND POCATELLO
Area code 208

Accommodation
MODERATE: **Best Western Cottontree Inn**, 1415 Bench Rd., Pocatello, Tel: 237-7650. 146 spacious rooms, breakfast included. **Cavanaughs**, 1555 Pocatello Creek Rd, Pocatello, Tel: 233-2200. New house with 152 spacious rooms, a restaurant, pool, jacuzzi and also a business center. **Ameritel**, 645 Lindsay Blvd, Idaho Falls, Tel: 523-1400, very well-equipped motel, partly with kitchenettes. *BUDGET:* **Super 8**, 705 Lindsay Blvd., Idaho Falls, Tel: 522-8880. Good value motel.

Sight, Museums and Parks
American Falls Dam, I-86, exit 40, Tel: 226-2688. **Bannock County Historical Museum**, Ross Park, S 2nd Ave., Pocatello, Tel: 233-0434. **Craters of the Moon N. M.**, Information Tel: 527-3257. **Experimental Breeder Reactor Number One** (First nuclear reactor in the world), 18 miles southeast via US 20/26, near Arco, Tel: 526-0050. **Idaho Museum of Natural History**, Idaho State University, 741 S 7th Ave., Pocatello, Tel: 236-3168.

Tourist Information
Greater Pocatello Chamber of Commerce, 427 N Main St., PO Box 626, Pocatello, ID 83204, Tel: 233-1525.

Idaho Falls Chamber of Commerce, 505 Lindsay Blvd, Idaho Falls, ID 83405, Tel: 523-1010.

GRAND TETON NATIONAL PARK JACKSON HOLE
Area code 307

Accommodation
LUXURY: **Jenny Lake Lodge**, Box 240, Moran, Tel: 733-4647. 37 historic guest cabins at the foot of the Tetons, breakfast, dinner, riding and cycling are all included in the price. *MODERATE:* **Colter Bay Village**, Box 240, Grand Teton National Park, Tel: 543-3100. Variety of comfortable log cabins or tents, with RV park. **Jackson Lake Lodge**, Box 240, Moran, Tel: 543-2855. Resort in the middle of the Tetons, with superb restaurants, but no TV. **Trapper Inn** , 235 N Cache St., Jackson, Tel: 733-2648, well-equipped motel right in the middle of town.

Guest Ranches
Flagg Ranch Resort, Box 187, Moran, on US Hwy. 89, Tel: 543-2861. Rustic log cabins beside Snake River, also a campsite and a wide range of sports available - from angling to whitewater rafting. **Heart Six**, Box 70, Moran, 5 miles est of Moran, on Buffalo Valley Rd., Tel: 543-2477. Dude ranch with herds of wild horses, lots on offer and accordingly high prices.

Camping
In Grand Teton Nationalpark there are five campsites: Colter Bay, Signal Mountain, Jenny Lake, Lizard Creek and Gros Ventre. Information and reservations can be made at the Park Superintendent's office (see tourist information), Tel: 739-3300.

Sights, Museums and Parks
Grand Teton National Forest, Information Tel: 733-2880. Recorded weather forecast: Tel: 739-5500. **Jackson Hole Museum**, 105 N Glenwood Ave., Jackson, Tel: 733-2414. Local and geological history of the area. **National Elk Refuge**, Jackson Hole, Tel: 733-9212. **Teton County Historical Center**, 105 Mercill Ave., Jackson, Tel: 733-9605, Exhibition on the fur trade and Indians. **Wildlife of the American West**, 110 N Center, Jackson, Tel: 733-5771.

Sports and Recreation
Hole Hiking Experience, Jackson Hole, Tel: 6904453, guided hiking, skiing and mountainbiking tours as well as adventure climbing. **Iditarod Sled Dog Tours**, Jackson Hole, Tel: 800/554-7388. Sled-dog tours. **Solitude Float Trips**, Tel: 888/704-2800, raft rides on Snake River. **Teton Wagon Train & Horse Adventure**, Box 10307, Jackson Hole, Tel: 7346101. 3 days riding in a covered wagon, accompanied by cowboys, camping in Grizzlyland: a real adventure!

Tourist Information
Grand Teton and Yellowstone National Park, Superintendent, PO Drawer 170, Moose, WY 83012, Tel: 739-3300. **Jackson Hole Tourist Information**, 555 E Broadway, Jackson, WY 83001, Tel: 733-3316.

YELLOWSTONE NATIONAL PARK

Accommodation
MODERATE: **Old Faithful Inn**, on Loop Rd., beautiful historic lodge. *BUDGET:* **Grant Village**, 18 miles southeast of Old Faithful, 2 miles south of Loop Rd., in the park, modern motel with 300 rooms. All accommodation in the N.P. is no-smoking. Bookings under **AmFac Parks & Resorts:** Tel: (307) 344-7311.

Camping
There are 13 campsite and RV parks. Some of these can be booked in advance, Tel: 344-7311.

Tourist Information
Yellowstone N. P. Headquarters Information, Tel: (307) 344-7381. **Buffalo Bill Hist. Center**, Cody, 720 Sheridan Ave., Tel: (307) 587-4771.

FROM
SAN FRANCISCO
TO SEATTLE

NORTHERN CALIFORNIA
OREGON
COLUMBIA RIVER / MT. HOOD
WASHINGTON STATE
MT. ST. HELENS / MT. RAINIER

Hardly any other coastal region in the world offers such a wealth of rugged natural beauty as the coastline of northern California, Oregon and Washington State. The drive begins north of San Francisco on the legendary Pacific Coast Highway, which runs along the Pacific Ocean. Merging into US 101 at Leggett, the road passes through remote bays and beaches in Oregon and Washington., and ends at two extinct volcanos shortly before reaching Seattle in the pacific Northwest. This is a long drive, almost 1,000 miles, and you should allow at least two weeks to cover the distance, especially considering the possibility of detours inland.

NORTHERN CALIFORNIA:
FOG BANKS AND GIANT TREES

The Pacific Coast Highway, or **State Highway 1**, winds northward from San Francisco, hugging the coast for a long while, bypassing steep, rocky cliffs and small, protected inlets. The combination of sand dunes and cliffs so typical of this region is perfectly displayed at the **Point Reyes National Seashore**, which lies

Previous pages: Mount Rainier. Left: The Chandelier Tree near Leggett is over 2,000 years old.

just a few miles north of the city. In winter and in early spring, **Point Reyes Lighthouse** is a good place from which to observe whales making their way up toward Alaska. In fact, they can be spotted all along the coast.

The wildly romantic coast, dotted with diminutive fishing villages, stretches all the way to **Mendocino**, which is a small and exclusive artists' colony that has unfortunately been overrun by tourists in recent years. This town is worth visiting for its carefully restored wooden Victorian houses, which look out over the ocean. Route 1 crosses **Westport** and **Rockport** before turning into US 101 near the town of **Leggett**.

The most significant and impressive attraction on the way to Oregon begins just a few miles to the north: California's **Redwood Parks**. In Leggett Valley you'll find the over 2,000 year old Chandelier Tree, which can only be described as simply amazing. A hole big enough for a car to drive through was chopped out of its trunk in the 1930s. Further north, **Humboldt Redwoods State Park**, can best be explored beginning in **Garberville**. The so-called **Avenue of the Giants**, an approximately 30 mile stretch of road running parallel to 101, is lined with these huge, centuries-old redwoods. But the oldest and largest spe-

cimens are to be found some way to the north in the **Redwood National Park**.

On the way there is the old farming village of **Ferndale**, a very pretty place which wears its 19th century origins on its sleeve. Route 101 then leads to **Orick**, and from there to Redwood National Park, where one can hike around for days and completely forget the passage of time. Redwoods, which can grow up to 280 feet tall with a diameter of up to 25 feet, are thought to be the oldest trees growing on earth. Some of them began their lives over 2,000 years ago. Hiking paths have been laid out throughout the park to guide visitors to the most special groves, such as **Lady Bird Johnson Grove** (named after President Lydon B. Johnson's wife, "Lady Bird"). The tallest trees in the world stand near **Redwood Creek**, whose king is the laconically-named **Tall Tree**, 368 feet tall and 44 feet in diameter. The trees are so dense at this

Above: Evening atmosphere in Mendocino, an artists' colony on Route 1.

point that their branches mingle to form a kind of roof worthy of a cathedral.

Yet, in spite of it all, there is another side to the redwood forests. In the past couple of centuries approximately 95 percent of the forests have been felled. The redwoods provide one of the most resistant woods with excellent insulating qualities. The logging industry, which owns old rights to the timber, is still hard at work cutting down these gigantic trees.

The primordial feeling of the landscape here, barring modern man's hiking paths of course, has been preserved, especially along the coast of the national park. The trail between **Gold Bluffs Beach** and **Klamath** explores some particularly natural scenery.

OREGON

The state line between California and **Oregon** is just a few miles north of Redwood National Park. Officially, the Pacific Northwest begins here, where nature is at its most untamed along the entire West Coast. Immense tracts of Oregon land are covered with forests, which provides the basis for the most important branch of industry hereabouts: the lumber business. Oregon was admitted to the Union relatively late; in 1859 it became the 33rd state. The settlement of Oregon began when a handful of fur dealers and daring trappers wandered over the Rockies and encountered Shuswap and Nez Percé Indian tribes with whom they went into business. The Gold Rush later brought more people into the region, mostly of the adventurer class.

A detour over **Grants Pass** and **Medford** takes you to an unusual natural phenomenon in west-central Oregon: **Crater Lake National Park**, which is accessible via Route 62. The main sight here is the 10,800 foot high **Mt. Mazama**, an extinct volcano whose crater has become a lake of dark and mysterious waters. The deep blue color of **Crater Lake** comes from its depth of 1,932 feet, making it the deepest lake in the U.S. **Rim Drive**, a 33 mile road that encircles the lake, allows you to go around the crater without leaving your car. Hiking trails begin at **Rim Village**. The most beautiful of these is **Cleetwood Trail**, which is at the northeastern edge of the crater. It leads down to the lake shore, where there are boats to take you out to the volcanic isle of **Wizard Island**.

The Coast of Oregon

The 30 mile stretch between **Brookings** and **Gold Beach** is one of the most beautiful along the Oregon coast. The little community of Gold Beach, which lies on the banks of the **Rogue River**, is a reminder of the days when gold fever struck this part of the country. White intruders looked for gold here over 150 years ago, and no sooner had they started than they ran into trouble with the Indians, for whom the salmon in the river was far more important.

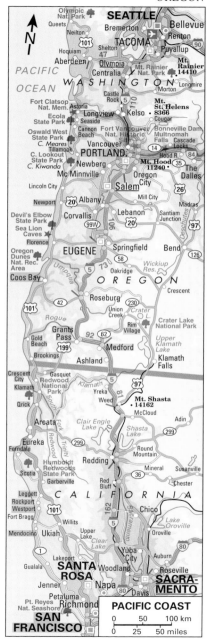

179

At **Coos Bay**, Route 101 begins making its way through the **Oregon Dunes National Recreation Area**, a 47 mile tableau of dunes shaped by wind and water that have been placed under conservation. These great masses of sand, some of which are in excess of 500 feet, represent the largest area of dunes on the West Coast. Paths through them lead to observation points, but many visitors prefer exploring the dunes by undertaking wild drives in motorized beach buggies or four-wheeled (ATVs). The softness of the sand is deceptive, by the way. The dunes are a considerable force of nature. The coastal winds blow them inland, and since the time of their creation, thought to be about 7,000 years ago, they have buried unbelievably large tracts of land. When the dunes moved on, they left behind oases of tree stumps and little lakes.

Above. The Pacific Coast Highway is one of the most impressive roads in the U.S. Right: ATV riding on the Oregon Dunes.

This dunescape continues as far as **Florence**, site of another worthwhile stop at the **Sea Lion Caves**, where hundreds of sea lions lounge about or play in the water, their roars echoing from the surrounding cliffs.

A little further along is **Devil's Elbow State Park**, followed by **Newport** in the north, actually an old port which derived its main revenue from the transportation of wood, and today the site of the **Hatfield Marine Science Center** (on Marine Science Drive) with its **Newport Oregon Coast Aquarium**. It displays a wide selection of wildlife from the local waters. This attraction is especially recommended for families with children. Another way to get a closer look at the fauna of the Pacific Ocean is to climb down to the **Undersea Gardens**, at 250 SW Bay Boulevard in Yaquina Bay. An ingenious "window to the sea" here allows you to view the underwater world in which Armstrong, a giant octopus, sometimes makes his rounds.

The next stop on the way is **Tillamook**, a town of 22,000 known primarily for its eponymous cheese, available in just about every shop here. A detour to the 22 mile long **Three Capes Scenic Drive** is well worth the time. The three capes referred to are **Meares**, **Lookout**, and **Kiwanda**, and their claim to fame is their particular combination of sand and rock, that is, dunes and cliffs. This is another good spot to do some whale watching from, in late fall and early spring.

Two classic seaside resorts lie to the north of Tillamook, Cannon Beach and Seaside, though it should be mentioned that the cold waters of the Pacific Ocean are hardly conducive to long, relaxing swims. **Cannon Beach**, named after the cannon of a ship that sank in 1846 was washed up on shore here, has miles of beaches and cliffs. The most prominent sight of the coast is the 235 foot **Haystack Rock**, a giant stone monolith that rears out of the water. For a while, Can-

non Beach was something of an artists' colony, but those days are long gone, and little of them remains to be seen.

Far more interesting for the visitor are the neighboring parks: **Ecola State Park** and **Oswald West State Park**. Both are conservation areas with extensive dune formations and lookout points that give a broad view of the surrounding bays.

The remoteness and solitude of the parks is a far cry from the old resort of **Seaside**, which has been the place where Portlanders have enjoyed rest and recreation since the turn of the century.

The Lewis and Clark Expedition

In the summer of 1792, Captain Robert Gray discovered the **Columbia River** at the spot where it spills into the Pacific near **Astoria**. He, like many of his forerunners and followers, was searching for the elusive Northwest Passage. This little town, nowadays a sleepy port, has had quite a history since its birth as a fort and

trading post for local fur traders. One of America's wealthiest families began its financial rise here. John Jacob Astor started out as nothing more than a hard-bargaining fur trader, but he laid the cornerstone of the Astor family fortune here. His modest beginnings are well documented in **Fort Astoria** (15th and Exchange Streets), the family's former warehouse.

Astoria also has the largest Victorian old town in Oregon. Worth seeing is **Flavel House** (441 8th St.), which once belonged to a seafarer of that name. The **Columbia River Maritime Museum**, which can fill you in on the history of the town, has exhibitions on specialized subjects, such as fishing, the advent of the steamboat, and navigation.

Five miles southwest of Astoria is the **Fort Clatsop National Memorial**, which is associated with two of America's greatest explorers: Lewis & Clark. Both officers spent the winter of 1805/1806 here. They had been commissioned by President Thomas Jefferson a

year and a half earlier to explore the West, a journey they undertook from St. Louis.

The nation was still young back then and it had just acquired from the French the entire area from the Mississippi River to the Rockies in the 1803 *Louisiana Purchase*. The country's surface area was suddenly more than twice what it had been, and Lewis and Clark's task was to find out more about this region and see if there was a possible shipping passage between the east and west coasts. In May 1804, with a company of 30 men, Lewis and Clark left St. Louis heading west. They spent one winter in South Dakota, and then continued, slogging their way through the western wilderness, over the Rocky Mountains, all the way to Oregon and Washington State. They explored the Columbia River, established friendly

Above: Logging is an important industry in the area around Portland. Right: Wine-tasting in the Willamette Valley.

contacts with local Indian tribes, and finally returned east in 1806. Lewis and Clark went down in the annals of American history as a pair of heros and great discoverers of the *frontier* era.

A Visit to Portland

Portland, which lies at the confluence of the **Willamette** and **Columbia River**, is not generally praised as much for its urban architecture as for its splendid parks and gardens. The city began modestly in the mid-19th century as a stopover on the way from San Francisco to Seattle, but rose to prominence thanks to its protected harbor, and to the fishing and logging industries in its immediate vicinity.

Portland proudly calls itself the "City of Roses," and during June, Portlanders celebrate the **Rose Festival**. Parades of color, hot-air balloon rides and car races thrill visitors from all over the West.

This is perhaps the best time to stroll through the city's parks, especially

Washington Park, with the **International Rose Test Garden**, where new varieties of roses are cultivated, and the **Japanese Garden**.

Pioneer Courthouse Square and the **Mall** are at Portland's center. Of interest to visitors is the new **American Advertising Museum** (9 NW 2nd Avenue) which is entirely devoted to the history of advertising in the United States. The **Portland Art Museum** (1219 SW Park Avenue at Jefferson Stree) has a very special collection of Indian art.

Still, the most interesting quarter of Portland is the **Old Town**, extending along both sides of Burnside Street from SW Front Street to 5th Street. The old warehouses and shops here successfully resisted the attempts of real estate speculators to turn the area into a modern nightmare. **Skidmore Market** is a weekly crafts fair which takes place on Burnside Street. The house of the most famous newspaper publisher of the city, **Henry Pittock**, built in 1914, is on Pittock Drive and is open to the public.

South of Portland is one of Oregon's most fertile wine regions, the **Willamette Valley**. Should time allow, you should visit this area, which is reminiscent of the Rhine Valley. Route 99W south passes about two dozen wineries, each of which offers wine tastings of Pinot Noir, Riesling or sparkling wine. In Vancouver, in Washington state north of Portland, the **Fort Vancouver National Historic Site** is a replica fort of the Hudson Bay Company, which used to trade in furs.

THE COLUMBIA RIVER AND MOUNT HOOD

The **Mt. Hood-Columbia Gorge Loop Scenic Drive**, a 163 mile well-built road, begins just beyond Portland. Some parts of it wind closely along the river, only to ascend high up into the mountains again. The Columbia River, the longest and mightiest in the United States after the Mississippi, springs somewhere in the mountains of Canada, and over the past 50 million years has eaten its way

183

into the mountains of the North Cascades. It flows into the Pacific near the town of Astoria. The river landscape along the Columbia is still very much as it always has been. After all, the region was just settled a century ago.

The journey eastward on the **Historic Columbia River Highway** (drive east of Portland on I-84 and take the signposted exit) provides spectacular views of the pristine, mountainous world on the Oregon side of the river. Every now and then a huge, gushing waterfall provides a charming distraction. The most famous is **Multnomah Falls**, crashing down a cliff 620 feet high, making it the highest in all Oregon and one of the highest in the United States. Multnomah is a favorite along the way because of the little bridge built opposite the falls; standing on it, you almost feel as if you were directly beneath the torrents of water.

Shortly beyond the falls, near **Bonneville Lock and Dam**, the highway leads back to Interstate 84. The 192 foot Bonneville Dam, completed in 1938, is one of ten built on the Columbia River in order to produce electricity. This interference with the natural flow of the river has had its consequences on the local ecology. The Columbia River serves as an annual breeding ground for about half a million salmon before they swim downstream to the Pacific Ocean. The fish have no problem swimming the rapids in either direction, or even jumping over smaller obstacles, such as rocks or snagged logs, but the great walls of the dam blocked their path eastward and proved lethal on their way west. Ecologists protested as early as the late 1930s because of the large number of salmon that were jumping to their deaths. After the war, the authorities built so-called fish ladders on the dams, allowing the salmon to follow their natural instinct without damage. Bonneville offers an excellent opportunity to closely observe this spectacle of nature.

To the south of the dam is a short hiking path called **Eagle Creek Trail**, which passes by more waterfalls and has a number of restful picnic areas.

Cascades Locks recalls a bit of genuine Wild West history. In the 19th century, pioneers making their way downriver from the Oregon Trail had to interrupt their journey due to the very dangerous rapids that suddenly developed at this spot. They were forced to unload, take their boats over land to a point farther west, and then re-embark. The **Cascade Locks Historical Museum** brings those difficult times to life again. Nowadays, the rapids have been tamed and can even be visited on an old paddlewheel steamer, the **Columbia Gorge.**

Today, adventurous spirits voluntarily take to the white waters of the Columbia near **Hood River**. This section of the Columbia is also a popular location for windsurfers, because the cold winds of the Pacific meet with the warm air of eastern Oregon and produce a great deal of hard and fast winds. Surfers from all over the world come here to test their skills on the river.

The Dalles, a small town situated a little to the west, is of no significance nowadays, but it did have its historic moments. It was the final stop on the legendary **Oregon Trail**, a path used by thousands of pioneers between the years 1843 and 1848, after news spread from missionaries and trappers that the new territories in the Northwest were a "paradise for pioneers." In Dalles, the prairie schooners were unloaded and the journey westward continued on the Columbia River. Statistically speaking, the process of settling Oregon was modest at best, but the convoys of pioneers that came here represented the last great thrust into the West, and, at the same time, signalled the demise of the Pacific Indian tribes.

Before crossing over to Washington State on a bridge farther to the west, try to make the detour up to **Mt. Hood**. Route

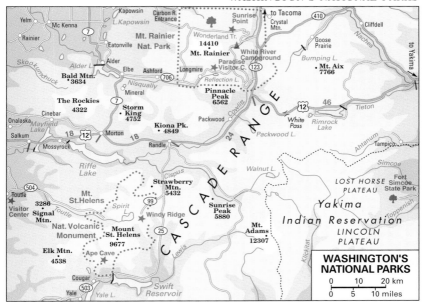

35 leads south to this extinct volcano, which is also Oregon's highest mountain at an altitude of 11,235 feet. The entire area around Mt. Hood is known for its winter sports, in particular downhill skiing. **Mount Hood Meadows** and **Mount Hood Ski Bowl** have a wide choice of slopes for any degree of expertise. The **Timberline Ski Area** even offers skiing all year round.

Heading back on Route 35, you cross the Columbia River to Washington State on the so-called **Bridge of the Gods**. The bridge's mysterious name is derived from an old Indian legend about a massive stone bridge built by the gods that once spanned the river at this very point. Highway 14 then heads back west, with a breathtaking view of the north side of the river and the mountain ranges around Mount Hood. A special stopover should be made at **Beacon Rock**, an 800 foot crag which is a veritable stone monolith. Interstate 5, however, takes you northwards to another monolith of sorts, but one that is not nearly so peaceful and if anything, rather frightening.

WASHINGTON STATE
MOUNT ST. HELENS

In 1987, **Mount St. Helens** was still a barren landscape that seemed dead to the world. For miles and miles trees lay about like matchsticks broken by an absent-minded hand. An entire forest had been flattened. Not a blade of grass sprang from the soil, not a single flower; there was no bird chirping to be heard, no insects buzzed through the air. The ground was either grey or black, and the breeze kicked a film of volcanic ash up into the air. In the past few years, **Mount St. Helens National Volcanic Monument** has been reforested to a great extent, and nature has recovered in many places, especially on the lava beds. Still, the overall bleak atmosphere vividly recalls the volcano's violent eruption over a decade ago.

On May 18, 1980, Mount St. Helens, considered until then to be inactive, suddenly errupted with incredible force, annihilating 250 square miles of the surrounding national park. The great masses

185

of lava and a steady shower of ash buried entire villages. Sixty people died during the three day eruption. The explosions tore a 1,300 foot chunk out of the northern side of the volcano, lowering the mountain's altitude to 8,364 feet. The climatic effect of all the ash thrown up into the atmosphere was felt all the way to the East Coast, reflected in a notably cool summer. The volcano has piped down in the meantime, and scientists are not expecting another eruption in the near future. As for the national park, it was re-classified as a national monument in 1982.

The **Mount St. Helens Visitor Center**, between **Castle Rock** and **Toutle**, east on I-5, provides a full documentation of this natural catastrophe. This is also the starting point for a detour on Route 504 that will take you right up to the northwestern slope of the volcano. The journey back south on I-5, turning off on Route 503 to Yale, goes

Above: Traces of the volcanic explosion of Mount St. Helens can still be seen. Right: Eunice Lake in Mount Rainier National Park.

through Cougar to **Ape Cave**. The latter, a cavern hollowed out in a lava flow, is the result of an eruption over 2,000 years ago. As the lava cooled it formed a hard crust in which hot lava continued to flow. It is a full two miles long, making it the longest lava cave on the North American continent. The observation terraces along the road south of Mount St. Helens are the starting point for hiking trails through the park, where you can get first-hand knowledge of the destruction wrought by the eruption. Over the centuries, enormous lava flows into the valley have left behind a barren, lunar-like landscape.

Route 25 makes its way across mountain crests all the way to **Strawberry Mountain**, which provides the best view of the collapsed crater and **Spirit Lake**, which lies before it.

The best view of Mount St. Helens is from **Windy Ridge**, which can be reached along Route 99. This is the closest you can get to the mountain by car. Toward the end of the traveling season, when few tourists are roaming around the park, the uncanny peace and quiet up here can be overwhelming. Steep trails lead from Windy Ridge up to spots where the volcano seems so near you can almost touch it.

The way from Mount St. Helens back to Interstate 5 is over **Randle** and **Morton**, neither of which are of particular interest, especially considering the dramatic scenery that has just been left behind. A short distance away, however, is Mt. Rainier, which, ironically, looks almost exactly like Mount St. Helens did before its 1980 eruption.

MT. RAINIER NATIONAL PARK

Incontestibly the greatest attraction in the state of Washington is this giant of stone, fire and ice. **Mt. Rainier** (14,411 feet), with its cool and distant beauty, dominates the landscape between Oregon and Seattle. The inhabitants of the city on

Puget Sound are often granted a colorful spectacle – especially when the weather is clear – when Rainier can be seen in all its glory 60 miles away in the distance: in the early morning the mountain slowly sheds its mists, gradually revealing its shape; at midday the snow-covered summit flashes in the distance; and when the sun goes down in the evening, it bathes the mountain in a deep red light. Mount Rainier is at this point in time considered to be an inactive volcano. It is permanently covered by ice and snow and is surrounded by about 80 glaciers, making this mountain area the largest glacial region outside Alaska.

Rainier's last eruption occurred about 150 years ago; though there are still occasional wisps of smoke coming from the hot interior of the mountain. Mount Rainier is part of an underground chain of connected volcanoes stretching all the way from Oregon (Mount Hood) to Mount St. Helens, Mount Adams and as far as Mount Baker in the North Cascades.

Millions of years ago, at the end of the Tertiary period, Mount Rainier was a perfectly normal mountain, a little taller than it is today. Over time, however, volcanic activity and gradual glacial erosion gave it a different shape. Here, as elsewhere in the North Cascades, glaciers carved away at the rocks in the region, even forming separate mountains, and their melting ice created numerous small rivers. This slow but consistent game of nature continues to be played in **Mt. Rainer National Park**, where three great glaciers still do their job of eroding the landscape.

The picturesque landscape of the park immediately explains why it was chosen as one of the first five national parks in the U.S. Its beauty was recognized as early as 1899. Route 706 makes access very comfortable, but unfortunately this means that during the summer months Mt. Rainier is completely overrun by "Seattleites" in search of recreation. The best way to get there is by driving to the southwest

entrance, through **Longmire** to the **Paradise Visitor Center** on the southern slope of Mt. Rainier. A number of trails begin next to the **Paradise Hotel**, some of which lead quite close to the glaciers. This applies to the somewhat short **Skyline Trail**, as well as to the **Nisqually Vista Trail**. Mother Nature has her way of showing strength in this region, especially in winter. In early 1972, at Paradise Point, 93 feet of fresh snow fell, a record for the United States.

Route 706 proceeds further to the southeast, bypassing **Reflection Lake**, whose clear, quiet waters reflect the towering mountain above it and the blue skies striated with white clouds: a picture-postcard view if ever there was one! Take Route 123, which hugs the mountain closely, and then take the fork to the north to **Sunset Point**, which is the best spot from which to view Mt. Rainier. At 6,600 feet,

this is also an ideal place to look out over the **Cascades Range**, as well as **Mt. Adams** and **Mt. Baker** in the distance. The most popular trail, the **Wonderland Trail**, some 30 miles long, leads from here around Mt. Rainier. This is by no means a leisurely hike; taking at least two days to complete, only physically fit hikers should attempt it. The **White River Campground** here offers space for overnight stays, but you will need to obtain a camping permit from a park ranger.

On some of the lonelier of these trails you might even forget what a popular destination Rainier actually is. Black bears and other wild animals live in the deep forests of the park. If you woud like to avoid well-trodden paths and crowded picnic sites, you are better off entering the park from the northwestern side by the **Carbon River**.

The densely settled coast of Puget Sound is not very far from here. In under two hours Interstate 5 takes you into Seattle, the much praised "Pearl of the Northwest."

Above: Mt. Rainier National Park is an ideal area for hikers.

NORTHERN CALIFORNIA
Area code 707

Accommodation
MODERATE: **Blackberry**, 44951 Larkin Rd., Mendocino, Tel: 937-5281. B & B in small houses like *Sheriff's Office* or *School House. BUDGET:* **Garberville**, 948 Redwood Dr., Garberville, Tel: 923-2422. 30 neat rooms, 6 miles south of the park entrance.

Sights, Museums and Parks
Humboldt Redwoods State Park, Weott, Tel: 946-2409. **Pacific Lumber Co. Museum**, 125 Main St., Scotia, Tel: 764-2222. Exhibition featuring old lumbering equipment. **Point Reyes National Seashore**, Point Reyes, Tel: (415) 663-1092. **Redwood National Park**, 1111 Second St, Crescent City, Tel: 464-6101.

Tourist Information
Crescent City Chamber of Commerce, 1001 Front St., Crescent City, CA 95531, Tel: 464-3174. **Fort Bragg-Mendocino Coast Chamber of Commerce**, 332 N Main St., PO Box 1141, Fort Bragg, CA 95437, Tel: 961-6300.

OREGON
Area code 503

Accommodation
LUXURY: **The Benson**, 309 SW Broadway, Portland, Tel: 228-2000. Elegant old hotel, centrally located. *MODERATE:* **Ebb Tide**, 300 N Promenade/3rd Ave, Seaside, Tel: 738-8371. Motel located on the promenade, some rooms with kitchenette. **Heron House**, 2524 NW Westover Rd., Portland, Tel: 274-1846. Classic old B&B in historical town quarter of Nob Hill. **Shore Cliff Inn**, 1100 S Hwy. US 101, Gold Beach, Tel: 247-7091. On the beach, many rooms with balcony. *BUDGET:* **Riverhouse**, 1202 Bay St., Florence, Tel: 997-3933. Good value motel beside the Siuslaw River.

Sights, Museums and Parks
American Advertising Museum, 9 NW 2nd Ave., Portland, Tel: 226-0000. **Pittock Mansion**, 3229 NW. Pittock Dr., Portland, Tel: 823-3624. **Cape Lookout State Park**, 12 miles southwest, via Hwy. US 101, near Tillamook, Tel: 842-4981. **Cascade Locks Historical Museum**, Marine Park, Cascade Locks, Tel: 374-8535. **Columbia River Maritime Museum**, 17th St./Marine Dr., Astoria, Tel: 325-2323. **Crater Lake National Park**, PO Box 7, Crater Lake, OR 97604, Tel: (541) 594-2211. **Ecola State Park**, 2 miles north via Hwy. US 101. **Flavel House**, 441 8th St., Astoria, Tel: 325-2203. **End of the Oregon Trail Interpretive Center**, 500 Washington St., Oregon City,
Tel: 657-9336. **Fort Clatsop National Memorial**, 6 miles southwest via Hwy. US 101A, Astoria, Tel: 861-2471. **Fort Dalles Museum**, 15th/Garrison Sts., The Dalles, Tel: (541) 296-4547. **Fort Vancouver Historic Site**, 612 E. Reserve Street, Vancouver, Tel: (360) 696-7655. **Hatfield Marine Science Center**, Marine Science Dr., Newport, Tel: (541) 867-0271. **Japanese Garden**, Portland, Tel: 223-1321. **Mount Hood National Forest**, 16400 Champion Way, Sandy, Tel: (503) 668-1700. **Oregon Coast Aquarium**, 2820 SE Ferry Slip Rd, Newport, Tel: (541) 867-3474. **Oswald West State Park**, 10 miles south, on US 101. **Portland Art Museum**, 1219 SW Park Ave./Jefferson St., Portland, Tel: 226-2811. **Rose Test Garden**, 400 S.W. Kingston Ave. **Sea Lion Caves**, in Yachats, Tel: (541) 547-3111. **The Dalles Dam and Reservoir**, The Dalles, Tel: (541) 296-1181. **Timberline Ski Area/Lodge**, Mt. Hood National Forest, Tel: (503) 272-3311. **Undersea Gardens**, 250 SW Bay Blvd., Newport, Tel: (541) 265-2206.

Sports and Recreation
Columbia River Cruises, Cascade Locks, Tel: 223-3928. Trips on a historic steamboat. **Jerry's Rogue River Jet Boat Trips**, Gold Beach Boat Basin (southern end of Rogue River Bridge), Tel. 247-4571.

Tourist Information
Columbia Gorge National Scenic Area, 902 Wasco Ave., Suite 200, Hood River, OR 97031, Tel: (541) 386-2333. **Portland/Oregon Visitors Association**, 26 SW Salmon, Portland, OR 97204, Tel: 222-2223. **The Dalles Chamber of Commerce**, 404 W 2nd St., The Dalles, OR 97058, Tel: 296-2231. **Tillamook Chamber of Commerce**, 3705 US 101 N, Tillamook, OR 97141, Tel: (541) 842-7525.

MT.ST.HELENS AND MT.RAINIER
Area code 360

Accommodation
MODERATE: **Paradise Inn**, PO Box 108, Ashford, Tel: 569-2275. Simple lodge in the NP. *CAMPING:* Campgrounds at Mt. Rainier, Tel: (301) 722-1257

Sights and Parks
Mount Rainier National Park, Tahoma Woods, State Rte., Ashford, Tel. 569-2211. **Mount St. Helens National Volcanic Monument**, Castle Rock, 3029 Spirit Lake Hwy, Tel: 274-2100.

Sports and Recreation
Information about mountain climbing around the Mount Rainier area is available at Tel: 569-2227 (summer) or 627-6242 (winter). For information on climbing at Mt. St. Helens, Tel: 247-3961.

THE PACIFIC NORTHWEST

SEATTLE
OLYMPIC PENINSULA
PUGET SOUND
NORTH CASCADES
AND MT. BAKER
VANCOUVER

Few European tourists make it out to this part of the U.S. and Canada. The Pacific Coast of the Northwest has maintained its unspoilt quality, revealing a world of mountains, great glaciers, and the ice-cold waters of the Pacific Ocean.

This itinerary begins in Seattle, or the "Pearl of the Northwest" as it is called by its admirers, steers a course through the islands of the Puget Sound, and ends in Vancouver, British Columbia. The two cities are only three hours apart by car, but you should allow for at least a week in order to cover all the interesting detours, which include a number of ferry trips. All in all, you will be driving around 400 miles.

SEATTLE

For a long time Seattle was touted as an inside tip for Americans on the lookout for new frontiers and willing to move. The city, which lies at the northwestern tip of the U.S., offered a quiet life, the amenities of any city and a natural wilderness beyond the city limits.

Shortly after their move, newcomers quickly became "Seattlites", and they

Previous pages: Seattle skyline with the Space Needle and Mt. Rainier. Left: Indian mask from the Burke Museum, Seattle.

would spread the news that the town was unpleasant to live in. This was designed to discourage the next wave of newcomerw. One of the most widely used complaints about the town was that it rained all year in Seattle. Now who on earth would ever want to move to such a place? Budding Seattlites always insisted that their move to the Northwest had been involuntary, a quirk of fate, done under economic duress, to find a job with, say, Boeing or Microsoft. The truth, however, has been revealed in the meantime. Seattle has even less rain than Boston and Washington, and its cultural array is just as important and of comparable quality. Indeed, Seattle has become so popular in the last decade that real estate prices have soared, the local government has ordered an end to the settling of certain parts of the city, and the first drug-related deaths have been reported in the suburbs.

City of Lumberjacks and Gold Miners

Seattle's popularity rests squarely on its natural setting. It is entirely surrounded by water, which determines its generally mild climate. In the west are the Pacific waters of **Puget Sound**, while in the east there is the gigantic surface of **Lake Washington**. And wherever you look, there seems to be a majestic snow-

193

capped mountain catching the rays of the sun: the sun rises over the Cascade Range of Mt. Rainier, and sets in the evening behind Mt. Olympus.

Seattle and its inhabitants seem both very natural and very casual, perhaps reflecting the youth of the town and its pioneer past. It was born in the middle of the 19th century as a small port where the Yesler Sawmill made lumber from the local forests, which it shipped down to California or off to Asia. At the time it was nothing more than a small agglomeration of log cabins representing an outpost of civilization, inhabited by lumberjacks and visited by the odd trapper seeking his fortune in the wilds of the Northwest. This changed rapidly in 1897, when the cry of "gold!" spread throughout the country. Within a few months, Seattle grew to a middle-sized town, as over 20,000 hopefuls flocked here to be

Above: Shopping bustle around Pike Place Market. Right: Inside the Seattle Market Hall.

shipped off to the Yukon Territories in Canada in order to profit from the *Klondike Gold Rush*. For Seattle it meant a brief, profitable economic boom.

Meeting Point for Asia and America

Until fairly recently, the Seattle harbor was still the embarkation point for ships to Alaska. Nowadays, its main business is loading and unloading container ships headed for Singapore, Hong Kong and other ports in Asia.

The **Waterfront/Alaskan Way**, a promenade-like street running along the dock wall, can be best investigated using the **Waterfront Trolley**, an old tram that has been refurbished for the comfort of modern tourists. To the north, near historic **Pier 57**, is **Waterfront Park**. Pier 57 is the place where the *Portland* docked nearly 100 years ago, carrying over a ton of gold from Alaska. Waterfront Park focuses attention on the underwater world, with the circular **Omnidome Theater** showing films made in

the depths of the Pacific, and with the superb **Seattle Aquarium**. Further to the north and set a little way from the waterfront, is famous **Pike Place Market**, an old two storey market hall built at the turn of the century. In those days, Seattle housewives complained of high prices in the shops. The city financed the market so that fishermen and farmers could offer their wares directly to consumers. Little has changed since: fresh salmon, mussels and Alaskan king crabs are available in abundance. A natural economic by-product of this trading activity are the many fish restaurants, shops and bars that have sprung up around the market.

Back on the waterfront, the path continues southward past **Ye Olde Curiosity Shop**, which is located in an architecturally fascinating building. It specializes, as the name suggests, in curiosities and oddities, including allegedly the smallest shrunken heads in the world and a perfectly preserved corpse discovered in the Arizona Desert. The old Yesler Sawmill, whose industry paved the way

for Seattle's rise to prominence, once stood to the left of the building; **Yesler Way** is named after the industrious businessman who founded it.

The street leads east to the historical center of town, **Pioneer Square**. The foundation stone of Seattle was laid in the middle of this plaza on the spot where the **Totem Pole** stands today.

The staid 19th century houses with artless façades that line the sides of the square now house fancy restaurants, cafés, shops and galleries. One of the tragic ironies of Seattle is that a lot of Native American crafts and art are traded here, while the descendants of the original inhabitants hang around Pioneer Square either sleeping or begging for a quarter.

Pioneer Square also has another side to it, which was for a while equally important for the homeless: after a city-wide fire in 1889, some parts of the town were rebuilt a little higher, namely above the ground floor of the old buildings in the city. **Underground Seattle** is a fascinat-

195

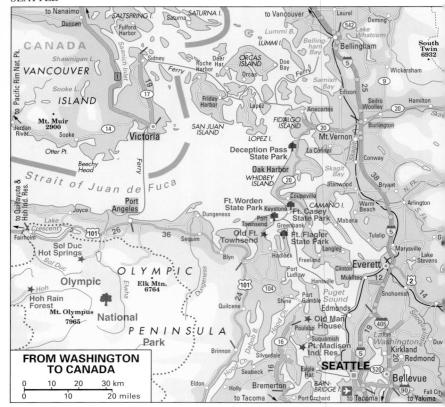

FROM WASHINGTON TO CANADA

```
0    10    20    30 km
0         10         20 miles
```

ing place to visit nowadays; a series of interconnected streets running under the town itself, a veritable city beneath the city. During the days of prohibition it served as a hideout for bootleggers and smugglers, and in more recent times, before it became a tourist attraction, as a warm refuge for the homeless.

To find out more about what made Seattle famous, make your way to the **Klondike Gold Rush Museum** at 117 South Main Street. To the southeast of Pioneer Square is the **International District**, a destination mainly for Korean and Chinese immigrants. Continue on through **Downtown Seattle** to the **Seattle Art Museum**, whose daring modern architecture succeeded in arousing the tempers of even the rather liberal Seatlites when it was built in 1992. Its most important exhibitions are the collections of Indian art from the Northwest and the modern art created in the region.

To the north of the downtown area is **Broad Street**, also known as Broadway, which cuts a diagonal swath through the city grid. This is the entertainment strip of Seattle, with numerous restaurants, bistros, bars and cafés all lying door to door. Young bands beginning what might be a promising career often try out their skills on the public in one of Broadway's rock cafés. If you tend to hear a great deal of "grunge," do not be surprised: Seattle was the birthplace of grunge in the early 1990s – and is proud of it.

196

The **Monorail**, an elevated magnetic train, begins its journey from the station at the corner of Pine Street and 4th Avenue through the highrises to the **Seattle Center**. The train looks perhaps a little on the old side, but consider that when it was built back in 1962 as part of the preparations for the World Fair, it was considered ultra-modern. What is left of that fair is the **Seattle Center**, a collection of museums and restaurants, the **Opera House** (the best-known Wagner productions in the entire U.S.A.) and, of course, the famous **Space Needle**, which has become the unofficial hallmark of the city. This nearly 600 foot tall television and observation tower, featuring a revolving restaurant, still seems

futuristic with its filigree architecture. It also gives the Seattle skyline its completely unique appearance.

The view from the top of the Space Needle stretches all the way over to the chain of islands in Puget Sound, to the mountain range of the Cascades, to Lake Washington and to Lake Union.

Washington Park, along Lake Washington, boasts a diverse **Arboretum** and an interesting **Japanese Tea Garden**.

Mountlake Boulevard leads to the campus of the **University of Washington**, where the **Burke Museum** offers a large collection of artifacts and crafts culled from the Northwest's Native American heritage. **Henry Art Gallery** on the campus exhibits modern 20th century art. Picturesque **Interlaken Boulevard** leads to **Lake Union**, on the shores of which a colorful collection of houseboats are moored.

THE OLYMPIC PENINSULA

Unfortunately, it is not possible to explore the beauties of Puget Sound in a houseboat. The next best alternative is to catch a car ferry from Pier 52 in Seattle Harbor which will take you to **Bainbridge Island**, which is off Olympic Peninsula. After a short crossing the ferry docks at **Eagle Harbor**, a small village with a host of souvenir shops, restaurants and wine bars.

Highway 305 bears north, passing through remote (and expensive) residential areas. The roads forking off to the shore offer spectacular views of Seattle with Mt. Rainier in the background.

Further north you reach **Port Madison Indian Reservation** with **Suquamish Museum**, which offer a vivid portrayal of Native American life in the area with live demonstrations of ancient Indian handicrafts (such as canoe making).

Another interesting sight is the so-called **Old Man House**, the largest longhouse in America. The grave of **Chief**

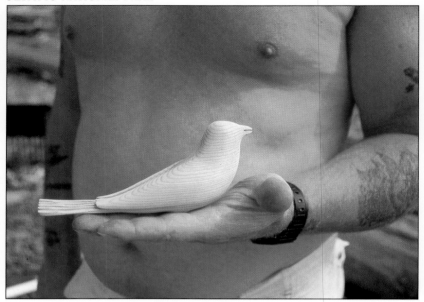

Above: Driftwood from the Olympic Peninsula makes good carving material. Right: The rain forests of Olympic National Park.

Seattle lies nearby, the Indian chief who gave his name to the city. In recent years, this Indian chieftain achieved considerable prominence, particularly among nature conservationists, for a speech he is said to have made more than a century ago in which he accused the white man of destroying nature, painting a bleak picture of an ecologically barren world.

The route leads further on to **Poulsbo**, a community founded by a group of Scandinavians, and on to **Olympic Peninsula** Here the road turns into Hwy. 101, which takes you into **Port Angeles**. As it did a hundred years ago, this little port town still lives primarily from fishing and the lumber industry, but is also home to **Visitor Center** of the **Olympic National Park**.

The fauna and flora of the park (a world cultural heritage site since 1981) is unique and paradoxical. Absolutely opposite climatic zones lie next to each other here, from dense, damp forests watered by nearly 120 inches of rain a year, to dry, barren slopes populated with elk, brown bears and other wild animals, and seals along the coast. A visit to this huge park (1,478 square miles) should only be undertaken in good weather, as a steady rainfall with dense fog would make any hike unpleasant. It is advisable to check the weather report before coming here.

In order to investigate the entire park, in particular the road along the coast, you might have to count on taking several days. But even a few short trips out from Port Angeles will give you an idea of the wild, pristine nature of the region. The route along **Hurricane Ridge** leads through a jagged mountainous area; a number of lookout points have been arranged along the road with excellent views of Puget Sound. To penetrate untouched nature, however, you will have to walk along some of the numerous hiking paths that crisscross the park.

The mountain ranges of the Olympic Peninsula, whose altitudes range from 4,800 feet to 6,700 feet, were created by glaciers during the Ice Age, a process that can still be observed to this day. Almost 60 glaciers are active today, most of them moving down **Mt. Olympus**, which at 7,965 feet is the highest peak on the peninsula. Since the discovery of the Olympic Peninsula in 1592, the Salish Indians who lived in the region have almost completely disappeared. Their descendants now live in the **Quillayute** and **Hoh Indian Reservations**.

Back on Highway 101, the journey heads westward past **Lake Crescent**, whose dark blue waters may appear ice cold, but are in fact warm enough to swim in – in summer, at any rate. Campers will find some very pleasant recreational opportunities at **Sol Duc Hot Springs**, a natural thermal water source which is said to be particularly good for people with back problems.

The crowning finish of a visit to the park should be to the **Hoh Rain Forest Visitor Center** (over Hoh River Road). There is a hiking path that begins here which takes you through an actual rain forest, with incredibly damp air and dense green vegetation.

CRUISING THE ISLANDS OF PUGET SOUND

Highway 101 leads back in an easterly direction to **Port Townsend** at the extreme tip of the Olympic Peninsula. Its obvious strategic location made it ideal for fortifying, and, in fact, a total of three forts were built here. **Old Fort Townsend** and **Fort Worden** (about a mile and a half north of town) have been turned into parks with a number of recreational facilities. Fort Worden also has several Victorian buildings on display.

A car ferry links Port Townsend to **Keystone** on **Whidbey Island**, the actual beginning of the island world of Puget Sound. It consists of a chain of virtually countless islands, many uninhabited, that stretches all the way up the coast to

Canada. The mainstay of the local population used to be salmon-fishing and logging. Nowadays, the little villages have become mostly vacation spots for stressed Seattlites who maintain secluded weekend houses here. Being relatively protected, these skerry-like islands are also a paradise for anyone enjoying watersports, be it sailing or canoeing.

There are two ways to reach the mainland from Keystone in the middle of Whidbey Island. The northern route leads over Coupeville to **Deception Pass**, Washington's most popular state park. The southern route is somewhat longer, but it passes through a number of quaint fishing villages that dot the southern coast of Whidbey. The way back to the mainland is by ferry.

Coupeville, just a few minutes drive north of Keystone on Route 20, is one of the prettiest and oldest of the fishing

Above. Fishermen gut their salmon. Right: Boeing in Everett is the most important employer in the region.

villages in the state of Washington. Its narrow streets are lined with carefully-restored Victorian houses. Visitors are made to feel welcome in the bed-and-breakfast inns and the excellent restaurants here. The neighboring **Rhododendron State Park** attracts nature lovers, and every June it turns into a veritable sea of red, pink and white blossoms. The rhododendron is also the state flower.

Deception Pass State Park is reached by way of **Oak Harbor**, which was originally founded by Dutch colonists. The park itself is beloved for its untamed nature, its forests and crystalline lakes, its jagged coastline providing long and dramatic walks. But what every visitor unanimously admires is actually man-made: a bridge connecting Whidbey and Fidalgo Islands at **Deception Point**. Below it, the dark Pacific waters flow into peaceful **Skagit Bay**, an incredible sight to behold. Route 20 then continues on to the mainland. After a short detour over **La Conner**, a remote and picturesque fishing village, you finally arrive at the town of **Burlington**.

The aforementioned southern route on Whidbey Island first makes a stop at **Langley**, which appears more commercial than Coupeville or La Conner. Nevertheless, it is the right place to shop for genuine antiques or local art and artifacts. The ferry to the mainland departs from **Clinton** and arrives after a short trip in **Mukilteo** to the south of **Everett**. Everett's main attraction, the **Boeing Works**, already makes its presence felt from afar. Great green jumbo jets without any tell-tale markings on the fuselage circle the skies as they are taken through their final tests before being sold. The world's largest hangar is adjacent to the factory's own runway, which can easily accommodate a dozen jumbo jets. A tour of this gigantic hall should not be missed.

With somewhere around 100,000 workers on its payroll, Boeing is the single largest employer in the Northwest.

The first Boeing aircraft took off from the waters of Lake Washington near Seattle in 1916. Nowadays, all the company's planes and parts are built in Everett and neighboring Reston.

The danger of having all one's economic eggs in one basket was made clear at the end of the 1960s when Boeing cut 50,000 jobs after a number of important military contracts had fallen through. Seattle was suddenly on the edge of ruin, as people flocked away from the city to look for work elsewhere in the country. Now, some 30 years later, the development of the Boeing 777 and new space-related contracts provide the company with a solid economic foundation in spite of recent competition from Airbus.

San Juan Islands

The **San Juan Islands**, an archipelago of 170 little islands, seem to invite you to be overcome by a bout of island hopping. But the ferries leaving from Anacortes (Northern Whidbey Island) often have to battle with heavy foaming seas and considerably strong winds.

Two islands worth stopping off at are **Orcas Island** and **San Juan Island**. In **Friday Harbor**, a one-time whaling station, the **Whale Museum** on 621st Street gives a regional rundown of the history of hunting these peaceful giants. Nowadays, they are left to sing their ocean songs in peace, and fishing boats docked in the harbor are used only for fishing salmon. In the distance, with a little luck, you might just spot the tailfin of a passing killer whale as it makes its way through the dark waters of the Pacific Ocean.

NORTH CASCADES AND MT. BAKER NATIONAL PARKS

The drive north on I-5 leads northward to Canada through the town of Burlington. Along the way you'll see **North Cascades National Park**, an elongated mid-sized mountain range that spans the border of Washington State and Canada.

The jagged summits of this world of rock and glacier can be seen all the way from Seattle, provided the air is clear. Mother Nature is still hard at work here, just as she has been for thousands of years, with glaciers carving away the mountains, forming new peaks, creating great waterfalls and leaving crystal-clear lakes in their wake. Highway 20 becomes the **North Cascades Scenic Highway**, which is only open from April to November. Some of the nation's heaviest winter snowfalls are registered here.

The landscape along the highway is among the most beautiful in the country. Even if you lack the time to attempt a thorough exploration, at least go as far as **Winthrop** in the eastern part of the state before turning around.

In **Marblemount**, the **Visitor Center** of the national park provides visitors with maps and brochures. The area south of

Above: Bald eagles can be seen in North Cascades National Park. Right: View of Canada Place and Burrard Inlet, Vancouver.

town, on both sides of the **Skagit River**, bald eagles can be sighted, especially during the winter months. The highway has plenty of parking spots with great observation areas on both sides of the road. Among the best panoramas are those at **Lake Ross** and **Diabolo Lake**. Near **Rockport**, a side road leads through a state park known for its 300 year old pine trees.

Take the fork heading north near the town of **Concrete** (which was indeed named because of its cement factory), and you will reach the **Mt. Baker-Snoqualmie National Forest**, whose main sight is the 10,778 foot high **Mt. Baker**. This extinct volcano is not as breathtaking as Mt. Rainier or Mount St. Helens, but it does have the advantage of generally attracting fewer tourists and hikers than its two colleagues to the south.

To get to Canada, take Route 9 from Burlington. Shortly before the border there is another opportunity to get to Mt. Baker, over Rte. 542. This side of the mountain is a favorite spot for winter sports.

VANCOUVER:
THE CITY IN THE MIST

The trip up I-5 from the south and then along Highway 99 to **Vancouver** gives one of the most spectacular skyline views of any city in the world. The tall, white, shiny skyscrapers of glass and steel seems to spring from the deep blue waters of the bay, and behind it rise the dramatic slopes of a mountain range.

Vancouver was founded in 1886, almost a century after the English captain George Vancouver discovered **Burrard Inlet** on his search for the Northwest Passage. Vancouver lies on the northern end of this inlet, on a natural peninsula. Like Seattle, Vancouver was a gathering point for adventurers, gold prospectors and trappers, who set off from here to explore new frontiers in Alaska.

Before driving into the city, make a stop at **Granville Island** (Highway 99, beneath the Granville Street Bridge), where restaurants and shops and an art college have nested in the restored industrial and shipyard buildings. Some of the best restaurants in town can be found here, serving the finest salmon, mainly Alaskan, which is tastier (and a good deal cheaper) than any European salmon.

Granville Street leads downtown to **Granville Mall**, Vancouver's main shopping street. At the north end of Granville Street, at **Waterfront Station**, the **Sea Bus Terminal** is located, from which ferries depart for Nanaimo and Victoria. The **Sky Train** runs between Waterfront Station and Surrey with stops downtown. West of here is famous **Canada Place**, with the **Pan Pacific Hotel**, restaurants, shops and an **IMAX** movie theater. This undeclared hallmark of Vancouver is remarkable for its harmonious design, reminiscent of a sailing ship.

Farther to the east is **Gastown**, Vancouver's charming old town, in which the **Steam Watch** – a steam-powered clock – and the narrowest house in the city, the **Sam Klee Building**, can be seen. The name of this quarter, with its numerous office buildings and shops, dates back to the year 1867, when "Gassy Jack" Deighton,(a talkative "gassy" sort of guy) opened a popular saloon here. South of **Hastings Street**, Vancouver's **Chinatown** market spreads exotic smells through the neighborhood.

Stanley Park, which occupies the western part of the city, is a forested area of almost 1,000 acres, with hiking paths, innumerable **totem poles** left by Native Americans and the **Vancouver Aquarium**, which offers special shows with killer and beluga whales. In late summer in particular, the great fins of these giant mammals plough their way quite visibly through the waters by Seattle, Vancouver and around the myriad islands in the region. The 230 foot high Capilano Suspension Bridge, which is also open to pedestrians, is located only 1 mile beyond the park.

Vancouver Island

The largest island along the Canadian Pacific Coast is **Vancouver Island**, which is about 300 miles long and can be accessed by car ferry. It is a perfect stage for nature's performances: sea lions sun themselves along the beaches backdropped by high and rugged cliffs with, behind them, vast, dark forests and snow-capped peaks. You get the finest panoramas from **Malahat Drive** (Highway 1) or along Highway 14 west.

Victoria, the capital of the Canadian province of British Columbia, lies on the southern tip of Vancouver Island. The city, which started out as a modest trading post and fort built in 1843 by the **Hudson Bay Company**, now attracts Canadians from colder climes who enjoy Victoria for its generally mild weather and also for the blossoms in the town's many parks and gardens, such as **Crystal**

Above: Whales are plentiful in the area (Whale Museum in Friday Harbor).

Gardens, with its tropical gardens, a monkey house and a waterfall, and **Butchart Gardens** approximately 15 miles north on the Seawick Peninsula. Due to its large number of Tudor-style buildinngs, Victoria has a certain British flair. Particularly worth a visit are the **Parliament Buildings** on Belleville Street and the luxury **Empress Hotel** on Government Street. The **Royal British Columbia Museum** provides information on the area's natural and cultural history.

From Victora, detours to the **Pacific Rim National Park** or **Strathcona Park** on the west coast are recommended. The drive takes you past **Duncan**, with over 60 totem poles, and **Nanaimo**, the island's second-biggest town. North of Duncan is **Chemainus**, where well-known artists have created some impressive outdoor murals. Ferries connect Victoria with Seattle (summer only) and Port Angeles; from nearby Sidney, ferries leave for the San Juan Islands and the U.S. mainland. In addition, Victoria offers whale-watching tours.

SEATTLE
Area code 206
Accommodation
LUXURY: **The Edgewater**, Pier 67, 2411 Alaskan Way, Tel: 728-7000. Superb first-class hotel located directly on the harbor.

MODERATE: **Pacific Plaza Hotel**, 400 Spring St., Tel: 623-3900. Restored hotel in the city center. **Tugboat Challenger Bunk & Breakfast**, 1001 Fairview Ave. N., Tel: 340-1201. B & B on a converted barge in Seattle harbor.

BUDGET: **Kings Inn**, 2106 5th Ave., Tel: 441-8833, good location.

Sights, Museums and Parks
Burke Museum, 17th Ave. NE/NE 45th St., Tel: 543-5590. **Japanese Garden with Arboretum**, Washington Park, Tel: 684-4725. **Klondike Gold Rush National Historic Park**, 117 S Main St., Tel: 553-7220. **Pacific Science Center** (with **Omnidome Theater**), 200 2nd Ave. N.,Tel: 443-2001. **Pike Place Market**, Information Tel: 682-7453. **Seattle Aquarium**, Pier 59, Tel: 386-4320. **Seattle Art Museum**, 100 University St., Tel: 654-3100. **Seattle Center and Space Needle**, 305 Harrison St., Tel: 684-7200 und 1-800-937-9582 (Space Needle). **Underground Tour**, 610 1st Ave., Tel: 682-4646.

Ferries
Ferries to Victoria and further destinations in Canada: **Washington State Ferries**, Pier 52, Tel: 464-6400 or Tel: 1-800-843-3779.

Tourist Information
Seattle-King County C & V Bureau, Washington State Convention & Trade Center, 520 Pike St., Suite 1300, Galleria Level, Seattle, WA 98101, Tel: 461-5840.

OLYMPIC PENINSULA, PUGET SOUND, NORTH CASCADES
Area code 360
Accommodation
MODERATE: **Katy's Inn**, 503 S 3rd St., La Conner, Tel: 466-3366. Comfortable B&B. **Lake Crescent Lodge**, 416 Lake Crescent Rd, Port Angeles, Tel: 928-3211. Lodge dating back to 1916, magnificent location. **Sol Duc Hot Spring Resort**, Sol Duc Rd., Hwy. 101, Port Angeles, Tel: 327-3583. Hotel and RV park near the hot springs. *BUDGET:* **Winthrop Inn**, on Hwy. WA 20, Winthrop, Tel: (509) 996-2217. Pleasant place with pool, idyllic setting, only for non-smokers.

Sights, Museums and Parks
Capilano Supsension Bridge, Vancouver. **Deception Pass State Park**, Tel: 675-2417. **Everett**

Industrial Tour at Boeing, via I-5, exit 189, Tel: 544-1264. **Fort Casey State Park**, near Coupeville, Tel: 678-4519.

Fort Worden State Park, Tel: (385) 4730-430. **Hoh River Visitor Center**, Tel: 374-6925. **Mt. Baker-Snoqualmie National Forest**, Tel: 856-5700.

Museum of Anthropology, 6393 N.W. Marine Drive, Vancouver, Tel: 822-3825. **North Cascades Scenic Highway**, Sedro Woolley, Tel: 856-5700. **Olympic Park Visitor Center**, 600 E Park Ave., Port Angeles, Tel: 452-0330.

Suquamish Museum (on Bainbridge Island, Sandy Hook Rd.), Sedro Woolley, Tel: 598-3311. **Whale Museum**, 62 1st St N, Friday Harbor, San Juan Island, Tel: 378-5240.

Sports and Recreation
Olympic Raft & Kayak, Port Angeles, Tel: 452-1443. Whitewater boat rides in the Olympic National Park. **Olympic Van Tours**, Coho Ferry Terminal in Port Angeles, Tel: 452-3858. Sightseeing trips on the waters of Olympic National Park.

Tourist Information
Washington State Tourism Office, Tel: 1-800-544-1800. **San Juan Islands Chamber of Commerce**, PO Box 98, Friday Harbor, WA 98250, Tel: (206) 378-5240.

VANCOUVER AND VANCOUVER ISLAND
Country code Canada 001 / Area code 604
Accommodation
LUXURY: **English Bay Inn**, 1968 Commox St, Vancouver, Tel: 683-8002. Romantic Tudor-style inn, only one block away from the sea and Stanley Park. **Empress**, 721 Government St., Victoria, Vancouver Island, Tel: 384-8111. Time-honored Victorian-style hotel with beautiful gardens, a highlight here is afternoon tea.

MODERATE: **Best Western Château Granville**, 1100 Granville St., Vancouver, Tel: 669-7070. Located in the heart of the city, good service.

Sights, Museums and Parks
Butchart Gardens, Benvenuto Ave., Victoria, Tel: (250) 652-4422. **Crystal Garden**, 713 Douglas St., Victoria, (250) 381-1277. **Parliament Buildings**, 501 Bellevue St., Tel: (250) 387-3046. **Royal British Columbia Museum**, 675 Belleville St., Tel: (250) 356-7226. Nature museum. **Vancouver Aquarium**, Tel: (250) 659-3474.

Tourist Information
Tourism Vancouver Info Centre, Plaza Level, Waterfront Centre, 200 Burrard St., Tel: 683-2000. **Tourism Victoria,** 1175 Douglas St., Suite 710, V8W 2E1, Victoria, Tel: (250) 382-2127.

FROM SEATTLE
TO YELLOWSTONE
NATIONAL PARK

YAKIMA
WENATCHEE AND COULEE
SPOKANE
IDAHO
MONTANA

The vast, boundless prairie crouches beneath the azure sky, the snow-capped Rocky Mountains glitter in the distance, and the highway snakes along endlessly. This 780 mile trip from Seattle to Yellowstone National Park is an encounter with nature at its purest, of a kind one can hardly ever get enough of. The road leads from Seattle through eastern Washington State, across the northern part of Idaho, through Montana, land of cowboys and prospectors, and on to the northern entrance of Yellowstone. This itinerary, which covers the northern section of the Rocky Mountains, is not as spectacular as a drive through Colorado. But then, you'll hardly encounter any fellow tourists (least of all Europeans) along the way. For want of a better description, Americans call this region the "Inland Empire":

YAKIMA

The eastern part of Washington State could not be more drastically different from the west of the state along the Pacific Coast. While the residents of the latter, in and around Seattle, feel they are

Left: Young Indian boy at a powwow – a tribal meeting with ritualistic dancing (Seattle).

being subjected to a continuous deluge, the inhabitants of the eastern part could not survive without expensive and complex irrigation systems. Its green hills belie its climate, which can only be described as desert-like. Without the largesse of the great Columbia River, whose waters prevent fields and orchards from drying out, agricultural pursuits in eastern Washington would never be possible. The reason for this climatic imbalance is the presence of the North Cascades Range, which forms a barrier against the weather fronts from the Pacific. The rain remains on the western side, while the east gets no more than ten inches of precipitation a year.

The drive begins in Seattle, on Interstate 90 heading eastward out of the city. Two detours can be undertaken at the intersection of I-90 and I-82. One goes in a southerly direction to Yakima. The other heads toward the north to Wenatchee, where you can switch to Route 2 heading east again.

Both towns are known above all for the great orchards surrounding them. In fact, they are in a sense the twin capitals of Washington State apple growing. The more significant of the two is **Yakima**. The growing of fruit, especially apples, began here in the 1870s, when farmers started irrigating this fertile, partially

volcanic soil. The erstwhile "fruit exchange" has been turned into a large shopping center known as **Yesterday's Village**. The history of the region is told at the **Yakima Valley Museum** (2105 Tieton Dr.), which also has other exhibits, including an interesting and curious collection of covered wagons.

If you have time and don't intend on driving a long stretch, stop in at some of the **Yakima Valley** cellars. In the past few years, Washington State wines have become increasingly popular, and nowadays it is the state with the second-largest wine production in the U.S. – after California. A key support of this industry are the 300 days of annual sunshine, which is vital for the cultivation of grapes. Some of these tasty wines are reminiscent of those of Greece or Turkey. All in all, the flavor of the Washington grapes, even though they might bear the

Above: Ascent into the mountain chains of the North Cascades. Right: Farm in the Wenatchee Mountains.

name Chardonnay or Riesling, for example, are somewhat different from the same varieties in Europe.

Most of the cellars with wine-tasting facilities are found in the villages around Yakima, including **Zillah**, **Sunnyside**, and **Grandview**. **Toppenish**, too, offers several wine cellars, and it also boasts the **Yakima Indian Reservation**. The **Cultural Center** on the reservation provides a look into the history of the Native Americans in the area. In the 1850s, the Indians started rebelling against the increase in white settlement, which is why the army built nearby **Fort Simcoe**. The descendants of the original tribes now live on the reservation.

WENATCHEE AND COULEE

A northern detour takes you from I-90 on to the town of **Wenatchee**, via Highway 97. Wenatchee is particularly beautiful in spring when the apple trees are in bloom. The beginning of the blossoming season is celebrated each year between the last weekend in April and May 1st with the **Washington State Apple Blossom Festival**. To the north of the little town lie **Ohme Gardens**, an enchanting idyll with waterfalls and bright green fields covered in a colorful tapestry of mountain flowers.

Should time allow for a longer detour up north, **Leavenworth**, at the foot of the **North Cascades**, should be put on the agenda. For Europeans, and Germans or Austrians in particular, this little town, made up to look like an Alpine village in Bavaria with all the trimmings, including a Maypole festival with brass bands, seems somewhat corny and terribly out of place in the midst of this typically American environment. But American tourists don't seem to mind, and it is, after all, a great deal cheaper than flying all the way to "good old Bavaria."

Route 2 leads on to **Coulee City** and the **Dry Falls State Park**, whose name

can be taken quite literally: the 400 foot chasm that greets visitors was once the receptacle of a huge waterfall that ran for nearly 3.5 miles. Once upon a time this waterfall was one of the largest in the world. At the end of the Ice Age, when the receding glaciers released the water trapped here, this section of the Columbia River ultimately dried up.

Another superlative can be found 26 miles farther east at the **Grand Coulee Dam**, which was considered to be the largest man-made construction when it was completed in 1941 after eight years of building work. It is over 550 feet high, with a base length of 500 feet. The engineers who designed it took ingenious advantage of the natural conditions of the area. The Columbia River was deviated into a gorge, which had been a river bed some several million years ago, and then dammed. **Franklin D. Roosevelt Lake**, formed as a result of this procedure, irrigates the entire surrounding region and supplies it with electricity. Leaving Grand Coulee on Route 174, and then

taking Highway 2 west, the trip continues on to Spokane.

SPOKANE

The "little big city" of **Spokane** (pop. 180,000) was long considered a provincial backwater lost somewhere out in no man's land between Minneapolis and the Pacific Ocean; though city dwellers from the sophisticated metropolises of the East Coast might point out that Minneapolis itself is in the middle of nowhere. Yet Spokane has a special charm of its own that even the twin cities of Minneapolis and St. Paul do not have. This old forward outpost for lumberjacks and trappers became one of the most important communities in the so-called Inland Empire toward the end of the 19th century, when it was a stop on the transcontinental railroad. As it happened, Spokane was the only pass along hundreds of miles of Rocky Mountain territory where the rails could be laid down.

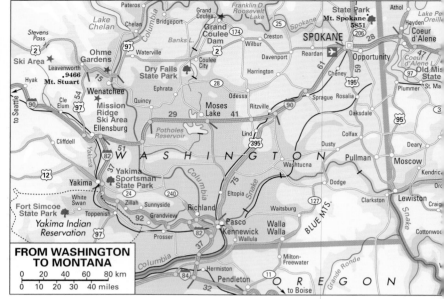

**FROM WASHINGTON
TO MONTANA**

| 0 | 20 | 40 | 60 | 80 km |

| 0 | 10 | 20 | 30 | 40 miles |

It experienced another spurt of growth when gold was discovered in nearby Coeur d'Alene. Parallel to this development, the local Indian tribes (Spokane means "Children of the Sun" in the local language) were gradually pressured into moving onto reservations.

Situated at an altitude of 1,900 feet, Spokane is seen by many as one of America's choicest residential areas, thanks to the beautiful forested hills that surround the city, its pleasant climate and its neat appearance.

The best place to get a taste of the old pioneering days is at the carefully restored **Riverfront**, with its office blocks and warehouses dating back to the end of the 19th century. The revival of the inner city followed in the wake of *Expo '74*. One special project was the restoration of **Riverfront Park**, a recreational area located on an island in the river. This 100 acre park has waterfalls, a historic carrousel, a ferris wheel, an IMAX large screen movie theater and playgrounds to keep the kiddies amused.

Pedestrian bridges connect the island to both sides of the Spokane River.

Spokane **Falls**, a modest waterfall on the river artificially illuminated at night, is visible from Bridge Avenue at Monroe Street.

Another aspect of local culture, one that is hardly visible any more in the area, can be inspected at the **Cheney Cowles Museum**, where artifacts from local Native American tribes are displayed.

But there are also other, beautifully laid-out parks and gardens in Spokane that are worth visiting, such as **Manito Park** (Grand Blvd./18th Ave.) and **Riverside State Park** (Downriver Dr.), which offers opportunities for hikers, anglers and campers alike. **Mt. Spokane State Park**, which lies about 40 miles to the northeast of town on Route 206, is another place worth seeing. It comprises, among other things, two of the highest mountains in the area: **Mt. Spokane** (5,881 feet) and **Mt. Kit Carson** (5,306 feet), which both offer splendid views of the valley.

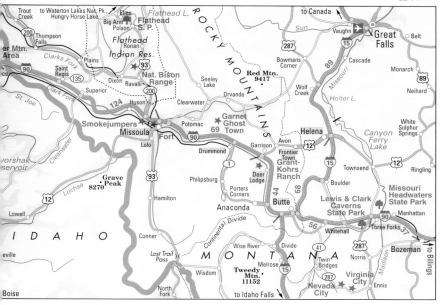

THROUGH IDAHO AND MONTANA

I-90 cuts through northern **Idaho**, one of the most beautiful and diverse landscapes in the U.S. (especially in the **Sun Valley** skiing region in the south of the state). No other single region of continental America has so many different geographical and climatic zones, from high mountains and warm, damp forests, to spacious prairies that stretch as far as the eye can see. Metals such as silver, zinc and lead are still mined here, particularly in the region between **Boise** and **Coeur d'Alene**. The latter is the center of a recreational area that lies along the shores of **Coeur d'Alene Lake**. Highway 97, which steers southward, and I-90 east are both particularly scenic. Boise is the starting point for trips toward Arco (Highway 20) to the solidified lava flows of the **Craters of the Moon National Monument** and toward Twin Falls in the southeast to **Shoshone Falls**, known hereabouts as the *Niagara Falls*

of the West. Furthermore, visitors should stop in at the **Museum of North Idaho** (115 NW Blvd. near the City Park) and at the **Silverwood Theme Park** in **Athol**, where the history of the Wild West is recreated in particularly vivid fashion.

Interstate 90 heading east leads through the old mining areas of the state. **Kellogg**, a community of about 3,500 people 35 miles east of Coeur d'Alene, still boasts America's largest lead and silver mines. In the late 19th century it was the site of a violent miner's strike that paralized the entire region. The history of the back- and soul-breaking work underground is recounted in the nearby **Wallace District Mining Museum** in **Wallace**. Silver mining is demonstrated live on tours of the now-defunct **Sierra Silver Mine** (also in Wallace).

Just a few miles to the east is the border with **Montana**, where flat prairie meets the foothills of the Rocky Mountains. At one time the state was the most important gold-mining region in the entire country, and even today, though somewhat more modestly, gold mined in the eastern part of Montana still represents a major economic factor in the state's finances. But what Montana is really known for is cattle: it has more cows than people. And then there are the cowboys, of whom there are more than most people think. The Wild West romance of tough guys riding the saddle day in, day out, herding cattle eastward, is still conjured up here. Men, even managers and bureaucrats, come to Montana to recover from their daily urban stress on the local *dude ranches* and on dusty riding trails. Webster's dictionary defines a dude as "a man excessively concerned with his clothes, grooming and manners"; while out West, a dude is simply a city slicker from the East.

On the dude ranch, people can get infused with toughness, sweat, leather and courage. Dude ranches offer week-long programs consisting of riding *quarterhorses*, cattle herding and grilling steaks over campfires. There are plenty of ranches in the region which offer this service, and adventures in the saddle can also be booked from as far away as Europe.

The real life of the cowboy of the past was quite different to how they were commonly portrayed. They were generally poverty-stricken cattle-herders, who seldom drew their Colts and shot up the town because ammunition was expensive. As for the gallons of whiskey they are alleged to have drunk (if we are to believe Hollywood), it, too, was expensive. By the end of the 19th century, many cowboys already lived in a "West" from which the "Wild" had been ruthlessly removed, thanks to technological improvements in ranching and the occurrence of a very simple event; the invention of barbed wire.

Right: The smell of animals, sweat and leather banishes thoughts of the office – guests on a dude ranch in Montana.

Near **St. Regis** you can take a trip along Routes 135 and 200 to the **National Bison Range**, where several hundred of this almost extinct species roam and ruminate freely under the endless sky on about 19,000 acres of prime prairie land. A little farther north (for those with some time on their hands) is **Flathead State Park**, where the mountainous landscape is striated with deep gorges, and the eponymous lake is lined with secluded bays. Boats depart from **Big Arm** to **Wild Horse Island**, a wildlife sanctuary which the wild horses indicated by the island's name share with eagles and bighorn sheep.

To the south of Flathead State Park, on I-90, lies the town of **Missoula**, a thoroughly unnoteworthy place with an interesting historical footnote. It was the first place in the U.S. to send a woman representative to Congress, namely Jeanette Rankin. This event took place in 1916, four years before women even had the right to vote in America. And this also occurred in what was has always been considered to be "men's country."

Today, as it was 150 years ago, Missoula is an intersection of a number of important routes. The **Historical Museum** at **Fort Missoula** is housed in several of the fort's restored buildings. If you are interested in finding out more about the rough job of "**smoke jumping**," you should pass by the **Visitor Center** seven miles westward on Highway 10. This is where forest firefighters are trained to parachute into the fires that devastate the western U.S.

Missoula is an important starting point for trips to **Waterton-Glacier National Park** to the north, passing **Flathead Lake** (on Hwy. 93) and on to **Hungry Horse Lake** (Hwy. 2). This park is connected to **Waterton Lakes National Park** on the Canadian side of the border. Hiking is available in both parks.

South of Missoula is a 17 mile detour along a twisting and turning scenic road

(Route 12) to **Lolo**. The Nez Percé Indians used this trail on their bison hunting expeditions hundreds of years ago. Later, it was explored by the **Lewis & Clark Expedition**, which left its traces all over Montana.

Route 12 joins Interstate 90 again, which in turn leads to **Drummond**, an uninteresting town. Not to be missed, however, is **Garnet Ghost Town** (ten miles west of the Drummond exit), one of the finest specimens remaining from the Montana gold rush of the last century.

Another detour worth taking is to **Helena**, the state's capital (via Route 12), which also recalls the good old days of gold fever. Appropriately enough, the city's main drag is still named **Last Chance Gulch**: in 1864, a band of weary and discouraged prospectors discovered a ravine here which they considered to be their last hope of finding gold. They turned out to be luckier than they expected, and in following years nuggets worth several million dollars were found in and around Helena.

The **Last Chance Tour Train** (at the museum at 225 N. Roberts St.) offers trips down this particular memory lane. For a look at some real gold, however, you will have to go to the **Gold Collection** (Norwest Bank of Helena, 350 N. Last Chance Gulch). That Helena, a town of only about 25,000 inhabitants, should be the capital of a state larger than Japan might amuse some foreign visitors, but its government buildings are worthy of its status, especially the **State Capitol**, with its copper dome, and the 1888 **Governor's Mansion**, located at 304 N. Ewing Street.

Fifteen miles to the west of town on Route 12, **Frontier Town**, a replica of an old log cabin settlement from pioneer days, offers some magnificent views of the surrounding valleys.

Back on Interstate 90 the route passes by **Deer Lodge**, the site of the **Grant-Kohrs Ranch**, a 23-roomed mansion that gives an idea of what life was like for a ranching family owning over a million acres of land.

The wealth of the mine operators, on the other hand, can be admired in nearby **Butte**, whose rise to prominence occurred thanks to copper and silver mining. **Copper King Mansion** (219 W Granite St.) was built in 1888 and testifies to the grandiloquent and opulent tastes of those boom times. What brought about this wealth, the nitty-gritty of mining, is demonstrated at the **World Museum of Mining and Hell Roarin' Gulch** (W. Park St.), including displays relating to silver and gold mining, and a reconstructed gold miners' camp.

Two routes lead from Butte to **Yellowstone Park** (see page 169). One steers a northward course and is far more scenically appealing, the other runs in a southwesterly direction, taking you through a number of old gold-mining locations.

The first stop on the northern route (I-90) is the **Lewis and Clark Caverns**

Above: Service station – a center of human civilization in the expanse of this countryside.

State Park near the town of Whitehall. This extensive system of caves carved into the limestone rock is considered the largest in the Northwest. A short distance away, near **Three Forks**, Lewis and Clark left signs of their passage when they came across the "birthplace" of the Missouri River, at the confluence of three rivers - then, as now, a grandiose sight! They gave appropriate names to the three source rivers: Jefferson, Madison and Gallatin. The road then heads to Yellowstone National Park, passing through **Bozeman**, named after John M. Bozeman, who was the leader of a group of pioneers from Wyoming.

The southern route follows Highways 41 and 287, and is a paradise for ghost town buffs. **Virginia City** and **Nevada City** were both once wild and dangerous mining camps after gold was struck in 1863. Within a few weeks the hungry and the greedy were streaming into the region. All that is left of these riches in the area today, however, are these two dusty and solitary *ghost towns*.

YAKIMA VALLEY AND SPOKANE
Area code 509
Accommodation
BUDGET: **Coulee House**, 110 Roosevelt Way, Coulee Dam, Tel: 633-1101. In this motel of some 61 rooms, some are also equipped with a kitchenette, there is also a pool. **Shilo Inn**, 923 3rd Ave., Spokane, Tel: 535-9000. Good motel with pool, gym room and restaurant.
Camping
Yakima Sportsman State Park, 3 miles east on Highway WA 24, Keyes Rd., Tel: 575-2774.
Sights, Museums and Parks
Central Washington Agricultural Museum, 4508 Main St., Yakima, Tel: 457-8735. Documents the history of agriculture and farming here in the 19th century. **Cheney Cowles Museum**, W 2316 1st. Ave., Spokane, Tel: 456-3931. **Coulee Dam National Recreation Area** (with Franklin D. Roosevelt Lake), Tel: 633-9441. **Grand Coulee Dam**, near the junction of Highways WA 155 and WA 174, Tel: 633-9265. **Manito Park**, Grand Blvd./18th Ave., Spokane, Tel: 625-6622. **Mt. Spokane State Park**, 25 miles northeast on Hwy. WA 206, Tel: 238-4258. **Riverfront Park**, Spokane Falls Blvd./Howard St., Spokane, Tel: 625-6600. **Riverside State Park**, near Downriver Dr., Spokane, Tel: 456-3964. **Wenatchee National Forest**, Tel: 662-4335. **Yakima Indian Nation Cultural Center**, US Hwy. 97, Toppenish, Tel: 865-2800. **Yakima Valley Museum**, 2105 Tieton Dr., Franklin Park, Yakima, Tel: 248-0747.
Sports and Recreation
Mission Ridge Ski Area, near Wenatchee, southwest on Squilchuck Rd., Tel: 663-7631. **Skiing Mt. Spokane**, 30 miles northeast on Hwy. WA 206, Tel: 443-1397.
Steven Pass Ski Area, 36 miles to the northwest on Hwy. US 2, near Leavenworth, Tel: (360) 973-2441.
Tourist Information
Spokane Visitors Bureau, 801 West Riverside, Ste. 301, Spokane, WA 99201, Tel: 624-1341.
Yakima Valley V & C Bureau, 10 North 8th St., Yakima, WA 98901-2515, Tel: 575-1300.
Yakima Valley Wine Growers Assn., PO Box 39, Grandview, WA 98930.

MONTANA AND IDAHO
Accommodation
LUXURY: **Coeur d'Alene Resort on the Lake**, 115 2nd St., Coeur d'Alene, Tel: (208) 765-4000. This large hotel is situated directly beside the lake and has 3 restaurants. *MODERATE:* **Townhouse Inns**, 2777 Harrison Ave., Butte, Tel: (406) 494-

8850. This motel is very well equipped and has a pool, sauna and a gym.
BUDGET: **Stardust Motel**, 410 Pine St., Wallace, Tel: (208) 752-1213. Tidy motel, good value for money.
Ranch Stays
Montana Dept. of Agriculture, Agricultural Development Div., PO Box 200201, Helena, MT, 59620, Tel: (406) 444-2402.
Sights, Museums and Parks
Copper King Mansion, 219 W Granite St., Butte, Tel: (406) 782-7580. **Flathead State Park**, US Hwys 200 and 93, near Kalispell, Tel: (406) 8495255. **Frontier Town**, 15 miles west on US 12, Tel: (406) 442-4560. **Gold Collection**, Norwest Bank Helena, 350 N Last Chance Gulch, Helena, Tel: (406) 447-2000.
Governor's Mansion, 304 N Ewing St., Helena, Tel: (406) 444-2694. **Grant-Kohrs Ranch National Historic Site**, Deer Lodge, Tel: (406) 846-2070. **Historical Museum at Fort Missoula**, 5 miles south on I-90, Tel: (406) 728-3476. **Lewis and Clark Caverns State Park**, 19 miles west on MT 2, near Whitehall, Tel: (406) 287-3541.
Missoula Aerial Fire Depot, 7 miles west on US 10, Tel: (406) 329-4934. **Museum of North Idaho**, 115 NW Blvd./near City Park, Coeur d'Alene, Tel: (208) 664-3448. **Museum of the Rockies**, S 7th Ave./Kagy Blvd. S, Bozeman, Tel: (406) 994-2251. **Old Mission State Park**, via I-90, exit 39, in Cataldo, near Kellogg, Tel: (208) 682-3814. Restored mission building.
Sierra Silver Mine Tour, 420 5th St., Wallace, Tel: (208) 752-5151. **Silverwood Theme Park**, on I-95 in Athol, Tel: (208) 6833400. **State Capitol**, Helena, Tel: (406) 444-4794. **Wallace District Mining Museum**, 509 Bank St., Wallace. **World Museum of Mining**, W Park St., Butte, Tel: (406) 723-7211. **Glacier N. P.**, West Glacier, Tel: (406) 888-7800. **Craters of the Moon**, PO Box 29, Arco, Tel: (208) 527-3257.
Sports and Recreation
Lake Coeur d'Alene Cruises, City Dock, east of the City Park, Coeur d'Alene, Tel: (208) 765-4000, Boat trips. **Lookout Pass Ski Area**, 13 miles east on I-90, near Wallace, Tel: (208) 744-1301. **Silver Mountain Ski Area**, via I-90, exit 49, near Kellogg, Tel: (208) 783-1111. **River-Rafting**: Glacier Raft Co., Tel: (406) 888-5454.
Tourist Information
Bovey Restoration, PO Box 338, Virginia City, MT 59755, Tel: (406) 843-5503.
Greater Coeur d'Alene C & V Bureau, PO Box 1088, Coeur d' Alene, ID 83814, Tel: (208) 664-0587.

215

THROUGH THE SOUTHWEST ON ROUTE 66

Get your kicks on Route 66, as the famous song goes. Route 66 was America's first national highway which, during the Depression, became an escape route from poverty into the Promised Land of sunny California so vividly described in John Steinbeck's *The Grapes of Wrath*.

This highway was used during the Second World War for transporting soldiers and military equipment, and was the favorite road of American adventurers on their way from East to West. Motels, truck stops, restaurants, diners and gas stations opened up along Route 66, many of which still exist and some of which are now in their third generation of ownership. Many took to this highway looking for freedom and fortune; a feeling that can still be captured today as the beauty and nostalgia of the landscape is experienced from the saddle of a Harley. The myth of Route 66 has been brought to life time and time again by singers, writers and filmmakers.

Route 66 was more than 2,500 miles long and passed through eight states, as well through a number of Indian reservations. Bobby Troup sang "It winds from Chicago to L.A.,", the starting and finishing points of the road. In 1926, 800 miles of the route were open to traffic, and the process of connecting individual stretches of road commenced, so that by 1937, America's first east-west highway came into being. Today, only several stretches of old Route 66 are still in existence; the rest has been incorporated into various interstate highways (I-10, I-15, I-40, I- 44, I-55).

The complete erasure of Route 66 from road maps had been planned for 1985, but the shutdown had the effect of

Previous pages: White Sands, New Mexico. Right: West of Kingman the nostalgia of Route 66 comes alive.

spawning a number of Route 66 associations hoping to preserve the old route, and membership is open to all interested parties. Texas, New Mexico, Arizona and California are the southwestern states where 66 can still be found – and Arizona boasts the longest drivable stretch of the road. Purists prefer the "classic" east-west journey.

In Texas, where about 90 percent of the frequently interrupted Route 66 is still intact, the road leads from Texola to the border and ghost town of Glenrio via Amarillo. **Texola** is the first "66 town" in Texas for people coming from Chicago and crossing Oklahoma who are looking for their "route." The next stop, the town of **Shamrock** which was founded by Irish immigrants, is known for its Art Deco buildings.

Heading west, the **Devil's Rope Museum** in **McLean** is a pretty original place to visit. This "barbed wire museum" exhibits different kinds of fences. McLean is also the home of the **Route 66 Association of Texas**, which features a small exhibition on 66.

Amarillo, made famous by Toni Christie's tune *Is this the way to Amarillo?*, is where the expression "Everything's bigger in Texas" is said to have originated. This is where the **Big Texan Steak Ranch** promises 72 ounce steak dinners free of charge – unfortunately only to those who can eat one in under an hour! Further highlights of Amarillo are the **Palo Duro Canyon**, a fascinating landscape of gorges, and the **Cadillac Ranch** (seven miles west of town on I-40), where this highway cruiser has been turned into a monument by artist Stanley Marsh: ten of the colorful cars have been planted end-up in the Texas soil, where they stand out comically against the horizon. The largest **Quarter Horse Association** is also based in Amarillo.

Tucumcari, Santa Rosa, Albuquerque, Grants and Gallup are the Route 66 towns in New Mexico, whereby a detour

to the pueblo-style city of Santa Fe (see pages 47-51) should be planned, as this route conforms to the old 1926 road.

Tucumcari was America's "motel capital" in the 1950s, with over 2,000 guest rooms at the time. Many of the motels from the Golden Age of Route 66 still operate today, offering good value accommodation. The old **Club Café** in **Santa Rosa** is a piece of history in itself, and is awaiting its grand re-opening.

Albuquerque has a few highlights to offer visitors: **Old Town**, founded in 1706, the **Indian Pueblo Cultural Center** (a Pueblo village in the middle of the city) and the **National Atomic Center** (documenting the history of the development of the atomic bomb). The **66 Diner** in the city might be named after the old route, but it is merely a reconstruction of a 1950's diner.

Grants, once the world capital of uranium mining, has brought the old Route 66 back to life with **East Santa Fe Avenue**, as well as with many of the motels from the old days.

In the one-time trading post of **Gallup**, Navajo and Zuni Indians still come to do their shopping. The landscape here is more interesting than the town itself, though. From 1929 to 1964, Gallup was a movie town; Hollywood stars liked to stay here at the **El Rancho Hotel**.

In Arizona, Route 66 passes through Holbrook and Winslow and on to Flagstaff. From there, it continues on to Ash Forks and Kingman.

In **Holbrook**, a detour to the **Petrified Forest National Park** in the Painted Desert is recommended (I-40, Exit 311). The colorful sandstone formations in the park are fascinating, as is the "forest" of petrified trees. From **Winslow**, where the **Old Trail Museum** is worth visiting, a road (I-40, Exit 233) leads to the one mile wide and five foot deep **Meteor Crater** – once a NASA training camp for "moon tourists" from 1969. In **Flagstaff**, there is a row of motels along the main route to the Grand Canyon; this stretch of the former Route 66 is now known as **Santa Fe Avenue**. From here the journey

continues to **Williams**, known as the starting point of the **Grand Canyon Railway**, a train ride to the Grand Canyon through some of the southwest's most beautiful landscapes. Passing **Ash Fork**, the route next leads to **Seligman**. Between Seligman and **Kingman**, the **Grand Canyon Caverns** can be visited. Somewhat further west, in picturesque **Truxton Valley**, is the town of **Truxton**, with the **Frontier Café**, a popular Route 66 meeting place.

There are a few 66 classics along **Andy Devine Avenue** in **Kingman**, such as the **El Trovatore** and the **Brand In Iron Motel**, as well as a further attraction: the **Mohave Desert Museum of History and Arts**, with an exhibition relating to the history of the region. The Wild West comes to life again in the **Oatman Hotel** in **Oatman**, when the **Oatman Gunfighters** put on their Wild West show on Main Street.

Above: Freedom on two wheels – Easy Rider on the move in the Southwest.

Needles, Amboy, Ludlow, Barstow, Victorville, San Bernadino, L.A. and Santa Monica are Route 66 cities in California.

Needles was named after the jagged peaks of the Black Mountains, and its **Broadway** helps preserve the memory of 66. The **Hungry Bear Restaurant** and the **Old Trails Inn** are well known destinations. **Roy's Café** in **Amboy**, well inside the Mojave Desert, is another popular Route 66 eatery. About two miles west of town is the **Amboy Crater**, the mouth of an extinct volcano and the Mohave Desert, used as a training ground by General Patton during the war, stretches out in the north. **Siberia** and **Bagdad** are nothing more than ghost towns. While the latter lent its name to the film *Bagdad Café*, the movie was actually shot at the **Sidewinder Café** in **Newbury Springs**.

There is a **Route 66 Museum** in California at **Rancho Cucamonga** (with a visitors' center). **Rialto** has a **Wigwam Village Motel** (as does Holbrook), a wigwam village of "petrified" teepees offering all the comforts of modern American motel rooms. In **San Berdadino**, the **Route 66 Rendezvous Festival** is celebrated every year in September.

Sunset Boulevard in **Los Angeles**, once part of Route 66, is a special attraction for "66 fans." **Barney's Beanery**, on **Santa Monica Boulevard** (also part of old Route 66), is a Route 66 classic; the Hollywood bungalow from 1920 was once a popular meeting place for stars of the silent screen, and is today a popular restaurant. At the end of Santa Monica Blvd., a plaque commemorates the popular American entertainer **Will Rogers**.

Santa Monica Pier marks the end of Route 66. The "always on the move" road-movie feeling that comes with a journey along the historic Route doesn't necessarily disappear when facing the tide of the Pacific – aren't the Hawaiian Islands out there somewhere... ?

ROUTE 66: THE SOUTHWEST

Accommodation
LUXURY: **Eldorado**, 309 West San Fransisco St., Santa Fe, NM, Tel: (505) 988-4455. 4-star hotel in Santa-Fe-style with a much-praised restaurant.
MODERATE: **El Rancho Hotel**, 1000 East Highway 66, Gallup, NM, Tel: (505) 863-9311. Charmingly old-fashioned historic hotel, in which stars of stage and screen used to lodge.
BUDGET: **Quality Inn**, 1400 East Andy Devine Ave., Kingman, AZ, Tel: (520) 753-4747, with a small Route 66 museum. **Wigwam Motel Holbroock**, 811 West Hopi Dr., Holbrook, AZ, Tel: (520) 542-3048. Great for kids, sleeping takes place in tipis!

Camping
Twin Lakes RV Park, 46200 Twin Lakes Drive, Newberry Springs, CA, Tel: (760) 257-3377. **Shady Lane RV Camp**, 36445 Soap Mine Road, Barstow, CA, Tel: (760) 256-5322. **Glen Helen Regional Park**, 2555 Devore Road, San Bernadino, Tel: (909) 880-2522. **Moabi Regional Park**, Park Moabi Road, Needles, CA, Tel: (760) 326-3831. **Mojave Narrows County Park**, 18000 Yates Road, Victorville, CA, Tel: (760) 245-2226.

Restaurants
Barney's Beanery, 8447 Santa Monica Blvd., Los Angeles, CA, Tel: (323) 654-2287. **66 Diner**, 1405 Central NE, Albuquerque, NM, Tel: (505) 247-1421. **Big Texan Steak Ranch**, 7701 E Interstate 40, Amarillo, Texas, Tel: (512) 372-6000, steak restaurant serving gigantic portions.
Frontier Cafe, Truxton, Route 66 in Truxton Valley, AZ, Tel: (520) 769-2238.
Hungry Bear Restaurant, 1906 Needles Highway, Needles, CA, Tel: (760) 326-2988.
Snow Cap Drive-In, Main St., Seligman, AZ, Tel: (520) 422-3291.
Cowboy Morning Breakfast, Route 1, PO Box 69, Claude, TX 79019, Tel: (806) 944-5562, Breakfast in the great outdoors, rides in covered wagons, for information: Tom and Ann Christian.
Roy's Cafe, 66 Old National Hwy., Amboy, CA, Tel: (760) 733-4263.

Museums
Indian Pueblo Cultural Center, 2401 12th St. NW, Albuquerque, NM, Tel: (505) 843-7270. **Devil's Rope Museum**, Old Route 66 / Kingsley St., Mc Lean, TX, Tel: (806) 779-2225.
American Quarter Horse Heritage Center & Museum, 2601 E Interstate 40, Amarillo, TX, Tel: (806) 376-5181. Horse museum. **Mojave Museum**

of History & Art, 400 W Beale St., Kingman, AZ, Tel: (520) 753-3195.
Old Trails Museum, 212 N Kinsley Ave., Winslow, AZ, Tel: (520) 289-5861. **Mining Museum**, 100 Iron St./Santa Fe Ave., Grants, NM, Tel: (505) 287-4802. **National Atomic Museum**, Kirtland Airforce Base, Albuquerque, NM, Tel: (505) 284-3243.

Sights / Parks
Cadillac Ranch, Amarillo CVB, PO Box 9480, Amarillo, TX 79105, Tel: (806) 374-1497. **Ki-Mo Theater**, 423 Central Ave NW, Albuquerque, NM, Tel: (505) 848-1370 (live shows every evening) **California Theater**, 562 West 4th Street, San Bernadino, CA, Tel: (909) 3867-361.
Pow Wow Trading Post, 752 North Nevgo, 86025 Holbrook, AZ (pictures, jewelry, stones, among othe things, are all sold here).
Meteor Crater, by Winslow, AZ, Meteor Crater Road, I-40 west exit 233, Tel: (520) 289-2362.
Palo Duro Canyon, TX, Hwy 217, 22 miles south of Amarillo, Tel: (806) 488-2227. **Petrified Forest N. P.**, Superintendent, Box 2217, AZ 86028, Tel: (520) 524-6228. **Petroglyph NM**, 6900 Unser Blvd. NW, Albuquerque, NM, Tel: (505) 899-0205. **Grand Canyon Railway**, Williams Depot, William, AZ, Tel: 1-800-843-8724.

Motorcycle Rental
Route 66 Motorcycle Rentals, 4164 Lincoln Blvd, Marina Del Rey, CA 90292, Tel: (888) 434-4473, http://caladventures.com/Rout66.htm **California Motorcycle Tours**, Tel: (858) 677-9892, tours@camotorcycletours.com

Tourist Information
California Historic Route 66 Association, 2127 A Foothill Blvd., Suite 66, La Verne, CA 91750.
Historic Route 66 Association of Arizona, PO Box 66, Kingman, AZ 86402. **New Mexico Route 66 Association**, 1415 Central NE, Albuquerque, NM 87106. **Old Route 66 Association of Texas**, PO Box 66, Mc Lean, TX 79057. **Route 66 Territory Visitors Bureau**, 7965-F Vineyard Ave., Rancho Cucamonga, CA, Tel: (909) 948-9166.
66 Association, contact address for membership: US Route 66 Assoc., PO Drawer 5323, Oxnard, CA, 93031. **Albuquerque C&V Bureau**, 121, Tijerros NE, 1st Floor, Albuquerque, NM 87125, Tel: (505) 842-9918. **Amarillo C&V Bureau**, 100 S. Polk St., Amarillo, Texas, 79101, Tel: (806) 374-1497.
Oatman Chamber of Commerce (for information on the Oatman Gunfighters), Oatman, AZ, Tel: (520) 768-7400.

AMERICAN CUISINE:
FAST FOOD AND ETHNIC FOOD

America's most successful export is neither Hollywood films nor pop music, but rather fast food. Hamburgers, chicken wings, chili and pizza are sold all over the world today. Junk food is the great equivocator, enjoyed by Texans and Chinese alike. The huge fast food chains, with McDonalds in the lead, began by conquering American cities before moving into the countryside and then beyond the nations borders. "Billions and billions served," is the proud proclamation under the golden arches of McDonalds' signs.

Fast food is a postwar phenomenon. Without cheap cars and well-developed highways, the hamburger could never have waged its victorious campaign on the American stomach. What more could the average travel-weary driver plough-ing through the endless miles of his country want but a quick snack by the side of the road. At the beginning, fast food was limited to sandwiches and hamburgers. The latter, a meat patty squeezed between the halves of a roll, was originally developed in the city of New Haven, Connecticut, in 1900, and was served with tomatoes and onions optionally, not ketchup. Sandwiches, long made with only cheese or ham, developed an endless number of variations thanks in great part to the Jewish delicatessen.

Industrially prepared, the hamburger tends to taste like fried cardboard. Its influence on America quickly became visible around the national midriff. The current statistics suggest that a third of all Americans carry around an extra 30 pounds. This is not only a result of the intake of junk food, but of the general attitude toward nutrition in the country. Americans eat too much of the wrong stuff, and they tend to get too little exercise. Anyone eating in a restaurant for the first time in America will be aghast at the sheer quantities Americans

Above: A fast food diet leads to becoming overweight in a third of the population.
Right: The motto is: Keep fit!

eat in a brief space of time. Some places advertise "all you can eat" specials, a genuinely American invention. Matching calorie intake with hard-earned dollars leads to a virtual eating craze. Americans consume on average twice as much as their bodies need for subsistance; around 3,700 calories per day.

But America would not be America if it did not also spawn a counter-movement. Since the 1970s, part of the nation has embraced a fitness craze, and since the Carter years, no American president has missed an opportunity to show his fighting spirit by going out for a jog every morning – even if the whole nation laughs at his wobbly thighs and thick calves, as in the case of Bill Clinton. Aerobics, bodybuilding, jazzercize and stretching are American inventions, developed and refined in the studios of New York and Los Angeles, and on the beaches of California. Health foods are the boom product in the food industry: diet products, from Coke to sausages, turn over about 50 billion dollars a year!

Of course, the U.S. offers a lot more than fast food. Beyond the highways and commercial strips there are dozens of delis and small ethnic food establishments. The immigrants brought their cuisine with them and it slowly became an integral part of America's gastronomic landscape. The pizza, born in New Haven as well, and chop suey are two examples. Frankfurters or wieners (better known as hot dogs) and kaiser rolls hark back to the days of German immigration, even if these products no longer have much resemblance to their original models.

In the 1990s, Latin-American and Mexican food rose to prominence. *Tex-Mex food* has appeared wherever Mexican immigrants have settled, and has made its way to Europe as well. Enchiladas, tortillas, tacos and quesadillas are part and parcel of American cuisine by now, and have even been incorporated into the fast food circuit.

Gourmets have a penchant for Californian cuisine, which is light and low in calories. It consists of a combination of American and European cooking, although Europeans might be a little surprised at the variations on their own themes: fresh, dry salad with fish or chicken breast, without oil or vinegar, accompanied by lots of fruit or lightly steamed vegetables. In California one can even sometimes be rendered thankful for the nearest junk food station.

And, finally, a mention of what there is to drink: with junk food, soft drinks of all colors and flavors are drunk, some purely artificial, others strangely experimental, or else milk shakes served in industrial-sized portions. Or, of course, there is the famous "bottomless" cup of coffee.

America's large beer companies cannot hold a candle to the small European breweries, but the recent craze in micro-brewing is beginning to turn the tide. And there are excellent wines available from California and Washington State.

THE UNITED STATES:
A SOCIETY OF IMMIGRANTS

A father with Scottish-Sicilian ancestors, a mother from Hong Kong, an aunt of Jewish origin with a touch of Russian thrown in: that is the kind of variety that can only be found in the United States. Americans are probably the people who have to spell their names most frequently for the benefit of their own countrymen. Read a telephone book in any big American city and you will find an anthology of the world's surnames. America is to this day the only true society of immigrants in the world.

No other country, no other society, no other culture entertains and organizes immigration quite the way the United States does. Every year 530,000 people arrive in the country legally. Some reasons for this are to be found in the history

Above: Barbed wire on the border to Mexico hardly hinders illegal immigrants. Right: Asians lead the immigration statistics.

of the country itself. America grew up on a social diet of colonists and immigrants. Until the middle of the last century most of these people came from Great Britain and Ireland. After the Civil War, the immigration from Germany and Scandinavia got going. After 1890, eastern and southern Europeans from very poor backgrounds and with inadequate skills began arriving in droves. This second great wave of immigration reached its climax in 1907, when more than a million people arrived on the shores of the New World. It ended in 1924 with a law introducing far more stringent measures for the immigrants; a law specifically aimed at the huddled masses from eastern and southern Europe, who were suspected of bringing in the germs of political radicalism. A quota system was set up for each country based on the number of its nationals living in the U.S. in 1890. The last major change in the immigration laws took place in 1965 with the introduction of a preferred status system, by which relationship to U.S. citizens and job qualifications counted most.

Illegal immigration happens parallel to this more organized form – especially from Mexico and Central and South America – which reached staggering proportions toward the end of the 1980s, when nearly 1.6 million Mexicans arrived in the country illegally each year.

Today's immigration policies are relatively liberal, but the laws governing political asylum are only gradually changing. During the days of the Cold War, refugees from communist countries were given preferential treatment, even if they were patently out for a buck like anyone else. Meanwhile, people fleeing right-wing dictatorships (notably from Latin America) were dismissed as "economic refugees."

About six percent of all Americans were born in another country. Some 47 percent of annual immigrants come from Asia, followed by 35 percent from Latin

America. European immigrants number less than ten percent. This shift in the make-up of new arrivals is definitely increasing the multicultural aspect of American society. America today consists of 71.3 percent whites, 12.7 percent African-Americans, 11.2 percent Hispanics, 3.9 percent Asians and less than one percent Native Americans (including Eskimos). By the year 2020, the Asian population is expected to reach at least the 7 percent mark and Latin-Americans the 15 percent mark.

Having said all this, it must be added that America was never a genuine melting pot. Most of the immigrant groups have mostly maintained their ethnic identity from generation to generation. Many Americans are still very proud of their ancestry. And the coexistence of various ethnic groups still functions rather well, considering the population densities of some areas. One reason lies in the promise of *equal opportunity;* every new arrival has a chance to climb up the social and economic ladder. In ad-

dition, new immigrants find large communities of their own people in most of the larger towns of the country. Races only mix in the poorest or richest neighborhoods. Yet in spite of these clearly defined borders, society does pressurize everyone to conform to a culture and language which are still primarily dominated by white Americans. It can happen that a Chinese child suddenly Americanizes his or her name after a few years in the U.S. The same applies to children of Mexican, Indian or Korean parents.

But the free marketplace does not really give equal opportunity to the immigrants of today. State-run institutions apply the rules of *affirmative action*, whereby every public institution has to fill a quota of minorities proportional to the quota in society when hiring. This system is the subject of heated debates in the United States. White conservatives complain about reverse discrimination, the idea that members of a particular minority might be hired because of racial status rather than ability.

THE NATIVE AMERICANS

"Indians," Columbus called them, supposing he had succeeded in finding a sea route to India; and settlers lumped them together ever after.

But the hundreds of thousands of people who inhabited North America before the Europeans arrived were members of different distinct civilizations with their own tribes, languages and customs. To settle their constant disputes, Iroquois tribes drew up an alliance called the Five Nations in the 16th century. Their democratic, state-like system of government was similar to that of the United States, except that it predated it by a couple of hundred years.

The attempts of early settlers to take advantage of the Indians for their land solidified into law under the fledgling U.S. Government. The Indian Removal Act of 1830 "allowed" members of the Five Civilized Tribes – "friendly" eastern tribes such as the Cherokees and Seminoles – to exchange their lands for territories to the west. The Five Tribes proceeded to create five nations in Oklahoma, each with its own government and its own capital. All this was ended by the Civil War. To "punish" the Indians for siding with the Confederate South, the victorious United States Government took away the western portion of their lands, settling them with various tribes from other areas, many of them bitter enemies.

The image most people have of an "American Indian" is of a Sioux, a warrior on horseback in war paint and a feathered bonnet, as depicted in films such as *Dances with Wolves*. It was the nomadic tribes of the Sioux who suffered most notably at the hands of the U.S. Government.

Currently, many Native American tribes are trying to get their own names back; for example, the word "Sioux" is

Above: Treasured art objects – the ceramic work of the Pueblo Indians. Right: Pueblo Indian in Taos.

Chippewa for "adder" – white settlers presumably learned it from Chippewa guides (similarly, "Apache" is the Zuni word for "enemy"). The Sioux call themselves the Dakotas. "Navajo" comes from the Tewa words meaning "cultivated field" and "mouth of a canyon." The tribe calls themselves "Diné," which means "the People."

The Pueblo tribes of the Southwest have been able to retain more of their heritage. New Mexico's 19 pueblos are some of the oldest settlements in North America. Remains of the adobe and brick buildings of prehistoric tribes – in Canyon de Chelly, Chaco Canyon and other sites – don't look very different from Acoma, Taos, or other pueblos inhabited today. Also in the southwest are the Navajo, the largest Indian tribe (numbering some 200,000); they started out as wandering sheep herders, but adopted many Pueblo customs and crafts when they settled in the area. Pots, jewelry, rugs and kachina dolls made by Pueblo tribes are sold throughout the Southwest. Some of these crafts were in fact developed after the advent of white settlers.

Today, there are two million Native Americans (0.8% of the U.S. population), struggling to keep their cultures alive in the face of overwhelming difficulties. Alcoholism is a terrible problem on many reservations, partly because of the limited opportunities for young people. Despite government reservation schooling, many children have to leave the reservation to get a high school education; some of them don't come back. Increasing numbers of young people are unable to speak their own tribal languages.

Attempts are now being made to reverse this trend; there was no system for writing down Native American languages until very recently. Today, scholars have produced Navajo dictionaries, and are trying to build up a body of Navajo language publications so that Navajo can be taught in schools.

Native American tribes have moved into the 21st century in other ways. Common tribal businesses today are gambling casinos and ski resorts. The Navajo have a number of industries, including sawmills, power plants and oil wells.

But tribal governments are not exempt from the kind of power politics and corruption common to governments the world over. The tremendous power tribal chiefs have over their constituents has led to excesses: former Navajo chief MacDonald is today in jail for embezzling tribal funds.

Meanwhile, tradition has moved into the present as well. Annual events in many parts of the United States are powwows, which are competitions for costumed native dancers and meeting places for the members of the widely scattered tribes. Everyone is welcome at these festivals, which are a happy compromise between catering to the tourist trade and adhering to traditional ways of life, which the dances of the powwow help to keep alive.

SPORTS IN AMERICA

Some Europeans stereotype America as a country of 250 million semi-educated, overweight materialists whose lives revolve around fast food and who tend to ignore the rest of the world. But this leaves out one major focus of attention: sports. Americans are proud of their Big Mac and of living in the good ol' U. S. of A., but an even greater source of national – and local – pride are the country's professional athletes. Due to popular demand, the national media offers even couch potatoes unparalleled access to a wide variety of sports – baseball, basketball, hockey, golf, skiing or surfing competitions – nearly every day.

The "purest" of these is the quintessentially American game of baseball. Baseball, like cricket in Britain, may be a game you have to grow up with to truly

Above: Sports create the heroes of the nation. Right: Whoever wants to be a cheerleader has to put in a lot of practice.

understand. Aficionados crave the leisurely pace of a summer afternoon doubleheader (that's two games played back to back): outfielders waiting for the ball to come their way, runners sweating in the sun, and spectators coming and going for beer and hot dogs at the concession stands. To the uninitiated, this whole process may just seem hot and boring.

But it's worth giving the game a second chance, if only because baseball, since Abner Doubleday invented it in 1839, has become a kind of American experience nothing else can quite emulate. Baseball, unlike football or hockey, is a literary sport, a setting for countless American novels and movies. Perhaps one reason so many baseball players have become American popular heroes – like Babe Ruth and Joe DiMaggio – is that the game, although a team sport, rises and falls with each individual on the field.

Basically, what happens in a baseball game is that a lone "pitcher" throws a ball at speeds of up to 100 miles an hour at a "batter," who tries to hit it. The pitcher can throw the ball in a number of ways: a "breaking ball," for example, comes toward the batter at one level and then curves sharply downward before it reaches him. Confronted with this, a batter often swings and misses – a "strike." Three strikes and he's out. If he hits the ball within the designated playing zone, however, he runs to first base; a player must run to all four of the "bases" to score a point for his team. The farther you hit the ball, the more bases you can run; and if you hit the ball out of the park altogether, you can circle all four bases in a triumphant "home run."

Beyond baseball, there's only one sport Americans truly crave: football. Each Sunday in autumn, football games attract crowds of 70,000 in the stands and several million more watching on television. In a listing of the highest-rated TV shows in the history of the world, the

annual championship known as the Super Bowl holds five of the top ten spots: some 38 million households watch this January spectacle.

Where baseball is elegant and literary, football is tough and down-to-earth – literally so, in fact, since most of the plays seem to end up in a huge tangle of bodies piled atop each other on the field. Each team tries to fight its way past the other team and carry the elliptical leather ball, or "pigskin," across the goal line for a "touchdown" (six points). For a sport called "football," there's not much footwork involved, although players do occasionally get to try to kick the ball high over the goal posts for a "field goal."

The winter member of the trio of great American sports is basketball (although hockey, too, has its passionate followers). While most professional sports in the U.S. have become increasingly color-blind since the first black American was allowed into baseball's major leagues in 1947 – Jackie Robinson, a star of the then-Brooklyn Dodgers – basketball is particularly the province of fine African-American athletes. Most inner-city districts in America boast outdoor basketball courts – no more than a cement surface with a hoop at each end – and for many gifted young players the sport has been a ticket out of the ghetto and into the limelight. Or the footlights, in the case of the show team The Harlem Globetrotters, who tour the world, not so much competing as performing their remarkable, quasi-acrobatic on-court antics.

It's not only professional sports that are popular in America. One reason sports are such a part of the national fabric is the widespread enthusiasm for college ball, at least football and basketball. College and university competitions get as much TV and media coverage as professional ones. And it isn't only college: go to any small town in America on a fall Friday night and you'll find most of the town's population turned out for the local high school football game – particularly if there's a crosstown rivalry with another local school.

229

METRIC CONVERSION

Metric Unit	US Equivalent
Meter (m)	39.37 in.
Kilometer (km)	0.6241 mi.
Square Meter (sq m)	10.76 sq. ft.
Hectare (ha)	2.471 acres
Square Kilometer (sq km)	0.386 sq. mi.
Kilogram (kg)	2.2 lbs.
Liter (l)	1.05 qt.

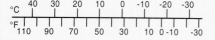

PREPARATIONS

The United States in Statistics

Population: 270 million. *Area:* 3.6 million square miles. *Population Density:* 17 per square mile. *Ethnic Groups:* White 71.3%, Black 12.7%, Hispanic 11.2%, Asian 3.9%, Native American 0.9%. *Religion:* Protestants 79 million, Roman Catholics 55 million, Jews 6 million, Mormons 4.6 million, Muslims 0.5 million, Buddhists 0.4 million, Hindus 0.2 million.

Climate

A rule of thumb is that the peak season, that is to say, the summer months from mid-July through September, is in many ways not the best time for foreign tourists. In tourist areas prices for certain things (hotel rooms, rental cars, etc.) can be up to 50 percent higher than during the rest of the year, and many of the best sights, notably the national parks, are completely overrun by American tourists between the end of May (*Memorial Day*) and the beginning of September (*Labor Day*). Furthermore, you might have to count on a lot of time waiting in line at popular tourist spots. In contrast, during the rest of the year, national parks and natural areas in general are fairly empty (with the possible exception of those in California) except for the odd retired couple or families with small children.

Some Europeans might also have difficulty coming to grips with the continental climate (300 days of sunshine annually) and extremely high temperatures of the southwestern U.S. Beware of the desert and its burning heat, keep enough water around for yourself and your car (which should be in top working condition before attempting crossings of Death Valley). On the other hand, in much of California and parts of the Pacific Northwest it is sunny and mild most of the year.

The Rocky Mountains are ideal for winter vacations. The area around Aspen, Colorado, is a great skiing destination, as is Vail. Taos, New Mexico, Jackson Hole, Wyoming and a host of others.

When traveling in the U.S., bear in mind that nature is often more violent here than elsewhere in the world. Pay attention to radio warnings about heavy storms, tornadoes, hurricanes and floods. This applies especially to Texas around the Gulf of Mexico. The wooded areas of the West are renowned for forest fires.

Money Matters

One basic rule is to carry as little cash around with you as possible. Between US $100 and $200 should be purchased before entering the country. Avoid carrying anything larger than a 50-dollar bill. Foreign currencies can only be changed in larger cities, and then only at some banks.

Better and safer are traveler's checks from, for example, American Express or Visa. They can be used in most shops and hotels, or cashed at any bank.

Even safer and handier are credit cards. Anyone with a Mastercard (Eurocard in Europe), a Visa card or an American Express card will be welcome anywhere, anytime. For car rentals and in some hotels a credit card is sometimes required.

Travel Expenses

The cost of traveling in the United States depends primarily on one's expectations and needs. There are, of course, certain basic considerations that can lessen the expense of a trip to the U.S.

Besides choosing the right time of year to travel, pre-booking rental cars and hotel rooms from Europe is generally cheaper. On top of that, the price levels vary greatly on the West Coast, in the Southwest and in the Rocky Mountains.

One rule of thumb in the West is that the farther east you travel (toward the prairies, that is), the cheaper life gets in general. The most expensive areas are the big cities, such as San Diego, San Francisco and Los Angeles. At any rate, California is more expensive than Texas or the Northwest.

The northern states (Idaho, Wyoming, Montana, Oregon and Washington State) as well as the southwest (Arizona, New Mexico) are all relatively inexpensive destinations for the European tourist. Colorado, especially around the large, famous resorts and more popular national parks, also experiences spontaneous inflation when tourists show up.

Travel Insurance

Traveling in the U.S. without travel (medical) insurance can be a passport to financial ruin. Compared with Europe, social standards are in their infancy in the United States, if born at all. Illness is considered a personal responsibility and the victim thereof is asked to come up with the cost of the repairs.

Many private insurance companies cover 80 to 100 percent of the doctors' bills and hospital bills abroad, as well as medication. If in doubt as to whether you are covered, ask your regular insurance company for information, or find out more from a travel agent; but whatever policy you take, make sure you are covered 100 percent while in the U.S.! The travel insurance often included with a credit card is generally not enough to cover medical costs.

In any case, doctors' and hospital bills in the U.S. have to be paid right away, either in cash, by traveler's check or by credit card.

Travel Planning and Information

Before choosing one of the routes described in this book, give careful thought to which itineraries or sights genuinely appeal to you. Brochures and further information are **no longer** available from the USTTA (the tourist offices of the United States).

Some individual states have offices abroad where you can find more specific materials. You'll find additional addresses and telephone numbers listed later in this chapter in the "Practical Tips from A to Z" section (see "Tourist Information" on page 249).

Visa Requirements

Tourists from England or the Commonwealth entering the U.S. no longer need a visa stamped in their passport, as long as they are not staying more than three months in the country as visitors, have a return or ongoing ticket, and have sufficient funds to support themselves during their stay (see also "Entry Requirements" on page 233).

It is strictly prohibited to work on a tourist visa (as an au-pair, for example) or even to study. Should that be your wish, you will need to obtain a special visa from a U.S. consulate in your country of residence.

Should you be traveling to the U.S. without a return ticket and/or be staying there for between three and six months (the maximum allowed), you will have to send a registered letter to the consulate applying for a visa or appear there in person. Generally, the visa is issued quickly and without too much bureaucratic red tape. During the peak season, before summer vacations, a waiting period should be expected, which can be as long as six weeks or more.

Visa application forms should be filled out carefully according to the best of the applicant's knowledge in order to avoid any later problems or misunderstandings. A tourist visa is seldom rejected, and then only in certain cases (i.e., a criminal record or drug-related offences).

Should you want to stay in the United States longer than six months, you can resort to a simple trick that is tacitly accepted by the authorities, namely traveling for a brief spell to Mexico or Canada, making sure your exit is stamped in your passport, and then reapplying for an entry visa at the nearest American consulate. To be absolutely sure of this method, you should prove you have enough money to survive on and be in possession of a return or ongoing ticket.

United States Embassies and Consulates Abroad

AUSTRALIA: U.S. Embassy, Consular Section, Moonah Place, **Canberra**, A.C.T. 2600, tel. (6) 270-5000; U.S. Consulate General, 553 St. Kilda Rd., P.O. Box 6722, **Melbourne**, Victoria 3004, tel. (3) 526-5900; U.S. Consulate General, 59th Floor, MLC Centre, 19-29 Martin Place, **Sydney**, New South Wales 2000, tel. (2) 373-9200.

CANADA: U.S. Embassy, Consular Section, 100 Wellington St., **Ottowa**, Ontario K1P 5T1, tel. (613) 238-5335/4470; U.S. Consulate General, Suite 1050, 615 Macleod Trail, SE, **Calgary**, Alberta T2G 4T8, tel. (403) 266-8962; U.S. Consulate General, Suite 910, Cogswell Tower, Scotia Square, **Halifax**, Nova Scotia, B3J 3K1, tel. (902) 429-2480; U.S. Consulate General, P.O. Box 65, Postal Station Desjardins, **Montreal**, Quebec H5B 1G1, tel. (514) 398-9695; U.S. Consulate General, 2 Place Terrasse Dufferin, C.P. 939, **Quebec**, Quebec G1R 4T9, tel. (418) 692-2095; U.S. Consulate General, 360 University Ave.,

Toronto, Ontario M5G 1S4, tel. (416) 595-1700; U.S. Consulate General, 1095 West Pender St., **Vancouver**, B.C. V6E 2M6, tel. (604) 685-4311.

NEW ZEALAND: U.S. Embassy, Consular Section, 29 Fitzherbert Terrace, Thorndon, **Wellington**, tel. (4) 472-2068; U.S. Consulate General, 4th Floor, Yorkshire General Building, **Auckland**, tel. (9) 303-2724.

UNITED KINGDOM: U.S. Embassy, Consular Section, 24/31 Grosvenor Square, **London** W1A 1AE, tel. (71) 499-1637; U.S. Consulate General, Queen's House, 14 Queen St., **Belfast**, Northern Ireland BT 1 6EQ, tel. (232) 328-239.

ARRIVAL AND ENTRY

Airlines / Airfares

The larger airlines, such as United, offer a variety of special or one-time fares. One thing is sure, however: the fares from mid-August to mid-May or mid-June are considerably lower than those during the summer holiday season (from mid-June to mid-August). Paying the holiday rate during the peak season allows the tourist (intending to stay for more than seven days and less than six months) to pick and choose his or her point of arrival and point of departure in the U.S. from the list of airports serviced by the airline.

Tickets must normally be paid in full within 24 hours of booking the flight. A penalty is usually charged for ticket alterations.

Special rates are generally available for students and young people (up to 26 years of age).

As a rule, the difference in price among the larger airlines is minimal. Since just about all European carriers have partnerships with U.S. airlines, travelers should investigate all network and fare options available for their destination: U.S. carriers often have special offers for passengers of their European partner companies.

Offering the most expanded flight schedule, the Lufthansa-United alliance is the only one of the major partnerships between airlines that links both continents with 300 flights daily to more than 70 destinations, thus covering the whole continental U.S. and Canada.

Among those flights are typical tourist destinations such as California or Florida, as well as flights to the Midwest, the South or Canada's remote regions. If you are a member of a frequent flier program (Lufthansa Miles & More or United Mileage Plus, for example), the partner airline will credit you with the points. In addition, many other partner firms, such as car rental agencies and hotel chains, will give you refunds on your miles.

If you want to travel around the country a bit, you might consider the kind of special stand-by ticket available to European residents from several U.S. airlines, such as United. For a rather low flat fee you can fly an umlimited amount within a 30 or 60 day period – although there's no guarantee you'll get on your first-choice flight. Also recommendable are coupon flights offered by United Airlines: you pay for a specific number of predetermined flights (up to twelve), which can be changed for a minor fee. You usually pay a base rate and then, depending on the number of coupons, subsequent fares.

These offers are valid within continental North America and only for tickets that were acquired in your country of origin.

Entry Requirements / Customs Requirements

Every traveler to the U.S. is given two forms in the airplane that must be filled out before reaching customs. The green entry form (the I94W) is for the usual bits of information about yourself. It also asks you for names and addresses of friends or relatives in the U.S., the reason for your visit, and whether you are a member of a prohibited organization or political party. The lower part of the form, bearing the date and place of entry in the United States, is attached to your passport by the immigrations official. On leaving the U.S. the slip is removed from your documents, generally by members of the airline staff. Be careful not to lose this part of the I94.

There are seldom problems at immigrations or customs. The officials are not particularly friendly, but are very efficient in processing the passengers of incoming flights. Occasionally, one of them will stop a traveler and ask how much money he or she is carrying, and what his or her destination in the U.S. is. Anyone with enough money in the form of cash or traveler's checks should have no problem getting through. Officials may get suspicious if your passport has stamps from communist countries, such as North Korea and Cuba, or from certain Arab states, such as Libya, Syria, Iraq, and Iran. Even in that case, though, they usually just ask a few questions, and a return ticket plus sufficient ready funds is enough to quiet them down.

A warning to those entering the country as tourists and then hoping to find au pair or restaurant work: if the immigrations watchdogs find out about your idea, you might find yourself on the next plane back at your own expense.

After clearing the minor hurdle of immigrations, you come to the customs part. If you are flying in from a western or central European state, then the procedure is usually a simple paper-stamping. This is where you show the second form you filled out in the airplane. It requires you to list various taxable items that are usually irrelevant for the tourist. Importing dollars (in the form of cash or traveler's checks) must be declared if the sum exceeds US $10,000. Importing fresh foods, such as meat or sausages,

233

bread, vegetables and fruit is not allowed. You might also be asked if you have recently spent any time on a farm.

If you take medication regularly, ask your doctor or hospital to provide a written verification of this in English prior to departure from your home country. This could help prevent an official from confiscating the medication in question during a routine search because it might violate American laws on narcotics.

TRAVELING IN THE U.S.

Airlines

All U.S. and European (and other) airlines keep offices in larger towns and at airports.

As with much of the shopping done in the U.S., bookings and payment can be easily taken care of by telephone using a credit card.

All airlines are accessible free of charge using their 800-numbers (from within the United States). Following is a list of toll-free numbers for selected airlines:

American Airlines (AA): 1-800-433-7300; **Continental Airlines** (CO): 1-800-525-0280; **Delta Air Lines** (DL): 1-800-221-1212; **Northwest Airlines** (NW): 1-800-225-2525; **Southwest Airlines** (WN): 1-800-435-9792; **Trans World Airlines** (TWA): 1-800-221-2000; **United Airlines** (UA): 1-800-241-6522; **USAir** (US): 1-800-428-4322.

Buying a Car / Driveaway Companies

If you are traveling for more than a month in the United States, you might consider the possibility of buying a used car. It's basically fairly easy. To register a car you need an international driver's license, or, better yet, an American one (easily available in one day by producing your international license and taking a test), providing an address in the state where you are, and producing the title of ownership for the car. Don't forget that, in several states, when a car changes

owners it must be taken to an inspection at a certified garage. This should be taken care of *before* registration.

Whether the seller is asking too much for the car can be checked in the *Blue Book* which is available at every garage. We recommend you purchase a *Collision Damage Waiver* in order to avoid ruinous expenses in case of an accident. Another thing to remember is the horrendously high insurance costs that are determined not only by the type of car, but also according to the age, sex, residence and status of the owner. Insurance can be about $300 cheaper with a U.S. license than with an international document!

A cheap alternative to buying or renting a car is the "driveaway service." These are companies which organize the transport of vehicles for people or companies who do not want to or are unable to make a long drive themselves.

Cars driven for a driveaway service must be delivered to their destination within a predetermined period of time. For the trip from New York to San Francisco, for example, allowing for around 400 miles per day of driving, the car would be expected for delivery on or about the eigth day. The driveaway company generally provides the first tank of gas and may request a security deposit.

For further information, contact **Driveaway Service** at 1-800-340-3793, or their branches in most big cities. For other companies, check the yellow pages under Driveaway Services or Auto Driveaway.

Breakdown Assistance

If you run into problems with a rental car, the first thing to do is call the rental agency. Another possibility is to get help from the American Automobile Association (AAA; generally called "Triple-A"), tel. 1-800-AAA-HELP. AAA also has reciprocal agreements with foreign automobile associations, so check with your own auto club to find out what services or wares (maps, brochures, etc.) are available to you for free.

Car Rental

It is generally cheaper to book your car from abroad (sometimes up to 60 percent cheaper) than to rent it in the U.S. The rates of the big rental agencies, such as Avis, Budget and Hertz, seldom vary greatly, but you should check into special offers, because they sometimes grant big discounts. To rent a car the driver must be at least 21 years of age and have a valid driver's license. Many rental companies add a surcharge for drivers under the age of 25. Some companies require an international driver's license even for rental periods of under four weeks. These are available at driver's license offices or automobile clubs in your country of departure.

When booking a rental vehicle, you should find out about additional expenses which are seldom mentioned. Among these are insurance costs, deductables, mileage costs (if mileage is not unlimited) and the cost for returning the car, should you be ending the trip in a different city.

Find out more from your travel agent about fly-and-drive packages, which include a car (usually for a week) with your flight – sometimes this can be a very good deal indeed.

Once you are in the U.S., you can make calls to the following agencies free of charge: **Alamo Rent-A-Car**: 1-800-327-9633; **Avis Reservations Center**: 1-800-331-1212; **Budget Rent-A-Car**: 1-800-527-0700; **Dollar Rent-A-Car**: 1-800-4000; **Hertz Corporation**: 1-800-654-3131 (1-800-654-3001 in Canada); **National Car Rental**: 1-800-CAR-RENT; **Thrifty Rent-A-Car**: 1-800-367-2277.

Campers and RVs

A number of rental agencies offer campers and RVs, or *recreational vehicles*, as they are known in America. Some European travel agents can arrange for the rental of these vehicles from abroad.

Motorcycles

Experiencing America on a motorcycle, preferably a Harley-Davidson, is the ultimate biker's dream. Harleys (or other makes) are available for rent at many locations. Should you want to buy a bike, you will have to purchase insurance in person (i.e., not via an agent) for example, from the **Dairyland Insurance Company, Berglund Insurance Company**, 5625 E. Indian School Rd., Studio B, Phoenix, Arizona 85018, tel. 1-602-949-1034, fax. 1-602-994-0321. You will need a credit card. Once the money has been transferred, you will receive your policy. Don't forget to request an application form.

Should you be traveling to the U.S. with your own bike, you will also need this insurance. A number of airlines offer a special "fly and ride" ticket for those who want to travel with their own motorcycles.

There are many places to rent motorcycles in the western U.S., with the classic American Harley-Davidson being the perennial favorite. Rates can vary greatly from state to state, or even from city to city; so it pays to shop around. The daily rental price of a Harley Sportster can be as low as $75, though other models average closer to $150.

Following is a list of selected motorcycle rental agencies by state:

ARIZONA: Arizona Sunriders, 3007 N. 73rd St., **Scottsdale**, tel. (602) 949-9153; Cruise America, 11 W. Hampton St., **Mesa**, tel. (602) 464-7300; Fun Time Rentals, 1207 N. Scottsdale Rd., **Tempe**, tel. (602) 968-2522.

CALIFORNIA: American Rentals, 2715 Hyde St., **San Francisco**, tel. (415) 931-0234; California Motorcycle Rentals (BMW 850Rs), 3304 Buena Vista St., **San Diego**, tel. (619) 581-6879; Classic

Motorcycle Adventures (Harley tours), P.O. Box 2817 **Truckee**, CA, tel. 1-888-339-4262 (toll-free); Eagle Rider, 20917 Western Ave., **Torrance**, tel. (310) 320-3456; Eagle Rider, 1555 Burke Ave., **San Francisco**, tel. (415) 647-9898.

COLORADO: Eagle Rider, 5440 N. Valley Highway, **Denver**, tel. (303) 295-7113.

NEVADA: Eagle Rider, 5012 S. Arville St., Suite 9, **Las Vegas**, tel. (702) 876-8687 or toll-free 1-888-916-7433; Iron Eagle Harley-Davidson Motorcycle Rentals, 5012 S. Arville St., Suite 9, **Las Vegas**, tel. (702) 257-6222.

VANCOUVER, B.C.: Coastline Motorcycle Tours and Rentals, #4 - 2720 Cliffe Ave., **Courtenay**, tel. (250) 338-0344; Coastline Motorcycle Tours and Rentals 240 - 2950 Douglas St., **Victoria**, tel. (250) 385-6199.

Driving in the U.S.

Driving in the U.S. is a lot simpler and a lot more relaxing than in Europe. The roads are wider, in rural areas they are more often than not quite empty, and Americans usually follow the rule of "safety first." They drive defensively, politely, and a good deal more reasonably than in, say, Germany or Italy. Perhaps one reason for this is that the car in America is by and large not a status symbol or an object to boost one's self-confidence, but rather a tool to be used regularly to get from point A to point B. Public transportation outside of cities is notoriously weak. Another reason for this careful driving is the fact that many Americans only have the lowest legal insurance coverage of $20,000 per person, which is nothing considering the cost of hospitalization.

Many of the daily plagues of European highways (flashing high beams on the slower drivers, tailgating and driving over the speed limit) are considered sheer rowdiness and rudeness in the U.S., and highway patrols are quick and efficient in dealing with such behavior. Americans expect civilized driving from their fellow Americans and from tourists, especially in the cities. It is expected (and in some states it is the law) that cars stop for pedestrians at crosswalks. That drivers come to a complete stop at stop signs goes without saying.

Parking is regulated by corresponding signs. Watch out for fire hydrants: keep at least twelve feet from them. Tickets and towing costs can be expensive!

Driving in America is on the right. The speed limit in towns and villages is 25 mph unless otherwise marked. Since December 1995, each state has been responsible for controlling its own speed limits on highways and interstates. The speed limit on these roads nowadays is generally 65 or 70 mph. These limits are by and large observed in America, as moving violations such as speeding are punished not only by a hefty fine, but also by an increase in insurance premiums.

Passing is generally on the left, but passing on the right is also tolerated. This is the rule for the large highways and interstates. Stick to your lane and expect to be overtaken on both sides.

Stop signs regulate traffic at intersections. If two cars stop at the same time, it's the car which comes to a complete stop first that has the right of way; when in doubt, this is the driver to the right. Lights turn from green to yellow (briefly) then to red, and then from red immediately to green. Unless otherwise posted, right turns can be made on red in most states. Pay attention to school buses. When one stops and flashes its red lights, traffic in *both directions* must come to a full stop and wait until the bus driver switches off the lights.

Two road signs that are probably unknown to Europeans are the "U-Turn," which allows you to perform that otherwise prohibited maneuver; and the "Crossover," which allows the same thing on a highway. "Xing" means "crossing," so if you see "Gator Xing," it means that alligators like to cross the road at this point.

Multi-lane roads in some of the larger cities are marked *HOV-2* or *HOV-3*, standing for *High Occupancy Vehicle*. Only cars with two or three people in them are allowed to use these lanes during rush hour.

Should you be stopped by a police car, stay calm, keep your hands on the wheel until asked for your papers, and then get them calmly out of your pocket; quick, nervous movements might appear like you are going for a gun. American police are not necessarily trigger-happy, but they can sometimes be overly cautious.

Greyhound Buses

A good way to get around, rub elbows with everyday America, and see a lot of highway and countryside, is to use Greyhound buses, which service the entire U.S. The buses themselves are not particularly comfortable, but are sometimes equipped with movies and always with a toilet. Foreigners can purchase an *Ameripass* in their country of origin before traveling to the U.S. This is a fairly cheap way of getting around. Smokers beware: there is no smoking on the buses, and the trips can sometimes be excruciatingly long.

Road Networks

The American highway and road systems have been conceived in a simple and logical fashion. They usually consist of two or four lane overland roads, whereby a highway usually applies to any four- or more-laned road. The wide highways leading from one state to the next are logically called interstates. On many highways, be they turnpikes, freeways, parkways or expressways, there are tolls; keep your change handy for speedier processing, especially during rush hour.

The number allotted to an interstate is not haphazard: even numbers indicate a road running east-west; odd numbers in-

dicate a north-south course. Three numbers (for example, Interstate 405 near Los Angeles) indicate either a highway leading into a city or else around it. If the first number is even, then it leads into the city, if it is an odd number then it circumnavigates the place. The last two digits indicate the highway or interstate it is coming from.

In many American cities, orientation is relatively easy, even for a first-time arrival. This is because streets are often organized in a grid beginning at the edge of town with either the last letter of the alphabet or a high number: W Street or 99th Street, for example. The closer you get to A or the lower the number, the closer you are to the center of town. House numbers are often given according to the length of streets: number 5605 is a house between 56th and 57th streets.

Gas stations are frequent in the U.S., many stay open all night or have at least automatic credit card service. At night you will usually have to pay first and then pump your gas.

Railways

In comparison to Europe, America's railroad network is poorly developed. The trains themselves are not particularly comfortable either. If you wish to make use of its service, however, find out more about prices, specials and the Amtrak Rail Pass from your local travel agent, or call their toll-free number in the U.S. at 1-800-USA-RAIL. Smokers be warned: there is no smoking anywhere on the trains.

A very special kind of travel are trips on historic or narrow-gauge trains. Among the great old-timer rides is the *Durango & Silverton Narrow Gauge Railroad*, in Durango, Colorado, tel: (970) 247-2733 and 8888725607. It runs from the end of April to the end of October. In 2000, the 3 hrs 15 mins trip costs $53, $27 for children. The *Grand Canyon Railway* in Arizona, tel: 1-800-

THE-TRAIN, trips lasting 2 hrs 45 mins cost $50 for adults (round-trip) in 2000.

PRACTICAL TIPS FROM A TO Z

Accommodation

Even in the peak season, finding accommodation should not be a problem. Motels, hotels and B&Bs are in good supply. The only crunch might come around the more popular national parks or during particularly busy weekends in such places as Yellowstone. That's why booking ahead of time is recommended if you are traveling, say, around July 4, Labor Day or Memorial Day.

Even the cheaper motels offer two beds (double, king- or queen-size), color television with cable, and often a swimming pool. If you are cooking for yourself, ask for a room with a kitchenette. Travelers over 55 years of age should ask for the senior rate, which can mean a discount of up to 20 percent. Children under twelve stay free of charge in some places, and can even eat for free in the hotel restaurant in some cases. Groups of three, four or five can ask for a double room with two large double beds and a fold-out bed without any problems; this works out much cheaper than taking two or three separate rooms.

The following "800 numbers" (toll-free) can be used for information or for making reservations.

LUXURY (over 120 US$): **Hilton Hotels**, tel. 1-800-HILTONS; **Hyatt**, tel. 1-800-228-9000; **Ritz-Carlton**, tel. 1-800-241-3333.

EXPENSIVE (90-120 US$): **Days Inn**, tel. 1-800-325-2525; **Holiday Inn**, tel. 1-800-HOLIDAY; **Mariott Hotels**, tel. 1-800-228-9290; **Sheraton Hotels & Inns**, tel. 1-800-325-3535.

MODERATE (60-90 US$): **Best Western**, tel. 1-800-528-1234; **Comfort Inn**, tel. 1-800-228-5150; **Howard Johnson**, tel. 1-800-654-2000; **Quality Inn**, tel. 1-800-228-5151; **Radisson Hotels**, tel. 1-

800-333-3333; **Ramada Inns**, tel. 1-800-2-RAMADA; **Rodeway Inns**, tel. 1-800-228-2000.

BUDGET (under 60 US$): **Budget Host**, tel. 1-800-BUD-HOST; **Econo-Lodge**, tel. 1-800-446-6900; **Hampton Inn**, tel. 1-800-HAMPTON; **Red Roof Inns**, tel. 1-800-843-7663; **Super 8 Motels**, tel. 1-800-843-1991/1-800-8000; **Travelodge**, tel. 1-800-578-7878; **Motel 6**, 1-800-4-MOTEL-6

Alcohol and Cigarettes

For many Americans, alcohol is something to be scorned. This has to do not only with the country's Puritan past, the excesses of Prohibition and the current drug problem, but also with the exaggerated cult of fitness. The dry Martini, the Daiquiri and other cocktails, though still available, have given way to vitamin pills, enzymes and other nutritional supplements. Alcohol, like tobacco, is simply considered unhealthy.

Anyone out for a drink has to be 21 years of age or older. ID (identification) cards are requested by bartenders. In fact, the same applies to anyone wanting to go into a bar or disco where alcohol is served. In some states, alcoholic beverages may only be purchased in special shops, so-called "Liquor Stores" or "Package Stores." But at any rate, salespeople are also required to ask for an ID. Consuming alcoholic beverages in public is strictly forbidden, which is why you may sometimes see people outdoors drinking from bottles concealed in brown paper bags. Drinking in a car or having an open bottle of alcohol is absolutely forbidden, so never keep an open bottle in the passenger compartment; lock it up in the trunk. Carrying alcoholic beverages onto an Indian reservation is forbidden as well.

Driving "while under the influence," or DWI, is not treated as a simple misdemeanor. Penalties are heavy (though sometimes novel: one judge had the defendants tour high schools to give lectures on DWI). Each state has its acceptable level, so the best bet is to avoid drinking and driving altogether. In an accident, the first thing the police do is administer a breathalyzer test or blood test. Breaking the law on this issue can land tourists in the local jail.

As for smokers, they will have a hard time in the U.S. Buses, trains, public buildings, most cafés and many restaurants simply prohibit it. Smoking sections in restaurants and bars are small. During the intermission at the cinema or theater you will have to step outside to enjoy a smoke.

Banks

Most banks are open between 9 a.m. and 4 p.m. They are closed on national holidays. To cash traveler's checks or obtain cash on a credit card, you should always have at least one source of identification with you, and in some cases even a second one (such as a driver's license). Some banks also impose a limit on the amount of cash you can take out.

Business Hours

American shopping hours are generally from 9 a.m. to 9 p.m., Monday to Saturday. Most shops and grocery stores are also open on Sundays – and even national holidays. Business hours for banks (9 a.m. to 4 p.m.) and post offices (8 a.m. to 5 p.m.) are slightly more limited; both being closed on Sundays and national holidays.

Camping and Youth Hostels

America is a paradise for campers. The national and state parks have established excellent campgrounds in the midst of the most pristine nature. Sites are usually available on a first-come-first-served basis. You generally pay a basic fee for a spot ($5 to $15, though often free of charge), regardless of the number of people. Barbecues, showers, toilets and washing machines are the norm at camp-sites. The camping places in the national parks are generally fairly crowded in the summer months, so reservations are recommended. Besides the phone numbers mentioned in the *Guideposts* at the end of each chapter, you can also try the toll-free 1-800-365-CAMP or http://reservations.nps.gov. Private campsites are an alternative to the state-run ones, though they are often more expensive (in some cases running up to $35 per night!). On the other hand, they offer motel-like luxury.

Youth hostels are not quite as widespread in the U.S. as in Europe, but they are nonetheless very cheap (in the $20 per night range) and clean. Information and a complete directory can be ordered from the **American Youth Hostels**,733 15th St., N.W., Suite 840, Washington D.C. 20005, http://hiayh.org or **YMCA** (Young Men's Christian Association), 224 E. 47th Street, New York, NY 10013.

Crime / Emergency Calls

Tourists in the U.S. should take the same precautions as in any other country they visit. Nevertheless, because of the high crime rate in the U.S. and the widespread availability and use of weapons, one should pay attention to certain unwritten rules.

Should your plane land at night, it is advisable to stay at a hotel near the airport and pick up your rental car the next morning.

Should you be purposely rammed on the highway or otherwise threatened, change lanes, keep driving, and accelerate. Go the the next well-lighted service area and call the police at 911 (which is also the emergency number for ambulances and the fire department). There are marked emergency phones along some highways.

In cities, pay attention to what locals say about dangerous areas; avoid them during the day if possible, and especially at night. Hotel and restaurant personnel

239

will give advice that should be followed. If you are not sure about an area, don't hesitate to ask. Americans live with crime and many know how to deal with it. At night, some inner cities are completely dead after about 9 o'clock. Find out where to go for nightlife, and drive or take a cab to that specific place.

Always make sure your car is locked and don't leave things lying about on the seats. On your strolls, take only as much money with you as you will need (carry it in your pocket; handbags are easy targets for thieves) and lock the rest away in the hotel safe. If you have two credit cards, only carry one with you at a time. If you are mugged, forget Hollywood antics and let the mugger have your cash.

If you have lost your way in a big city, ask a policemen for directions or find the nearest hotel or restaurant and inquire there. If your car breaks down, park it by the side of the road, open the hood and wait in the car until a police car or a tow-truck comes.

Avoid brandishing large sums of money or wearing expensive jewelry. Don't open your hotel or motel room door if you don't know who is knocking. If the person knocking says that he or she is on the hotel/motel staff, call the reception desk to verify this.

Don't forget to keep the telephone numbers where you can cancel your credit cards or travelers'checks handy. The numbers and addresses of embassies and consulates are also important, as well as a photocopy of your passport. Remember, too, that Americans themselves have become a little paranoid on the issue of crime. The free sale of weapons means that an unusually high number of regular citizens own firearms, and many of them are quick on the trigger. If you must go to a house for help or address someone on the street, try to be non-aggressive.

While these precautions are important, we would like to add that there is no point in ruining your holiday by extreme fear.

Crime in the U.S. is also fairly focused on poorer areas of big cities. In the sleepy, close-knit communities of villages and small towns in the countryside, on the other hand, some people never even lock their cars or front doors (although such a feeling of security is on the wane of late). Travelers, of course, are well advised to lock their own cars at all times.

Currency

The American dollar, or "greenback," as it used to be referred to, is not only the most important currency in the world, but also one with great symbolic value. It immediately calls to mind pure and unadulterated capitalism, rapid fortunes, wealth and financial daring.

The dollar is printed in bills of the same size (make sure you know which bill you just handed someone). It comes in denominations of 1, 5, 10, 20, 50, 100, 500 and 1,000 – though you may occasionally encounter the odd $2 bill and will rarely see one larger than $100. Most business transactions only use bills up to $50. Some shops and restaurants, especially in rural areas, will balk at a 50-dollar bill, so it is advisable to change larger bills at a bank.

A dollar breaks down into 100 cents, minted in the following sizes: 1 (penny), 5 (nickel), 10 (dime), 25 (quarter), 50 (half-dollar, rare), one dollar (also rare). Quarters and dimes are important for pay phones, parking meters and vending machines.

Doctors / Pharmacies

Any tourist with the proper insurance coverage can visit any doctor, provided he or she has enough cash or traveler's checks on hand to pay the bill, or a credit card. Payment must be made immediately. What percentage of the fee will be covered by your insurance company should be cleared up before starting your trip. Should a doctor refuse treatment, for whatever reason, try the local Medical Center. These organizations have several doctors working together, and they also provide a kind of out-patient emergency service.

Those on medication, especially of the stronger type, should make sure their regular doctor gives them a letter verifying this (in English) for customs officials. A doctor's prescription is also handy. Medication can be purchased at the prescription counter of drugstores, in some larger supermarkets and in pharmacies.

The emergency telephone number for the police, ambulance or fire department is 911.

Electricity

Electricity in the U.S. is 110 volts, so European appliances will require a voltage adaptor that should be bought in your home country. Even though many modern appliances feature a voltage switch, you will still need a plug adaptor because American plug outlets are different.

Embassies and Consulates

BRITISH CONSULATES: Suite 1900, First Interstate Bank Plaza Building, 1000 Louisiana, **Houston**, TX 77002, tel. (713) 659-6270; 813 Stemmons Tower West, 2730 Stemmons Freeway, **Dallas**, TX 75207, tel. (214) 637-3600; c/o Davis, Graham & Stubbs, Suite 4700, 370 17th St., **Denver**, CO 80202, tel. (303) 893-7300; Suite 400, 11766 Wilshire Blvd., **Los Angeles**, CA 90025-6538, tel. (310) 477-3322; Suite 850, 1 Sansome St., **San Francisco**, CA 94104, tel. (415) 981-3030; 820 First Interstate Center, 999 Third Ave, **Seattle**, WA 98104, tel. (206) 622-9255.

AUSTRALIAN EMBASSY: 1601 Massachusetts Ave., **Washington, D.C.** 20036, tel. (202) 797-3000. *AUSTRALIAN CONSULATES:* Suite 800, 3 Post Oak Central, 1990 South Post Oak Blvd., **Houston**, TX 77056-9998, tel. (713) 629-9131; 611 North Larchmont Blvd., **Los Angeles**, CA 90004-9998, tel. (213) 469-4300; 1 Bush St., **San Francisco**, CA 94104, tel. (415) 362-6160.

CANADIAN EMBASSY: 501 Pennsylvania Ave., NW, **Washington, D.C.**, 20001, tel. (202) 682-1740. *CANADIAN CONSULATES:* St. Paul Place, 750 North St., Paul St., Suite 1700, **Dallas**, TX 75201-3261, tel. (214) 922-9806; 300 South Grand Ave., 10th Floor, **Los Angeles**, CA 90071, tel. (213) 687-7432; 412 Plaza 600, Sixth and Stewart, **Seattle**, WA 98101-1286, tel. (206) 443-1777.

NEW ZEALAND EMBASSY: 37 Observatory Circle NW, **Washington, D.C.**, 20008, tel. (202) 328-4848. *NEW ZEALAND CONSULATE:* 12400 Wilshire Blvd., Suite 1150, **Los Angeles**, CA 90025, tel. (310) 207 1605.

Etiquette

Many European tourists, especially German and British, are considered excessively aggressive and rude in the U.S. This has to do with a misconception and misunderstanding of the different cultures. The apparently loose and informal American society in fact invites this kind of behavior. However, social intercourse in the U.S. is governed by a few subtle rules and regulations that are barely visible to the foreigner. In order to enjoy your holiday without any sudden and unpleasant experiences with Americans, here are a few tips on the correct behavior with your host country.

Americans keep careful watch on physical distance, that means the moment you get too close to someone, you should utter an *"excuse me."* Americans wait in line, and trying to cut in line is considered highly improper. Banks, post offices and other such places where lines are common often have an ingenious funneling system to keep the first-come-first-served rule operating without hitches.

Casual meetings seldom involve shaking hands. However, a salesperson or businessperson may well insist on shaking your hand after a successful transaction. Greetings are otherwise fairly informal, involving a casual "Hi, how are you," which should be answered by a "Fine, thanks, how are you."

Even in department stores one finds this question being asked of customers, whereby a thorough and truthful answer concerning your state of being is neither expected nor desired.

Americans tend to talk loudly, a fact you will notice at the latest during your first visit to a restaurant. But they seldom raise their voices or use a cutting tone. Therefore, in case you have to complain about something, avoid becoming gruff, and instead use a quiet, factual tone to register your complaint. Anything else would be seen as gratuitously aggressive and the reaction would be the same. In shops and restaurants, in businesses where you are the person paying, remember that the customer is *always* right. You will generally be treated with courtesy.

The general puritanism of American society extends to the whole issue of relations between the sexes as well. The established form of meeting up with someone of the opposite sex is to "date," which essentially implies an invitation to a restaurant, a movie, a cup of coffee, and so on. This highly contrived game is obnoxious to someone raised in Europe, but it should be played. If you are in business, and you are male, beware of making flirtatious remarks and giving the "eye" too much. There have been many cases of sexual harassment in recent years, some apparently based on what some Europeans might consider perfectly normal intra-sexual behavior.

Food and Drink

The United States still has a reputation abroad for being backward when it comes to the culinary arts. When most people think of American food, they think of hamburgers, hotdogs, steaks and chili. Americans like to have a hearty breakfast, a light lunch (often cold) and a hot meal for dinner.

Breakfast in America, which is, incidentally, rarely included in hotel or motel stays, is best enjoyed in a coffee shop. Breakfast normally starts with orange juice and cereal, followed by eggs with bacon or sausage and toast or pancakes. Lunch, generally between noon and 2 p.m., is usually a sandwich and soup or salad. Dinner is the biggest meal of the day.

Restuarants in America are somewhat different to those in Europe. Even in more exclusive restaurants, no one seems too concerned about jackets and ties or formal clothing. The relationship between staff and customers is more relaxed and familiar than in Europe, and etiquette is more lax (it is not uncommon to see women putting on their makeup right at the table, for example).

Customers are normally greeted by a host or hostess – or by the maître d' – on entering an establishment, and are almost always asked if they want to sit in a smoking or non-smoking section. If the restaurant is full, your name will be taken and added to the list of those already waiting for a table. As tables become free, guests are called in the order in which they appear on the list. While waiting for a table, guests can go to the bar or cocktail lounge (in restaurants that have them) for an aperitif.

Once you are at your table, the waiter or waitress will bring you the menu, and will generally introduce him- or herself ("Hi, my name's Brandy and I'll be your server this evening..."). Portions in the U.S. are considerably larger than in Europe, so you might want to pass on the appetizer and order the main course straight away.

Ice water (tap water) is always on hand in American restaurants. Coffee refills are free, as many as you want, as refills often are for soft drinks. American coffee tends to seem sort of watery to foreigners, and it may take a few days for you to get used to it. If you don't want ice in your Coke of Fanta, make sure to order it that way.

Most restaurants offer a Daily Special meal at a special price. Most restaurants have self-service salad bars, which are much bigger and more complete than any you'll have seen in Europe. For those who are really hungry, a lot of places have all-you-can-eat specials. Most restaurants also have a special children's menu and senior citizen's menu, with smaller portions at smaller prices.

American beer has a bad reputation abroad. While it is true that some of the beers made by the mega-breweries are not especially good, there are dozens if not hundreds of smaller breweries and so-called micro-breweries that produce extremely palatable beers. Better-known import beers (e.g., Heineken and Beck's) are available just about everywhere. While European wines are on offer in many restaurants, California wines prevail, some of which are quite good.

On Sundays and bank holidays it might just be that alcohol will not be made available to customers. You may have to settle for alcohol-free. Even in restaurants, if your appearance belies your age, you may have to show ID.

After dinner, you will almost always be asked if you'd like dessert. The assortment of these sweet delicacies is generally extensive, and many restaurants have their own home-made special treats.

When the check is brought to you, it is generally put on the table. In some restaurants you pay at the table, though in general you pay at the cash register on your way out. The tip, which should be between 15 and 20 percent, is left on the table, not handed to the waiter or waitress. Keep in mind that service is not included in the bill; food servers in the U.S. earn most of their money from tips – their hourly wage is negligable. If paying by credit card, there is a space on the form for the gratuity.

Once your bill has been brought, you are expected to pay and leave within a few minutes: especially if the place is crowded and others are waiting for a table. Again, keep in mind that the service personnel make their money from tips, and the longer a table is tied up, the less money they will earn. In some instances, if it is thought that you are spending too much time relaxing after a meal, you might even be asked to leave. This is not necessarily being unfriendly, it is simply a matter of business.

Those who want to forego dining out and prefer to fend for themselves will find more than they could ever want in supermarkets, almost all of which have their own bakeries and delicatessen.

If you want to try some indigenous cheeses, New York and Vermont cheddars are excellent, especially the sharp ones, as are most varieties from Wisconsin (known as America's Dairyland).

A number of foods are much cheaper in the U.S. than in Europe, especially beef and seafood. Although Americans tend to eat mostly white bread, a variety of whole grain breads are available; albeit these are generally pre-packaged.

Ground coffee, sold in cans, is extremely coarse and not very good. Instant coffee is commonly drunk in many American homes. Good fresh ground coffees are generally available in bigger supermarkets, and in natural food and specialty shops.

Americans don't drink much mineral water, especially since tap water is free.

Hiking and Trekking

Most of the national parks have extensive trails that can be explored alone or accompanied by a park ranger (who can tell you volumes about the park in question). These guided tours last anywhere from 20 minutes to several days and usually start daily during the summer months. Accommodation is either at camping sites or in simple huts that have to be reserved in advance either at the local visitor center or from the park ranger. Those who want to wander through a national park alone, must, for their own safety, register with a park ranger and, upon returning, de-register.

Watch out with campfires! Especially in summer; forest fires can start easily and spread rapidly ! There are some very stringent regulations on this.

Language

Volumes have been written about the American language and how it is spoken. The debate as to whose is better still rages on to this day between the old colonial masters, the British, and Americans, whereby the latter seem a lot more relaxed about the wagging of their tongues. In fact, Americans are simply more relaxed when they speak, both in terms of pronunciation and grammar. As long as the meaning is out there, who cares what form it takes? At any rate, anyone wishing to find more information and thousands of linguistic tidbits should pick up a copy of H. L. Mencken's *The American Language*. Though written in the 1930s and 40s, it gives the background to the development of euphemisms, of expletives, of surnames and place names, of cant and argot. It compares British and American English and examines (with typical Menckenian sarcasm) the differences between them.

The American language is very lively. New words appear out of the blue and spread across the country like wildfire; the expression "to be psyched," for example, meaning prepared for or excited about something, or "megabucks," meaning extremely rich or expensive.

Time is money, as Ben Franklin said, so things have to be shortened in America to save on both. The President is called the *Prez*, the suburbs are known as the *burbs*, parents are the *rents*. Acronyms have a field day as well: BYOB = Bring Your Own Bottle (or Booze); SNAFU = Situation Normal All Fouled Up; PDQ = Pretty Damned Quick; ASAP = As Soon As Possible; SASE = Self-Addressed and Stamped Envelope; TLC = Tender Loving Care. And that is only the tip of the iceberg. Simplifying language also takes on another appearance. Through becomes *thru*, *4-sale* means "for sale," *Ped Xing* means "pedestrian crossing," and *Xmas* is Christmas.

With all the linguistic freedom taken, however, Americans are beginning to suffer from the constraints of PC, which in this case means not "personal computer" but rather "political correctness." In some cases the changes are indeed justified, but one must be careful not to offend a social group or minority by using the wrong word by accident or by habit. Syntactical acrobatics are now required to deal with the gender issue (male or female: waitperson, chairperson, etc.). Manning a telephone is a no-no. The list goes on. The result of all this is that the emotional quality of the language is beginning to disappear in certain quarters, to be replaced by objective sterility. And whether these mighty efforts are truly getting rid of discrimination is a wide open question.

Media

Foreigners traveling in America will realize without a shadow of a doubt just how insular this gigantic nation is. Television, radio and the print media stick mainly to local topics, and world news is often given merely cursory treatment.

To stay in touch with international events you can turn to the *Los Angeles Times*, the *New York Times*, the *San Francisco Chronicle* or the *Wall Street Journal*. All others, even the most important print media, report almost exclusively on national topics. Even the main news magazines, such as *Time*, *U.S. News and World Report* or *Newsweek*, are sold in their American version, which is different from the European one.

International newspapers and magazines are not easy to come by either once you get beyond the big cities. Television offers little relief from the innate isolationism of the American media. The 99 percent private ownership of the broadcasting stations means that they have to sell their product as if it were shoes or doughnuts, and the American public, long used to using the media as means of switching off its gray cells, will not necessarily turn to news or news programs. As any bout of channel surfing with an American television set proves, the percentage of sheer bilge being broadcast on the major networks is extremely high.

Even news programs, such as those on CNN and Dan Rather's evening news on CBS, have an overtone of perfectly contrived hype to them that removes a lot of their credibility. Somewhere and at some time, the networks got a message that their anchorpeople had to be more aggressive, and hence we have the image of a perfectly harmless fellow, Dan Rather in this case, performing such acts as cutting George Bush (then Vice-President) off in an interview because he was talking too much about Irangate. The model here seems to be the talk show, during which such self-propelled high and windy priests as CNN's Larry King go about verbally bashing anyone in sight or earshot, usually by means of aggressive interruptions. It's part of the game of making information interesting by turning the anchors into stars and the news into show biz. And, as already suggested, much of the news deals with national events. International events must either be of extreme importance, and possibly with a tie to the U.S., or blood must be flowing or threatening to do so.

There are naturally some redeeming shows, even on CBS: *Eye on America* makes an attempt at social commitment, and Ted Koppel on *Nightline* (ABC) has a more intelligent and profound way of conducting interviews. The best news show by far, however, is on PBS, the publicly-funded network. Every weekday evening one can tune into the *MacNeil-Lehrer Report*, a one-hour news program on the British model. PBS should also be mentioned in connection with the public radio stations that cover the nation from coast to coast. No advertising is only one aspect of the relief. Their programming covers a wide range, from classical music, to news and public affairs. *Morning Edition* (in the morning of course) and *All Things Considered* (in the evening) give excellent coverage with good interviews. Some stations even broadcast a half hour of BBC World Service news. Though conservative Americans constantly fire broadsides at PBS for its allegedly liberal stance, in truth the views expressed are often quite balanced.

Finally, to be fair, one should mention CNN as a source of news as well. And if you are a news addict, or need to follow the daily life in your home country, we can only advise you to purchase a short-wave radio (see under "Shopping" on page 246).

The entertainment offered by the networks consists mostly of series, soaps, glossy shows that border on vulgarity, and lots and lots of commercials. To get a good feel for American culture, tune into some of the specialties, such as *Late Night with David Letterman* on CBS or its forerunner on NBC, *The Tonight Show*, hosted by Jay Leno, who took over from the legendary Johnny Carson. Then there are the countless talk shows that often start first thing in the morning. The stars are Oprah Winfrey, Phil Donahue and Geraldo Rivera, among others. They demonstrate how the public mind can be influenced and provide a deep view into the nature of the American psyche. They are also inadvertently comical.

Otherwise, American TV is characterized by great variety and by its technical proficiency. When booking a hotel room, ask if some of the movie channels are available in the room, HBO, Showtime or Movie, for example. These channels broadcast relatively recent films with few breaks for advertising. If you are a sports addict, tune into ESPN, a channel exclusively devoted to sports. Note, however, that the focus is on the U.S. Even during the World Cup soccer matches in America, ESPN favored baseball over some of the soccer games.

Post Offices

The United States Postal Service is government-operated, and it functions relatively well, considering. Postage is also generally cheaper than in Europe.

Although not exactly abundant, their business hours are basically from 8 a.m. to 5 p.m. on weekdays, and from 8 a.m. to noon Saturdays. Stamps are also available at supermarkets, in drugstores, in convenience stores (small supermarkets), and at hotel and motel reception desks. Some stores also offer fax service, but fees to Europe can be quite high. A normal airmail letter to Europe currently costs $1.00, a postcard or aerogramme costs 50 cents. A letter within the U.S. costs 35 cents, a postcard costs 20 cents.

Public Holidays

Besides the usual holidays known to Europeans, America has several national holidays that have, to some extent, greater meaning to the general public than Christmas and Easter. This is true in particular for residents of big cities, where Christians and citizens of European origin form only a part of a multicultural society. Government offices, post offices, banks, other public institutions and some businesses are closed for the following holidays:

January 1: **New Year's Day**.

Third Monday in January: **Martin Luther King Jr. Day**, celebrating the birthday of the slain civil rights leader.

February 21: **President's Day**, celebrating the birthdays of George Washington (Feb. 22), the first president of the U.S., and Abraham Lincoln (Feb. 12), the 16th president. Their birthdays were formerly celebrated separately.

Last Monday in May: **Memorial Day**, a day of national remembrance for Americans killed in foreign wars. The main vacation season begins after this.

July 4: **Independence Day**, the most important national holiday, celebrates the signing of the Declaration of Independence. Parades, fireworks and barbecues are the order of the day.

First Monday in September: **Labor Day**, the American equivalent of May 1 in Europe. It officially ends the vacation season and prices for tourists drop accordingly in certain sectors.

October 12: **Columbus Day**, celebrating the discovery of America.

November 11: **Veteran's Day**, honors the veterans of the United States armed forces. Formerly called Armistice Day, it originally celebrated the end of World War One.

Fourth Thursday in November: **Thanksgiving Day**, a harvest feast. It is second in importance to July 4.

December 25: **Christmas Day**.

Shopping

Stores are generally open from 9 a.m. to 9 p.m. Monday through Saturday, and Sunday from 9 a.m. or noon to 6 p.m. There are, however, no official opening hours, and many stores stay open 24 hours per day. For Europeans, this is a true shopper's paradise. Many things are much cheaper in the U.S. than they are in Europe, especially goods "Made in the U.S.A.," of course.

You will hardly ever encounter an unfriendly salesperson in the United States. American shopping malls, some of which can house hundreds of shops, as well as department stores, restaurants and cafés, are like cities unto themselves.

Besides the usual arts, crafts and souvenirs, electronics goods (TVs, stereos) tend to be cheap, as do CDs, videos and music casettes. Computer goods and peripherals, cameras and accessories, and select clothing can also be much cheaper. Some electrical goods, in fact, can be up to 30 percent less expensive than in Europe (check to make sure these can be switched to 220 volts!).

Televisions and VCRs are not much use to Europeans, as the American system (NTSC) is not compatible with the European ones (PAL and SECAM), although some are multiple system. For the same reason, NTSC videos cannot be played on European systems.

Cameras, on the other hand, can be excellent bargains here – and you don't have to worry about whether it's the right system or voltage. All brand name cameras and accessories are noticeably cheaper in the U.S. than in Europe.

When buying clothing, the biggest bargains are those made in America, like Levi's or Lee's, for example. American designer wear is also much cheaper here than in Europe.

A U.S. tradition is the Factory Outlet Store, where clothing and other goods with slight flaws, or last years fashions, can be purchased directly from the factory at a big savings.

Telephoning

No other country in the world has such a dense telecommunication network, and so many telephones available that actually work. Furthermore, the service is efficient and fairly inexpensive.

Before reaching for the receiver, keep in mind that the system is in private hands, and the service is taken on by a number of competing companies; and with competition come advantages to the consumer. There are regional companies and long-distance ones. If phoning locally within an area code, just dial the seven digits. If phoning outside your area code, dial 1, then the area code of the region you are phoning to, followed by the seven digit phone number.

If calling from a coin-operated telephone with coins, an operator will automatically come on the line to tell you how much money you have to put into the slot and the duration of your call. Should you lose money in a coin-operated telephone, call the operator (0) and give a U.S. address where the phone company can send the refund. Even a dime comes back!

Operators make life very easy, though using their services is more expensive than direct dialing. If you are at a public phone that can't make international calls, an operator can help; they also perform such services as reversing charges.

The easiest – and probably cheapest – way of telephoning is to use a "calling card." Several companies offer them, AT&T, MCI and Sprint, for example. It costs nothing to get one, and the fees are charged either directly to your bank account or to a credit card. Furthermore, the companies offer special discounts for frequent phone users. If you have a great deal of phoning abroad to do, you can usually get a special discount. Just shop around for the best deal.

Using a calling card: The AT&T card, for example, has a number and a PIN (Personal Identification Number) that you should memorize. Dial an AT&T operator direct, or ask the regular operator to connect you. It's very simple and efficient. The service can be used in your hotel room to avoid high phone bills (you will be charged only for a local call, that is, up to 75 cents). Operators can also charge your calls to a credit card. All of this eases the hassle of juggling with coins at a street corner.

Two other peculiarities of the American phone system that you might come across are pagers and voice-mail boxes. Pagers are known in other countries, but in America they are more widespread

247

than elsewhere. The voice-mail box is a kind of answering machine service offered by telephone companies, which switches on if no one answers the phone or the line is busy. Leave a message and the person will get back to you. All they have to do is pick up their phone and dial a number for the message to play back.

So-called "800 numbers" (and 888 numbers) are another American specialty. They are toll-free for the user (i.e., there is no charge). Sometimes they come with a combination of letters, such as 1-800-345-ALEX. Look at any American telephone, and you will see letters next to each digit. The rest is a question of spelling. In the case of ALEX you would have to dial 1-800-354-2539.

Beware of the 900 numbers, however, they are very expensive for the user!

Directory assistance is 555-1212 nationwide. If you are in Los Angeles and need to know a telephone number in, say, Seattle, you dial 1 + 206 (the area code for Seattle) + 555-1212.

Calling abroad: The international access number from the U.S. is 011.

Country Codes: Australia – 61; New Zealand – 64; Ireland – 353; U.K. – 44.

To call the U.S. Embassy in Canberra, Australia, for example, you would dial: 011 + 61 + 6 (area code of Canberra) + 270-5000.

Time Zones

The continental U.S. is divided into four time zones. On the east coast it's Eastern Time (ET), which is five hours behind Greenwich Mean Time (noon in London is 7 a.m. in New York). The next zone is Central Time (CT), one hour behind ET. Then comes Mountain Time (MT) and Pacific Time (PT), each minus one hour respectively. At noon in New York it is 11 a.m. in Chicago, 10 a.m. in Colorado Springs and 9 a.m. in San Francisco. Keep this in mind when making phone calls across the continent.

Daylight Saving Time in America begins on the last Sunday in April and lasts until the last Sunday in October.

Departure and arrival times for flights are always given in local time.

Tipping

Service is not included in the bill at restaurants and bars. Waiters and waitresses therefore expect tips, generally between 15 and 20 percent, which can be left as cash on the table or written into the space on your credit card receipt.

The reason for this is that the minimum wage for restaurant service help is negligible, and waiters and waitresses live primarily from their tips. Furthermore, an amount of around seven percent of a waiter's or waitress' turnover is automatically earmarked as income by the International Revenue Service; so even if they are not tipped, they still have to pay income tax on money they theoretically should have earned. Also, tips are generally shared with busboys (the people who clean the tables and assist the waiters and waitresses) and bar staff, which is something else to keep in mind

A by-product of this system is very polite, friendly and helpful service personnel. If the food isn't great, or the cook is slow preparing your meal, don't take it out on the person serving it to you; be a fair tipper and address your complaints to the management.

Tipping is also appropriate for cab drivers. Rounding off the fare to the next logical sum is usual ($6.35 to $7, for example, or if in doubt between five and ten percent). For a great driver (they can be very entertaining) you may want to give a larger tip. The same applies to extra services, such as waiting until you have entered your home at night.

Tipping at hotels can become expensive, and the more luxurious the place, the more one tends to give larger tips. This can become ruinous. Bellboys, doormen, room service, parking attendants and others will all have their hands out. A couple of dollars per bag for bell-boys, per taxi being hailed by the door-man, or for room service dropping some-thing off at your room is expected.

Otherwise, tipping is not one of the great economic factors on a trip to the United States. Keep in mind, though, that it might leave a good impression with a particularly good guide or for a service rendered beyond the call of duty.

Tourist Information

The tourist in America is cared for in exemplary fashion. Besides dozens of *visitors' centers* usually posted at the main sights, there are also numerous toll-free telephone numbers than can be made use of to request more information or brochures. Here is a list of state tourism offices:

WEST COAST: **California**, Califor-nia Department of Tourism, Tourism In-formation Offices, 801 K Street, Suite 1600, Sacramento, CA 95814, tel. 1-800-TO-CALIF.

Oregon, Oregon Tourism Division, 595 Cottage St. N.E., Salem, OR 97310, tel. 1-800-547-7842.

Washington State, Tourism Develop-ment Division, 101 General Administra-tion Building, P.O Box 42500, Olympia, WA, 98504-2500, tel. 1-800-544-1800.

British Columbia (Canada), Tourism British Columbia, 1117 Wharf Street, Victoria, B.C. V8W 272, tel. 1-800-548-8016.

ROCKY MOUNTAINS: **Colorado**, Colorado Tourism Board, 1625 Broadway, Suite 1700, Denver, CO 80202, tel. 1-800-433-2656.

Idaho, Idaho Division of Tourism De-velopment, Idaho Department of Com-merce, 700 W. State Street, Boise, ID 83720, tel. 1-800-635-7820.

Montana, Travel Montana, 1424 Ninth Avenue, Helena, MT 59620, tel. 1-800-548-3390.

Nebraska, Nebraska Division of Travel, 301 Centennial Mall South, Lin-coln, NE 68509, tel. 1-800-228-4307 (in state: tel. 1-800-742-7595).

Utah, State of Utah, Utah Travel Coun-cil, Council Hall, Capitol Hill, Salt Lake City, UT 84114, tel. 1-800-448-8355.

Wyoming, Wyoming Division of Tour-ism, Frank Norris Travel Center, Cheyenne, WY, tel. 1-800-225-5996.

SOUTHWEST: **Arizona**, Arizona Office of Tourism, 1100 W. Washington Street, Phoenix, AZ 85007, tel. 1-800-842-8257 (toll free).

Nevada, Nevada Commission on Tourism, Capitol Complex, Carson City, NV 89710, tel. 1-800-2370774.

New Mexico, New Mexico Depart-ment of Tourism and Travel, P.O. Box 2003, Santa Fe, NM 87503-2003, tel. 1-800-545-2040.

Texas, Tourism Division, Texas De-partment of Commerce, Box 12728, Aus-tin, TX 78711-2728, tel. 1-800-88-88-TEX.

AUTHORS

Jürgen Scheunemann, is a Berlin-based freelance journalist and translator. He studied U.S. history at the Free University of Berlin's John F. Kennedy Institute, and taught American history at the University of Maryland. He was proj-ect editor of *Nelles Guide Berlin and Potsdam*. For this guide, he wrote the chapters "Go West! – A Journey through the Promised Land," "From Los Angeles to Las Vegas," "From Las Vegas to the Grand Canyon," "Through Navajo and Hopi Country," "From Los Angeles to Yosemite National Park" (with Arturo Gonzales), "From San Francisco to Seattle," "The Pacific Northwest," "From Seattle to Yellowstone National Park," "American Cuisine: Fast Food and Ethnic Food" and "A Society of Immigrants."

Margarete Batt, an art historian and tour guide, wrote "Through the South-west on Route 66."

Arturo Gonzalez has written for U.S. magazines and newspapers for forty years. He wrote the chapters "From the Grand Canyon to Denver," "From Los Angeles to San Francisco," "From Los Angeles to Yosemite National Park," "From San Francisco to Salt Lake City" and "From Salt Lake City to Yellowstone National Park."

Sara Hare is a San Francisco-based freelance journalist. Since completing here studies in socio-economics, she has written for a number of magazines in the United States and Europe. She wrote the chapters "From Los Angeles to Phoenix" and "From Phoenix to Santa Fe."

Anita King, a former copy editor of the *San Francisco Independent*, contributed to Sara Hare's chapters.

Gary McKechnie, a travel journalist, wrote, together with Anne Midgette, the feature "Sports in America."

Anne Midgette, who spent twelve years living in Munich, now lives in New York from where she writes about music and the arts for the *Wall Street Journal, ARTnews, Opera News* and other publications. Her published travel writings include a guidebook to Bavaria. She was also co-author and project editor of *Nelles Guide New York*.

For this book she contributed the chapters "From Santa Fe to San Antonio," "From San Antonio to Houston," "Native Americans" and "Sports in America."

PHOTOGRAPHERS